❧ *The Wine Revolution in France*

The Wine Revolution in France ❧ ❧ ❧

THE TWENTIETH CENTURY

❧ *Leo A. Loubère*

PRINCETON UNIVERSITY PRESS

PRINCETON, NEW JERSEY

Library of Congress Cataloging-in-Publication Data
Loubère, Leo A.
The wine revolution in France : the twentieth century /
by Leo A. Loubère.
p. cm.
ISBN 0-691-05592-0 (alk. paper)
1. Wine industry—France. 2. Wine industry—France—
Technological innovations. 3. Viticulture—France.
4. Viticulture—France—Technological innovations. I. Title.
HD9382.5.L68 1990
338.4'56632'009440904—dc20   89-70154

This book has been composed in Linotron Garamond

Princeton University Press books are printed on acid-free paper,
and meet the guidelines for permanence and durability of the
Committee on Production Guidelines for Book Longevity of the
Council on Library Resources

Printed in the United States of America
by Princeton University Press,
Princeton, New Jersey

1   3   5   7   9   10   8   6   4   2

TO NICHOLAS AND SOPHIE

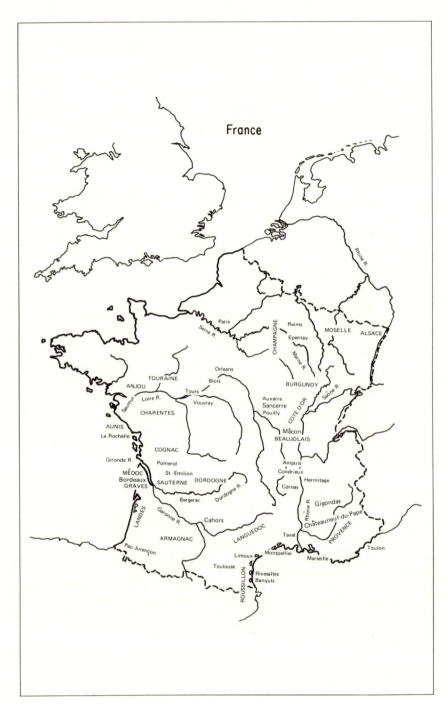

MAJOR WINE AREAS OF FRANCE

❧ CONTENTS

❧ ILLUSTRATIONS

❧ TABLES

❧ ACKNOWLEDGMENTS

I wish to thank the following persons for reading one or more chapters of this book, and for freely offering advice for improving it: J. Harvey Smith, Jay Freer, Harry Paul, Kirby Moulton, Etienne Montaigne, and Peter Amann.

Several research, statistical, or commercial institutions and their personnel have also graciously gathered recent quantitative data for me or sent me up-to-date publications: Institut National de la Recherche Agronomique, Department of Economics and Rural Sociology, Montpellier; Office International de la Vigne et du Vin; J. Laurent of La Confédération Nationale des Coopératives Vinicoles; the interprofessional committees of Bordeaux, Burgundy, Touraine, Champagne, and Alsace; François Bonal of Epernay; Jean Malvoisin of Mâcon; Jean Nollevalle of Aÿ; M. Marcellin of the Chambre d'Agriculture de Roussillon; Jacques Loyat of the Agriculture Ministry; René Engel of Vosne Romanée; Yves Rinaudo; André Brunet of Violès; Gabriel Delhomme and René Faure of Vinsobres; M. and Mme C. Savès of Bouzy; M. Hilzer and Mme Maigret of Epernay; Max L'Eglise of the Lycée Viticole at Beaune; Wendel C. M. Lee of the Wine Institute of San Francisco; and Mme C. Ourvouai of the Office National Interprofessionel des Vins; Pierre Poupon of Meursault, and Mm. Baret and Bernard of Beaune. For the gift of photographs I wish to thank three cellar equipment manufacturers: Thiéron, F. Valentin, and Grilliat-Jaeger.

AO	Appellation d'origine
AOC	Appellation d'origine controlée. The V sometimes preceding these initials simply means "Vin"
DES	Diplôme d'études supérieures. Roughly equivalent to a master's thesis
EEC	European Economic Community (CEE in French)
GIE	Groupement d'Intérêt Economique
ITV	Institut Technique de la Vigne et du Vin
INRA	Institut National de la Recherche Agronomique
OIV	Office International de la Vigne et du Vin
ONIVIT	Office National Interprofessional des Vins de Table
SAFER	Société d'Aménagement Foncier d'Expansion Rurale
SICA	Société d'Intérêt Collectif Agricole
SMAG	Salaire Minimum Agricole Garanti
SMIG	Salaire Minimum Interprofessionnel Garanti
SOPEXA	Societé pour Encouragement d'Exportations Agricole
VCC	Vin de consommation courante (ordinary table wines)
VDQS	Vin délimité de qualité supérieur (one step above the VCC)
VQPRD	Vin de qualité produit dans des régions déterminées

❧ *The Wine Revolution in France*

About This Book and the Metric System

This book is a continuation of my first study on wine, *The Red and the White: The History of Wine in France and Italy in the Nineteenth Century*. It is, I am sad to state, an incomplete continuation because it does not include Italy. This absence was not planned in advance; it is, rather, the result of the theft of all my notes from my car when it was parked at the University of Bordeaux in June 1983. Six years of research simply disappeared. When I discovered the robbery I think I shared the same feeling of hopeless despair of the saloon keepers as they watched astounded when Carrie Nation went about breaking their bottles of various alcohols. This analogy is not an idle one, since the thieves who stole my notes also carried away everything save four cases of excellent wine given me by growers whom I had recently interviewed. They did not smash the bottles; they simply ignored them. In this case ignorance was bliss, not theirs but mine, yet a bliss that hardly compensated for the monstrous dimensions of my loss.

Happily for me I was able to reread the materials concerning France during two years of continuous residence there. But I never found time to recover the data on Italy. The history of the peninsula will be the subject of Volume Three.

As in my first volume, I use the metric system to designate the area of vineyards and quantities of wine. Some of my American readers, in consequence, may believe that they will not be able to follow my text. Frankly, I do not believe that they would be more mystified if I gave dimensions in the American system, now unique in the world. If the term "a hundred liters of wine" leaves a vague impression, would the statement "one hundred six quarts" be more enlightening? To conceptualize large magnitudes of any liquid or space is not easy for most people because in their daily life they deal in small quantities: pints, quarts, and more rarely, gallons. Not even many wine drinkers handle cases of twelve bottles, and who among them could tell how many gallons there are in a case? The vast majority, according to merchants I have questioned, buy a few bottles at a time, or bring home larger glass or plastic containers equivalent to three or four bottles, or else resort to jug wine by the gallon for a gathering of fun lovers who are not overly concerned about the quality of their drink. I exclude here youngish academics whose taste in food and beverage is generally more embellished than their wallets.

Perhaps the most effective means to form an idea of magnitude is to envision a hectoliter as the contents of a rather smallish barrel or cask roughly nineteen inches in diameter and two feet long, holding a little over twenty-six gallons or 10.9 cases. To a modest consumer this is a lot of wine, about a year's supply. To a producer of simple table wine of about ten degrees alcohol, it is scarcely enough to feed, house, and clothe his family for more than two days. To a vineyardist of fine grapes, it would allow him a decent living for perhaps seven days if the harvest were of high quality.

Volume, therefore, must be viewed not only as magnitude but also as sustenance, as wherewithal. A crop resulting in the production of two hundred hectoliters would not enable the grower of common wine (*vin ordinaire* or *gros rouge*) to survive for a year, save at the meanest level, yet this represents 5,200 gallons, 26,667 bottles of seventy-five centiliters, 2,222 cases, a lifetime supply for our modest imbiber—if he lived two hundred years. The most widespread barrels for maturing wine contain from 220 to 225 liters, or 2.2 to 2.25 hectoliters, the equivalent of fifty-seven gallon jugs, with a little left over for sipping. Were the contents of this barrel a true margaux or vougeot or champagne, it would be worth its weight in gold. Were it an ordinary from some Mediterranean coastal vineyard, it could be used for washing oneself in a dry summer when the price of pure water surpasses that of ordinary wine.

Vines are planted in land measured in hectares and ares. One hectare equals 2.47 acres; one hundred ares equal one hectare, and roughly forty of them make one acre. When most independent French grape growers purchased land, they accumulated it by ares rather than by hectares because of its high price. The average American suburban house lot of 65 by 150 feet encloses approximately one are. A hectare consists of ten thousand square meters or twelve thousand square yards, about two and a quarter

American football fields. That space represents a very small parcel by to-day's standards in a region of *vin ordinaire*, a middling property if located in an area of fine growths. A vineyard of ten hectares, suitable for a family devoted to common wine, is the equivalent of twenty-five football fields. In terms of planting, that space could accommodate fifty-three vine rows 7,500 feet long (1.4 miles). Such a vineyard could contain from 70,000 to 130,000 plants, depending on the distance between rows and between vines in each row. In Champagne this would constitute an enormous property, in Languedoc a rather small holding allowing a family of four or five to live decently, provided there were not more than two seriously deficient grape harvests in each decade.

To sum up, see table A for a list of American equivalents of metric measures.

All these efforts to measure space and volume may seem infelicitous for a creation as mysterious and romantic as wine. To the person who has never thought of it except as a beverage given to men by the gods, a divine nectar, such data detract from the values that really count: color, aroma, bouquet, body, taste, aftertaste, and their harmonious balance. If I were writing this history exclusively from the drinkers' point of view, I would agree. But the universe of wine is far larger than the wine lover imagines, and observed from the producer's point of view, measurement is a constant factor, from harvest to the final act of bottling and selling. This history has been written to a large extent from the grower's perspective, with some attention to commerce and consumption, both of which are major determinants of production. Growers, however poetic they wax about their creation, do not on a day-to-day basis live in a setting of the mysterious and the wonderful. They make wine for the mundane purpose of selling it, and they are guided, if not to say driven, both by the quantity and quality of their wine bought by the public. They stand at the center of this universe, sometimes creating, sometimes innovating, ever searching to introduce a beverage excellent in every respect, and this in return for a price that will

Table A.   Metric and standard U.S. equivalents

1 liter = 1.06 quarts liquid, or 0.26 gallons
100 liters (1 hectoliter) = 26.4 gallons or 11.1 cases
1 meter = 1.1. yards
1 hectare = 2.47 acres
0.4 ha. (40 ares) = 1 acre
1 kilogram = 2.2 pounds

cover the costs of their material and labor. That there is wine to savor rather than merely to drink has been the result of the devotion, the skills, and the hard work of a cultured minority among them.

Yet they, as a professional group, have rarely appeared in most books about wine, and enjoy at most a few lines among the myriad pages printed in English. Even the finest tasters and the most knowledgeable journalists focus their attention first on the merits or defects of the wine, then incidentally on the wine maker. Not even the technical specialists who turn out thick manuals on the science of vine training and enology give more than passing mention to the human factor. A few journalistic writers, like Eunice Fried, give a far more humanistic account of the people who labor in the vineyards and the cellars, and provide some useful insights about the vignerons (grape growers) whose way of life is intimately bound to the vine and the vat. The very nature of their writing, however, limits its scope to a few examples. This book, I hope, bridges the gap between the two views, the scientific and the personal, and borrows from both. It concentrates on the history of a profession, as well as on a product and the persons who make it.

My research consisted of the usual reading in printed sources in many libraries, chiefly in France. I have not spent much time in public archives, in part because recent collections are not yet open to the public, in part because the documents that are accessible, chiefly quantitative data, have appeared in publications located in national and local agencies of the state. Departmental chambers of agriculture, specialized research centers, especially those of the Institut National de la Recherche Agronomique (Montpellier above all), and CIRVIN of the Geography Department of the University of Bordeaux, as well as the many interprofessional committees of growers and merchants have provided me with their publications and with information that is not obtainable in archives. My sources also include numerous interviews with vignerons, and sometimes with their wives and working children.[1]

As in my previous work I capitalize the names of grapes, use lower case for the names of wines, and continue to hope that this usage dispels confusion between the two. I list my sources in notes at the end of the volume, and when no place of publication is indicated, then Paris is understood.

ABOUT THE WINE REVOLUTION

The term "wine revolution" will seem pretentious or even erroneous to some specialists in the field who contend that changes, when they occurred, did not happen with the suddenness that the word "revolution" suggests, but came about slowly, requiring generations to spread from their starting point and to have a widespread effect on the industry as a whole. Winemen, after all, have traditionally been cautious, sticklers to old ways of going about their business, and unwilling to innovate until they could be sure of success. The same argument can and has been made about the industrial revolution. The issue, in part, is one of time: how many generations have been required before methods of production changed extensively enough to be no longer recognizable to prerevolutionary producers. As regards grape growing, change of considerable magnitude began in the 1880s. The destruction of old vineyards by the phylloxera in the last third of the nineteenth century hastened the pace of change when new vines were planted in parallel rows, and concrete vats began to replace wooden ones in some large wineries. But while row planting became universal, concrete vats did not. The pace of innovation—new insecticides, pasteurization, more efficient horse-drawn plows, hydraulic presses—steadily quickened and prepared the way for more rapid innovation, without many growers going very far until after World War I. These early steps may be compared to the first inventions carried out by a few English spinners and weavers in cotton textiles during the eighteenth century. These artisans were the harbingers of the industrial revolution. Most of their implements were used in the domestic industry and had to be reinvented in the changeover to steam power. The introduction of this novel source of energy began the precipitous rise of the textile industry, just as the selective breeding of animals and the expanded use of fertilizers had prepared the way for the agricultural revolution of the seventeenth century.

The processes of viticulture and wine making before 1914, like those in textiles and general agriculture, marked a prerevolutionary phase.[2] The true champions of progress extended their activities less to theoretical and more to practical research and teaching that benefited a few hundred sons and other heirs of large owners, or sons of modest families preparing for careers in government or in private bureaucracies specializing in grape and wine growing. Save for methods of combatting the phylloxera, which were extensively known and whose use were a matter of survival, few vignerons of middling and small properties were able to benefit from the accumulation of knowledge that appeared in articles in learned journals and, to a lesser extent, in more popular publications such as the *Revue de viticulture*. Far too many vignerons were insufficiently trained to comprehend new techniques or to trust them. They were nearly all literate by 1914, thanks to compulsory primary education, but their literacy often diminished after they left school or was never truly functional enough to enable them to understand texts above the simplest level. The fat manuals published by professional scientists were both too expensive and difficult for most of them. As Harry Paul put it, the government's sponsored research and teaching "programs concentrating on agriculture could not compare in achievement with those devoted to industry. Although by no means stagnant, French agriculture was far less innovative in its structure and methods than industry."[3] At least before 1914.

The great conflict that began in that fatal year was more than a war, it was a revolution. Not only did thrones topple, but so did age-old ideas and practices. Unlike most French politicians who hoped to restore the past, the generation returning from the trenches was different; they were more sympathetic to novelty, more familiar with machines, and more mature in outlook. Their knowledge of pure science had hardly improved, but such knowledge was not germane to their professional life immediately after the peace. After all, major economic changes in the past had come first to Britain, later to France, at a time when pure science had only minor, indirect importance for artisan inventors. And they were innovative in well-established economic sectors with an almost primitive technology that, applied pragmatically, had brought about numerous small modifications over a long period of time: textiles, metallurgy, cereals, herding, and viticulture. Historians have recently divided man's history largely according to innovations in these sectors.

My method of periodization, I hope, is not too rigid; it assumes overlapping periods or time zones of transition. In the artisanal phase before 1914, scientific invention was by no means absent. The men who discovered that grafting European vines onto American root stock in order to combat the phylloxera were highly trained scientists connected with the University of Montpellier. And in Bordeaux, during the 1890s, an enological research institute was created by Ulysse Gayon, a student of the great Louis Pasteur. These important innovations notwithstanding, the influence of pure scientific research was too limited to mark the period; indeed, certain paths of investigation seem to have lost ground after 1900, such as the seeking for a means of destroying the phylloxera without destroying the vines. Efforts continued on a pragmatic basis to discover the most effective root stock to serve different varieties of scions in various ecological conditions. But the phylloxera has survived all the assaults upon it, and still lives. Apparently scientists have run up against the wall of natural resistance, and have found that efforts to destroy the aphid are no longer compelling, either to their requests for funding, or to furthering their careers. An explanation of this standoff between scientist and insect is perhaps the belief that even if an effective insecticide were found, it would not be more cost effective than grafting as a means of control. Problems, then, transcend time periods.

A new period began after World War I as the pace of innovation accelerated rapidly enough to merit the adjective "revolutionary." There did not as yet occur a truly mature transformation—first, because the indispensable financial support was not fully in place, given the long crisis of those years; and second, because the growers' mentality was not yet ready. Nonetheless, the introduction of a few steam-driven tractors in several very large vineyards and of electrical power in a far larger number of cellars signaled the first stage of what has become, to use Leon Trotsky's expression, a "permanent revolution." And this is precisely how more recent innovation differs from that of earlier centuries. Acceleration was the key word here; once underway, change acquired a momentum of its own. The result was that the grower of the 1860s, indeed of the early 1900s, was not at all familiar with the modern techniques that go far beyond age-old basic processes. Less than a century of notable transformation after millennia of classical techniques is very rapid change—not an evolution but a revolution. The meaning of the latter term assumes more than new technologies; it is a code word for mutations of vast extent, well beyond the vineyard and the cellar.

Undeniably the basic mutation began in the vineyards, where time-honored practices were carried out unquestioningly for centuries. Viticulture was the creation of man's empirical approach to cultivation of the soil. Although former monastic vineyards were often models of efficiency, the cultivation of grapes was scarcely a science until highly trained, increasingly academic specialists began not only to discover how to adapt the many varieties of grapes to soil and climate in a much shorter time than was previously possible, but also to penetrate the hitherto mysterious structure and nature of the vine as a species. Botany, and particularly ampelography, the science of identifying vines, accompanied and reinforced this great leap forward. Equally important were the experiments carried out in trial vineyards and in the laboratories of chemical companies to develop and test the sprays and powders needed to defend vines more effectively against their natural enemies. The discoveries of botanists, biologists, and nurserymen who were able to create virus-free stock were another dimension we must not ignore. Likewise, the achievements of manufacturers of machine-driven equipment for the cultivation of vines were demonstratively compelling. Mechanization of vineyards has, it can be argued, introduced a second phase of the revolution in the 1950s. Animal power gave way to tractors and, more recently, manpower to computers.

At this point it is useful to ask what forces have motivated these persistent efforts to understand and to improve viticulture. Some scholars argue that growers have been "pushed" ahead by scientists and innovative technicians who, in their laboratories and trial vineyards, have made major discoveries about vines. Especially important were the breakthroughs on the genetic influences on the health and heartiness of each variety; on the biochemical means of producing healthy, virus-free stock; and on improved soil conditions. By hybridizing and cloning, scientists have even created new varieties that are more resistant to pests and disease than older ones. Indeed, a few specialists have even undertaken the almost utopian task of creating a vinifera hybrid variety that will be resistant to the phylloxera. These laboratory experiments have been carried out under the auspices of the Institut National de la Recherche Agronomique since World War II, and by other research centers that have sprung up since then.[4] So far growers have accepted only the most readily applicable and least expensive of these innovations. Very few have undertaken the Herculean task of fully replacing traditional varieties with new ones. Since under normal conditions only about 2 percent of vineyards are replanted each year, new varieties will be slow to appear. Rather, growers continue to treat their aging vineyards with chemicals from firms that test and produce more effective sprays in their own laboratories. They also look actively to the government-organized open-air demonstrations of innovative machines turned out by private firms. In addition, they go to the annual international and regional wine fairs to discover what products are new and useful for the cultivation of vines. There is, it is evident, some push toward innovation by both public and private agencies. I am inclined to believe, however, that the "pull" of the market has been and will remain the stronger force, drawing vineyardists toward new technologies and cultural practices, if only because they cannot compete in the market without them. The market has existed for thousands of years, and changes occurred piecemeal and pragmatically as sales demanded. It is the recent changing market for wine that has directly influenced the goals and therefore the methods of grape growing.

Wine making, or viniculture, has also gone through a similarly rapid transformation in our century. Indeed, there would be little incentive to grow superior grapes if one did not wish to produce superior wines. In time, the training of an army of skilled enologists and technicians brought into both government and private laboratories the array of specialists capable of analyzing the chemical components of grape juice, their interaction, and the changes the juice underwent on its way to becoming wine. This process was markedly facilitated by the introduction of new materials for the fermentation and storing of wine, in particular the substitution of glazed masonry or stainless steel for wooden vats. Large oak tanks, especially the open type, are now more nearly the stock of museums than of commercial operations. Some small growers, especially those in Burgundy, still use the wooden vats—and swear by them rather than at them—but they are surviving on the margins of modernization. It is their sons or sons-in-law who will eventually renovate the cellars.

Most large-scale producers did not have to await a new generation. In fact, what they were not able to learn through their own professional sources of information they picked up from the INRA and from manufacturers of products for other beverages. They became familiar with high-speed assembly line bottling from soda pop and fruit-juice makers: machines invented to clean, fill, and cap bottles of soda or juice were easily adapted to wine bottles, especially to those of one-liter capacity stoppered with plastic caps. Imaginative entrepreneurs—merchant-blenders first of all—reached out to other economic sectors to enhance their own technology. Known as *négociants-éleveurs*, they blended the wines that they matured (*élevé*) in their own cellars, then commercialized them under their own labels. It was at this level of quality that the wine revolution has had its greatest impact. Producers of great wines were too conservative; those of cheap wines were usually too poor.

The wine revolution spread far beyond these early technical innovations. It included a political dimension in that the governments of the Third Republic (1875–1940), composed of deputies and senators who traditionally were committed to the doctrine of laissez faire, really initiated a kind of planned economy in the 1930s as well as the financial resources to make it viable. The transformation of public policy was another aspect of rapid modernization. Under the pressure of events, and of grape growers as voters, liberal politicians began promulgating laws that made the wine industry the most closely controlled of all industries in the French economy. A huge ministerial bureaucracy emerged to regulate various processes, and

an even larger academic bureaucracy took up the task of training generations of students who, with diplomas in hand, returned to their vines and
cellars with more legal and technical knowledge than was ever imagined
by their forebears. Research and instructional centers were set up as quasi-
independent entities or in high schools and universities where state-paid
faculty and other specialists carried forward the scientific aspects of the
revolution.

Like the industrial revolution, the wine revolution signified a recourse
to science and modern technology in production on a national scale. The
major result, apart from the greater flow of wine, was an enormous increase
in costs. Advanced technology has never come cheaply, and neither has the
specialized equipment without which it cannot advance. If wine may be
viewed as the blood of the new industry, then test tubes, centrifuges,
stemmer-crushers, refractometers, pH meters, chromatographic equipment, ebulliometers, filters, and so forth are its bones and integument.

The enormous expense of so much apparatus has put the small producer
at a great disadvantage. His search for survival has led him to organize
wine-making cooperatives. From the initiative of little vignerons have
come forth mighty collective wine cellars which, in turn, created mighty
collective wine sales operations. Within three generations, cooperative
production and sales have visibly and deeply transformed the entire industry, and saved from extinction a multitude of small grape growers.

This salvation has, until recently, nearly maintained the numerical
magnitude of the people who depend on wine. Because of their ability to
modernize within their means, they number roughly 5 to 6 percent of
French society, if the total includes all those involved in growing and
sales, their families, the manufacturers who supply the tools of their trade,
and the vast bureaucracy that has grown to supervise everyone's activities.
The demographic consequences of the revolution are of considerable proportions.

The social aspects are varied in their impact. Some growers benefited
from the changes, while others suffered and were ultimately displaced because of their inability to adapt to the exigencies of a new, increasingly
selective market. The beneficiaries opted to use the new technology to
enhance quality. But then there were those who sought to adapt by seeing
in viti-viniculture the equivalent of metallurgy and coal, of cereals and
other food crops readily transformed and increased by scientific and technical innovation. They have been up to now the losers. To them, innovation on a vast scale would lead to a highly profitable rise of yields and

productivity, as it had in industry and cereals. The market would simultaneously expand as new drinkers chose wine to enhance their gaiety or to drown their sorrows. In their calculations they were right, but only partially. Consumption did increase, but not to a level that absorbed all the common or jug wines that these growers poured into the market. There simply were not enough drinkers seeking joy or solace from mediocre beverages. On the contrary, the increase of consumption that brought in profits occurred among an increasing population of middle-class professionals whose high levels of taste demanded superior wine. Changing class structure has had a marked impact on the market for all beverages. Unfortunately, enhanced production did not magically lead to improved quality. Too many growers confused magic and science, and discovered the limitations of both.

It was precisely in this respect that the wine revolution differed conspicuously from the industrial and general agricultural revolutions. The participants of the latter augmented production while lowering cost per unit and, over time, have turned out preferred goods. But when vines have been forced to enhance their yields beyond a certain limit, the quality of their juices and the wines made from them steadily deteriorated. The industrial and agricultural revolutions were mistakenly perceived as models for viticulture. Therefore modernization assumed different forms. Availing themselves of enological research and technical breakthroughs, both grape growers and wine makers applied the innovations in different ways: some to enhance value by limiting yield, others to expand quantity at the expense of quality. In so doing they created a series of problems of such proportions that they have resolved them only imperfectly even today. And recently-created vinifera hybrids capable of giving yields over 100 hl/ ha with adequate alcohol and acceptable taste may put an end to the old ratio of yield and quality for ordinaries, but they will most likely worsen an already intolerable situation.

My wording here may run the risk of dividing the people engaged in the wine industry into two distinct and hostile factions. This view is not entirely erroneous; there have always been several classes of wine, just as there have been classes of wine makers. Remarkably, like social classes in general, they rarely marry outside of their assigned strata. As for wine itself, a château lafite commingling on the same shelf with a jug wine of the lower south would be considered slumming, and if blended, miscegenation. But between the lofty and the base, and their respective producers, there are hoards of growers who, like their forebears in the past, turn out a range of medium wines, neither highly prized nor scorned as "plonk," an appropriately expressive English term for low-grade jug wine. Between the two extremes, most growers and blenders have acquired and come to rely on advanced cultural and enological techniques that have enabled them to offer buyers a great variety of sound but not always inspiring beverages in corked bottles with fancy labels—the kind that white-collar workers drink daily with meals and that blue collar workers look upon as a treat for their Sunday lunch, if only because they have a cork in the bottle. Most of this middling wine, incidentally, is marketed by merchant-blenders, who buy young wines, mature them, usually blend them to create a brand style, and then sell them under a house label. It is at this level of the trade that modernization has had a truly revolutionary and profitable impact.

Increased profits have resulted in large part from increased yields, a phenomenon that is almost universal and one of the most financially beneficial results of advanced viticulture. Augmented yields have not in themselves created a hierarchy of wines; that is due to the amount of the increase, the specie of grapes, and the care and skill exercised in production. Quality-minded vignerons have augmented their yields moderately, mass producers more heavily. The latter, blindly driven by a domestic market that diminishes each year, have lost sight of reality and, in their desperation, try to force the French to drink their wine by using violence to keep out all competing wines of foreign origin.

Fine growers have been more subtle. They too are market driven, and are incredulous when anyone mentions the rise of yields above historic levels. At times, when reading their advertisements, it is easy to believe that the wine revolution somehow by-passed the great Bordeaux estates and their exiguous Burgundian equivalents. Indeed, several great Médoc châteaux were still using oxen to draw plows long after World War II had ended. This persistence, however, was not merely a technological anomaly, but also excellent publicity. Managers of the first-rate vineyards and wineries were circumspect as well as pragmatic. They knew that their wines were world renowned and had enjoyed two hundred years or more of fame. Why, then, change? Yet, with some trepidation, given the traditionalism of their profession, they began to introduce new devices and techniques in their cellars already a decade or so before World War I. Even then, some of them resorted to concrete vats with interiors covered by acid-resistant enamel or glass. The changeover, however, was slow until the 1960s and '70s. During these two decades the viti-vinicultural transformation attained truly unprecedented proportions, which resulted in part from the greater accessibility of financial credit and the willingness of a new generation to use it.

The magnitude of the wine revolution can be better understood by the five dimensions that I will discuss more fully later in this book. (1) In *science* there was the discovery of vast areas of knowledge that dissipated many of the mysteries shrouding the wine-making process. (2) *Technology* brought the introduction of a vast array of new machines, and a rapid shift from simple, hand-operated to fully automatic models. (3) *Economically* there was a considerable increase of wealth accruing chiefly to the makers and sellers of fine wines. (4) This increase was closely associated with the *social transformation* of the French and European population, in particular the rise of an affluent bourgeoisie and the decline of the industrial and rural proletariat, which also occurred in the viti-vinicultural population. (5) Finally, the reversal of *governmental policy* became conspicuous and was a great stride away from the traditional "hands-off" attitude and toward control and regulation.

None of these changes occurred in a vacuum. Rather, the revolution of the wine industry was simply another aspect of the transformation of France—and all of Europe—since the beginning of the century. Inevitably, as in every kind of revolution, mutations in life-styles affected various grape and wine producers differently and decided the destinies of those who profited and those who lost out.

CHAPTER ONE

General Trends and Conditions since 1914

WINE IN WORLD WAR I

It was unfortunate that Europe was not ruled, in the late summer of 1914, by men who tended vines. They would never have made war. How could they have contemplated any activity other than the preparation of their baskets for grape harvesting and their vats for wine making? They were not lacking in patriotism, nor were they all averse to violent collective action, as they had revealed on several occasions in the past. Their desire for peace in August and September would have resulted rather from their personal interests. As a vintage year 1914 was promising of grapes of ample quantity and good quality. Of course there had been spring frosts, some loss of flowers, attacks by insects and powdery mildew, but these adversities had merely reduced the crop, making for higher prices, and had not lessened the richness of sugar, which would also boost value by increasing the alcohol level. When August came, all growers were eagerly prepared to harvest a fine crop of grapes, not to make war. A generous fate, however, was not on their side. The nations of Europe were ruled by nationalists whose attention and territorial appetites were fixed on boundary lines, not vine rows, and who threw Europe into a war that unsettled or destroyed the peaceful ways of life learned during most of the nineteenth century.

The conflict, breaking out just as the grape harvest was scheduled to start, had an immediate effect: nearly all the healthy males over eighteen were called to the colors. Peasants, among whom were a large contingent of vignerons, filled out the ranks of foot soldiers, the *poilus*, the cannon fodder, as they came to be called. They did not depart alone. Their animals—horses and mules—were also conscripted to transport provisions, draw artillery, and provide mounts for the cavalry. Left at home were women, children, and old folk, and it was they who picked a record crop of grapes and who produced nearly sixty million hectoliters of wine, well above the forty-four million of 1913. This harvest undertaking was of truly heroic proportions.[1]

Of equal magnitude was the problem of marketing the wine. Here was a dilemma unique to vignerons. Growers of cereals, green crops, meat, and wood did not find their markets so suddenly disorganized by conscription and by the ferocious battles resulting from national hatreds. The government and its need to feed millions of troops replaced their foreign markets. These troops, it must be noted, marched on the strength of their stomachs rather than that of their bladders. Although a small serving of alcohol (one-sixteenth liter) had been issued daily until 1901, wine did not enter soldiers' rations until 1908, when the Chamber of Deputies voted two million francs for wine, to help distressed producers. By 1914 the ration for troops on maneuver came to a mere quarter liter, hardly enough to improve the market.[2] Worse, with the outbreak of war, producers, especially those in the Midi and the west, suddenly faced a loss of European markets as well as a lack of vehicles and rail transport, both monopolized by the government for military needs.

A solution emerged from the Midi where nearly everyone accepted as gospel the notion that wine is a health-giving beverage. There was no doubt, growers affirmed militantly, that wine-drinking soldiers are more valiant in battle and resistant to typhus.[3] Whether myth or truth, this belief, along with a combination of patriotism and self-interest, induced some Languedocians to send about 200,000 hectoliters of their *gros rouge* to military hospitals and camps, asserting that all soldiers needed a wine ration. They even paid the taxes on it, and the *Revue de viticulture* could hardly be less than a vigorous advocate of this proposal.[4]

Alexandre Millerand, the minister of war in late 1914, decided to initiate the distribution of wine to soldiers. He reasoned that perhaps Pasteur was right in claiming that wine is a healthy drink, certainly safer than the local water supplied in the trenches. The ration began roughly as twenty-five centiliters per day, then rose to fifty centiliters in 1916, when the army bought six million hectoliters, and to twelve million the next year. This supply consisted of ordinary wine, *vin de consommation courante* (VCC), and government purchases absorbed vast portions of it, especially after the terrible vintage of 1915. Lack of manpower, fertilizer, chemical sprays, and animals, combined with adverse weather, had reduced that crop to a mere twenty million hectoliters, worse than the 1910 vintage. The problem of transport and storage of such large quantities was overcome by professional merchants who were in the army, the hiring of railway tank cars from private companies, and the creation of distribution centers at Montpellier, Narbonne, Nîmes, Marseille, Bordeaux, Rouen, and Paris.[5]

The producers of VCC in the south and Bordeaux were saved. They were more than saved; they were enriched. Money now flowed into the countryside as the price of wine and numerous other foodstuffs went up sharply. Before the war, ordinary wine sold for about twenty-five francs per hectoliter and degree of alcohol; by 1918 the average price was close to ninety francs for military purchases and over one hundred francs in the civilian market.* Inflation eroded some of this gain, yet vignerons were able to pay off debts contracted in the 1880s and after, when they or their parents had borrowed to replace vines killed by the phylloxera. This was a boon for those who escaped death or mutilation in the trenches. For the lucky, the brave, and the clever who survived, favorable changes had taken place during their absence and after their return. Most notable was the increase in wine consumption after the war. Men who had rarely or never tasted wine had acquired a penchant for it, and they, added to the number of long-standing drinkers, provided a sizable market during the decade following hostilities, when consumption climbed to seventy million hectoliters, an average of 136 liters per head by the mid-twenties. Given the terrible experiences of *poilus* during the four years of slaughter, those who returned home had an almost unquenchable thirst.

Even before the armistice brought an end to fighting in November 1918, grape harvests were falling short of demand. Women, adolescents, and old men could not maintain the vineyards. Their weaknesses were compounded by the scarcity of work animals and of chemical sprays. After the skimpy crop of 1915 the government, concerned that low supply caused prices to rise unduly, began importing wine, two to four million hectoliters, from Spain and Portugal, and even from Argentina until the Atlantic crossing proved too expensive. Imports from Algeria rose to eight million hectoliters in 1915, then fell to two million in 1917 and 1918. In places where native Moslem workers were numerous and cheap there was no labor shortage. Spain, on the other hand, exported not only wine but

* Ordinary wines have long been priced by their alcoholic content, usually the only element differentiating them. A hectoliter with ten degrees of alcohol selling at 25 francs brought a revenue of 250 francs.

also thousands of workers, because the labor shortage became increasingly acute. German prisoners were sent to farms and vineyards to help with harvests, but only large estates could use them because the war ministry required a contingent of at least twenty workers, and seven soldiers to guard them. I know of at least one case in Vosne-Romanée in Burgundy where a prisoner was an expert vigneron; he overhauled the property, improving it beyond the capability of its owner.[6] Indeed, growers in eastern France, nearer the front, were lucky inasmuch as they could hire off-duty soldiers to help out. The army even released many men at harvest time precisely so they could pick grapes.

The major wine regions of France underwent various experiences in wartime. It seems likely that growers of VCC benefited more than those committed to the production of fine wines. The Languedoc-Roussillon vineyards profited on a grand scale, although in economic, not human terms, for numerous vignerons never returned from Flanders fields and were buried far from their vines. Before 1914 many of them had cried out against the excess of political centralization in Paris and the cultural imperialism of the north. Once war broke out, however, they rallied to the tricolor with unstinting patriotism and fervor—and paid the price.

The region of Bordeaux, on the other hand, passed through a more traumatic experience. No less patriotic, the Bordelais, as the region and natives of Bordeaux are called, was less economically fortunate. Its VCC sold well. It was an army supplier second only to Languedoc, but its viticulture differed dramatically from that of the south. Its VCC fetched a higher price as a product of more solid quality, 46.50 francs per hectoliter as compared to 35 and 42 francs for seven- to twelve-degree wine of the Midi. Yet the Bordelais hardly broke the long cycle of depression that had followed the phylloxera of the 1880s. There was a persistence of adverse weather and mediocre harvests, and when the army began requisitioning supplies it took huge quantities, nearly a fourth of the crop in 1917, and fixed prices too low. Loud protests began, and representatives of the Gironde department called for an end to requisitioning.[7] Regional producers were adversely affected because they grew a larger amount of grapes for fine wine than those of the lower Midi. The army was not interested in fine wine for its soldiers and therefore provided neither a significant labor supply nor tax incentives; it just waited for the protests to dissipate. Meanwhile, Bordeaux fine wines, which constituted a significant part of the region's total production, were usually more profitable than simple wines, but still in serious difficulty.

The reasons for this result are not complex. First, all growers complained that the economics ministry was taxing French wines "out of existence." The ministry, however, looked upon fine wines as a luxury of the rich who should help pay for the war. This was not a very menacing "soak-the-rich" fiscal policy. The government simply did not intend to weaken private property and family wealth by a policy of highly progressive taxation on income, so the men in power relied on indirect taxes. It is true that a majority in the two chambers, deputies and senators, passed a progressive income-tax law during hostilities out of the need to finance the war, but they neglected to insist on its vigorous enforcement. That is, the fiscal bureaucracy did not see eye-to-eye with the legislature about taxes on income, and it preferred sales, transport, and property taxes as a means of augmenting revenues to wage an inordinately expensive war. Such impositions severely affected all wines, but superior ones in particular. Second, fine wines ran into protective tariffs and heavy internal duties in friendly countries such as Great Britain, which had the effect of raising retail prices and limiting consumption. Finally, major prewar markets, such as Germany, were closed or, as in Russia, curtailed by political turmoil that ended in revolution.

Burgundian wines suffered similar problems. There, as in Bordeaux, government prices were too low to cover all expenses, and although requisitioning was limited, it imposed storage costs on growers who had to keep the wine until the army could arrange for its transfer to the troops, an enterprise that could take months. During that time losses through evaporation consumed between 7 and 10 percent of the crop per year in estate cellars that were not sufficiently humid, and where small oak barrels were used for storage. Loss through evaporation was much less serious for VCC producers who used glass-lined brick vats with airtight covers, which curtailed losses during fermentation and storage.

It does not seem that the winegrowers of either the Loire or the Rhône Valley were in a position to benefit seriously from army acquisitions. They had only belatedly begun to replant after the phylloxera wiped out their vineyards, and had turned to other crops. Reconstitution in the Loire Valley made little headway as long as vignerons remained convinced that grafted vines would produce an inferior wine. Consequently there was little vine surface in either valley before 1914. Grape and wine growing were supplementary crops—really cash crops—but only part of a polycultural regime in which fruit (Loire) and olives (Rhône) were just as important—even more important as prices for wine declined after 1900.

The vineyard region that did not at all benefit from the war was Champagne. When Alsace fell into German hands in 1870–71, along with much of the Moselle vineyard, France's most northerly vines were suddenly those of Champagne. Although one of the most prestigious wine areas, it was relatively small in size, only fourteen thousand hectares in the Marne department. Most of the vineyards were owned by individual growers who had one or two hectares and sold their grapes to the more than one hundred champagne firms. They were the men who rioted in 1911, full of anger against the firms that blended southern wine into the *cuvées* that were labeled as pure champagne. At the height of their fury they destroyed several wineries and spilled the contents of vats, barrels, and bottles into gutters until the towns reeked of the acrid odor of stale wine. The first battle of the Marne, however, made that destruction seem trivial. The Germans launched a massive campaign through the Ardennes, a maneuver that convinced Champenois like Monsieur Moreau-Berillon that the "Huns" had not been satisfied with robbing France of her Alsatian vineyard in 1871—they started the war in 1914 to take over Champagne as well. When French artillery finally halted the German advance, Monsieur Moreau-Berillon, like all other winegrowers, was convinced that the soldiers' wine ration, their *pinard*, had instilled in them the ferocious fighting spirit that saved these precious vines.[8]

Well, not the vines, merely the land. When the Battle of the Marne ended in the stalemate of immobile trench warfare, the vineyards of Champagne became part of a long battlefield. And on the battlefield, where civilization was doggedly struggling against barbarism, champagne was the *vin de civilisation*, as Talleyrand had once put it. The old vineyard was thoroughly destroyed, largely by fighting and trench-digging, but also by the inability of vignerons to defend their vines against another old enemy: the deadly aphid, phylloxera. When this plague had struck in the 1890s, growers, aided by the larger firms, had sought to defend their own-root vines by the use of carbon bisulfide (or disulfide), a powerful chemical injected into the soil near the roots, which killed enough of the aphids to save the plant. It was a terribly costly process but enabled growers to replant slowly so that they could continue to harvest the fine grapes of old vines while new vines matured. Delay of reconversion was also the result of highly chalky soil in which pure American rootstock, resistant to the phylloxera, suffered from chlorosis.

The vignerons of Champagne displayed a remarkable heroism. They often tried to tend the vines that did produce a crop during the war years, and to harvest them while under fire from the enemy. These were the vignerons who lived in the countryside. The city of Reims had been evacuated early in the war, and for good cause: it was a favorite target of German artillery. In 1918, when the Germans tried an advance on Château-Thierry, far from the vineyards, they bombed these vines, as well as the city of Reims, mercilessly. The result, over four years, was catastrophic: nearly 40 percent of the prewar vineyard died, and no one knows how many bottles of wine were either destroyed or consumed by both German and French troops. The former were never forgiven. French troops, on the other hand—often stationed in the deep cellars of the firms—were forgiven even though they had well fortified themselves with sizable quantities of wine. The rationale was that "they had kept it from falling into German hands," or rather, into their gullets, and surely they had been incited to fight more heroically by the invigorating qualities of French wine. When the armistice was signed in November 1918, over half the buildings of Reims had been fully or partially destroyed, including the cathedral, whose towers, the Germans claimed, were used as military observation posts. Whatever the truth, the vineyards of the Marne, and most of the champagne firms of Reims, were in ruins. The huge cavernous cellars deep underground were untouched, but their contents were diminished.[9]

This was not the first time that Champagne had played an unwilling host to foreign invaders. In 1814–15 Russians, Prussians, and some English had, in their fight against Napoleon I, passed through Reims. They did not destroy vineyards. There was no trench warfare. There were no artillery duels. Army officers simply helped themselves to bottles. In this case, they developed a taste for the product and, after the war, ordered sizable quantities of it for their festive occasions. Losses were easily recouped within less than a generation. This was not to be the case after 1918: the Russian nobility was overthrown, Prussian nobles were seriously weakened by the creation of the Weimar Republic, and the English aristocracy as well as the upper bourgeois suffered economic setbacks in the early 1920s, dampening their enthusiasm for the "bubblies." The champagne industry, at least for a while, did not benefit much from the peace, even though it had suffered so much from the war.

THE INTERWAR: PROSPERITY

The First World War marked an important step in the history of winegrowing. Most important and tragic was the massacre of many cultivators, men in the prime of life who did not tend a few vines merely to provide the family with a mediocre beverage that was safer then water, but those who put most of their wine or their grapes on the market. This does not mean that a majority of growers were exclusively vineyardists; most of them raised other crops as well, and still sought to grow much of their own food and the fodder required by their animals. Wine was an important cash crop in their budgets. They and the vignerons who relied entirely or more heavily on viticulture were about half a million in number, a calculation that I shall return to later. Possibly 10 percent of them were killed in battle and as many were maimed to the point where they could no longer farm their land. After 1918, therefore, a good deal of land was put up for sale, and widows and mutilated veterans tried to live on meager pensions augmented by the income from their land sales.

Except for the filled cemeteries, the situation after the war was somewhat similar to the one following the phylloxera crisis. It was a boon for the lucky men who came back in good health, with a bonus from the government and some savings at home, and who were daring enough to buy additional parcels at reasonable prices and to equip themselves to cultivate these additions. These men became independent within a few years. Borrowing to buy land was still frowned on as an imprudent step in the rural world, and, as in the past, farmers tried to conceal their debts. Yet more and more of them turned to the mutual credit banks that played an increasingly important role in the modernization of farming in general and of viticulture in particular. Loans were long term and rates a mere 2 percent.[10]

As the years passed, an increasing number of growers saved or borrowed to buy land to plant vines and ignored the need for wine-making equipment. Rather, they began to establish wine-making cooperatives. The coops borrowed money to build wineries, enjoyed government subsidies, and proved to be the savior of small producers. The result of these changes was the near doubling of the average vineyard during the interwar years (1918–39) from two or three hectares to five or six.

On the whole, army service and the horrors of war had a maturing effect in the industry. Demobilized vignerons recognized their need to know more about their markets and how to influence them. From this need emerged the Office International de Vin (oiv, International Wine Office), which had been long in the making because of foot-dragging by several European governments. It began to gestate in the early 1920s and was finally given legal status in 1927. Member states sent delegates to meetings and paid dues, for a sizable budget was required to carry out propaganda in favor of wine, to root out fraudulent labeling, and to encourage heads of state to sign treaties helpful to wine sales. By 1928 membership included twenty-five nations.[11]

The interwar also witnessed a good deal of scientific study of viti-viniculture. Highly sophisticated research was carried on in the enology centers at Montpellier and Bordeaux, but many learned growers undertook research in their own vineyards and home laboratories. With regard to viniculture or wine-making, these efforts sought to discover the many chemical components of wine, as well as the ways to preserve wine during fermentation and storage. As to viticulture, scientists studied the efficacy of various chemicals to control insects and fungi, and the effect of various pruning systems on grape quality. Agricultural machinery was also tested. This research was not confined to theory; it was practical in its aim, and it was put to use rapidly by means that I shall discuss later. The immediate result was an increased yield, that is, more grapes and juice per hectare. This bounty, combined with worldwide expansion of vine planting, led to an inordinate amount of wine, not merely in France, but all over the face of the earth. Table 1.1 shows the trend.

The vineyard area shown in the table is too large because it includes the areas between vine rows used by farmers in Italy and elsewhere to plant other food crops. A more accurate estimate of actual vineyard area at each time period reduces the numbers by at least three million hectares, which shows that the total area did not increase excessively during the interwar. Active planting was undertaken mainly in southeastern Europe, South America, and North Africa. But the quantity of wine itself came as a great flood, hitting a world population whose customs and religions often did not encourage alcohol or absolutely forbade it. The interwar period therefore was a time of recurring overproduction, with only short intervals of prosperity for vignerons.

Such a short period occurred immediately after the armistice. The world now had abundant reason to celebrate, and by 1918 a bountiful harvest contributed to dissipating all economic inhibitions. In a sense, the three

Table 1.1. World vineyard area and wine production

Area (in hectares)		Production (in hectoliters)	
1909–13	1935	1909–13	1935
8,949,800	9,623,400	142,183,900	217,994,000

SOURCE: J. Masson, *Crise viticole en Gironde* (Bordeaux, 1938), 57.

or four years following the war were really a continuation of the active sales and high prices of wartime, at least for ordinary wine. Prices reached their peak in 1919–1922. As noted earlier, the millions of returning soldiers had acquired a taste for wine. Per capita consumption rose from about 100 liters in 1913 to 136 liters in 1926. But this increasing thirst did not buoy prices, and they began to ebb in 1920. According to Rémy Pech and Augé-Laribé, growers suffered decreasing profits, and if inflation is factored in, their revenues tumbled by two thirds after 1920.[12]

Before this reversal became catastrophic, however, cultivators of vineyards of all sizes enjoyed prosperity in an inflationary economy. Inflation in France was mild compared to that in the new German republic, and French wine drinkers were not as severely affected as German ones. The French republic was far wiser in managing economic problems than the Weimar government, but the fall in value of legal tender was still an irresistible force everywhere. In France rising prices consumed a good 25 percent of the franc's value in the early and mid-1920s. This period was just long enough to enable growers to pay off long-standing debts that were made trivial by the falling value of money. And with cheap money available, growers were able to renew their equipment, fix up their housing, and, more important, replant large sections of their vineyards, thus enhancing yields with young vines. Most of them survived the lean years of 1926–27. They thrived visibly in the few following years of rising prices, after Raymond Poincaré finally stabilized the franc at one-fifth of its prewar value.

In order to paint a more detailed picture of the 1920s, let us move from the general to more specific observations, and discover the great variety of conditions in French viticulture. From the Gallic point of view, one of the happiest outcomes of the war was the recovery of Alsace and the parts of Lorraine that had been taken by Germany in 1871. Vignerons of the old province of Alsace, however, may have had mixed feelings about the return. Under German rule they had enjoyed adequate markets in the non-beer-drinking section of the population. German officials were complacently lax about grape selection, sugaring, and chemical additives, with the result that the local wine had lost much of its earlier reputation. After 1918, when local producers had open access to the French market, they were nearly drowned by a tidal wave of cheap wine from the Midi. Their prices fell and they faced ruin. There was only one path to salvation, and that was to improve quality. This was a difficult path, however, because the vineyard had truly deteriorated during the war. Under the leadership

of the wine grower and deputy Gustave Burgur, vignerons began replanting with superior vines, such as Riesling and Traminer, uprooting hybrid
stock, limiting yields, and giving greater attention to vinification. Vineyards in the plains disappeared. In general, the more stringent laws of
France governing viticulture were beneficial, and the agriculture ministry
even sent experts to teach the locals how to improve their cultivation.
Wholesale merchants began to augment their budgets to include advertising. The French were persuaded that buying Alsatian wine was an act of
patriotism, and they responded. In 1927 the Syndicat des Propriétaires
Viticulteurs de Vignoble Alsacien opened a wine fair at Colmar, which
became an annual event. Because the vineyard area fell from 23,900 hectares in 1913 to 12,000 hectares in 1938, the latter including only the
best sites, the wine recovered much of the reputation it had enjoyed in
earlier centuries and even began to find buyers abroad.[13]

Moving southward, we change not only geography but general conditions as well, and the story is less happy. It was necessary almost to completely replant the Champagne region, and the growers, like the government, expected the Germans to pay for repairing the damage, but this did
not happen. Growers had to borrow heavily to restore their vineyards, and
the wine companies themselves were in no financial position to help as
much as they had been able to in the long struggle against the phylloxera.
Vignerons, many of whom had never resorted to American rootstock but
were now forced to do so, discovered that the costs of replanting had at
least tripled since 1914, and that costs of cultivating their vines had also
spiraled upward at the same rate. But the price the firms were willing to
pay for prime grapes amounted to only double their prewar offers. Fortunately, the harvests of 1919, 1920, and 1921 were excellent, though the
yield was way down in 1921. Heavy frost struck the young vines in April,
killing or wounding so many that four-fifths of the eventual crop was destroyed. Even with satisfactory prices, the vignerons would have suffered
a severe financial setback. But prices offered by the firms were low—only
2.50 francs per kilogram, whereas the growers demanded double that
amount. The firms were very exacting in the type of grape they would
accept: chiefly grapes from vines with a short trim, and absolutely no hybrids or vinifera grapes not listed in the appellation rules. The champagne
firms, almost all of which were still owned and managed by a family,
insisted on high standards. They wanted the same quality of product that
had enriched them before the war—a necessity to recapture their clients.

The export market, where most of the money was made, had declined during hostilities. In 1913–14, over 18 million bottles were sent abroad, in 1919–20 only 13.5 million. Sales in France, which rose from 8 million to about 9.7 million bottles, could not compensate for the loss since French consumers, preferring and investing more heavily in red wines from Bordeaux or Burgundy, favored the less expensive brands of white champagne.[14]

Both growers and shippers were hampered in their sales efforts by too many adverse conditions: the loss of the Russian market when the Bolsheviks captured power; the loss of the United States market because of Prohibition and a general return of protective tariffs, which affected luxury items such as sparkling wine; and, finally, rising national taxes on alcoholic beverages in Great Britain and even in France. England in particular had been the major market for the finest and most expensive champagnes; but English taste was soured by the postwar general economic decline, hastened as it was by the financial strains of four years of hostilities and the loss of numerous foreign buyers of textiles and metals. These unfavorable market conditions notwithstanding, the companies began to thrive once more, and sales efforts concentrated more heavily on domestic buyers and in finding new buyers in Canada, non-Bolshevik Europe, and Latin America. The later 1930s became increasingly prosperous.

Moving southward into the valley of the Saône River, we penetrate the great province of Burgundy. Unlike Champagne with its relatively small vineyard centered between Reims and Epernay, with the Côtes des Blancs hanging like a tail, and with a wine that was classified as fine, finer, and finest, the large vineyard of Burgundy turned onto the market some of the world's finest as well as some of its worst alcoholic beverages.

The truly great burgundies, which had been in competition with champagne for several centuries, suffered from the same adverse market conditions in France and worldwide; like makers of the sparkling product they, too, relied heavily on foreign markets. The best beaujolais growths fell into this situation as well. These wines had not benefited from military purchases and emerged from the war with serious problems. Unlike Champagne, Burgundy never became a battleground, save in the eternal war against insects, fungi, and bad weather.[15]

A sizable amount of ordinary burgundy, including much beaujolais and mâcon, consisted of wines consumed by the lower classes: coach drivers, grass bowlers, porters in the huge food market of Paris, artisans. These wines competed with the *gros rouge* of Languedoc, consumed at zinc-covered bars and bistro tables shabbily laid with oil cloth, where it was served in thick glass pitchers to men more interested in their card games or dominoes than in their drink. Local growers of this wine were usually general farmers who reserved some of their arable land for vines—more and more the hybrids that required less care—and sold either their grapes or newly fermented juice to *négociants-éleveurs*. These Burgundian negotiants formed over many decades, not so long ago, a close link between Burgundy and the Côtes-du-Rhône to the south by buying up the more alcoholic, deeply colored grenache and carignane wines from the Vaucluse and Châteauneuf-du-Pape, which they secretly blended into the common wine called *passe tous grain*, officially a mélange of Gamay and some Pinot Noir grapes. This wine managed to hold its own against the flood of jug wine from Languedoc. Rhône grapes were eventually prohibited in the blend, and their producers now prefer to sell the wine in bottles for a superior profit.[16]

In western Burgundy red grapes had given way to white before the phylloxera crisis. Just beyond Burgundy's borders, local growers in Sancerre, Chablis, Pouilly-sur-Loire, and Quincy decided, like those in Alsace, that their future depended on their ability to produce fine wines. Those of Chablis retained the Chardonnay grape; but those in the other localities experimented with the Sauvignon and succeeded in launching it on a brilliant career as the source of dry fruity beverages. They found it difficult, however, to create an image of excellence because numerous general farmers planted hybrids and vines of lesser quality to produce a mediocre mixture that unprincipled merchants sold under communal labels.[17] This same situation existed in the southern sector of the Côtes-du-Rhône, in Châteauneuf-du-Pape, and in lower Provence, where rosé was still a simple thirst quencher for vacationers during the heat of summer.

None—or very few—of the vignerons engaged in producing these simple wines found their efforts worth the labor. Therefore more and more of them uprooted their vines in order to use the land for other crops, or they sold their holdings altogether and left for the cities. The war itself contributed to this tendency, for while the killed-in-action *could* not return, many survivors *chose* not to return. Hence the interwar was a period of vineyards that declined in quality, if not in size, and of fewer vignerons.

The massive vineyard of lower Languedoc-Roussillon had, economically at least, benefited from the high prices paid by the war government. Returning veterans enjoyed about two more years of relatively high prices and were about to reconvert and modernize their holdings. But as elsewhere, prices began falling seriously in the early 1920s, a phenomenon that provoked vignerons to ask whether the investment could ever pay off.

Worse: as prices declined, costs rose, thanks to the weakness of the franc that began not long after the war. And vignerons everywhere were caught in this scissors grip: low prices for their produce, high prices for the articles they had to buy. For those who hired workers, wages made up half the total costs, and yet these wages were not sufficient to retain workers on the land. Since growers could not control prices, their only recourse was to cut costs. A few managed to obtain free labor by lending equipment and work animals to needy neighbors who performed various jobs in return. Most, however, simply reduced the frequency of plowing, spraying, and other work, and hoped for the best. If mildew or insects reduced the crop, then at least less wine would push prices up.

The ordinaries of Bordeaux had also benefited from massive military purchases during the war, but as in Languedoc, prices began to fall soon after hostilities ended. And while a weakening market was a sharp disappointment to peasant growers, it was even more disconcerting to the classed estates of upper Médoc, home of the great bordeaux. Unlike the vcc's they did not benefit from the war; to the contrary, they had not recovered from the prewar marasmus, and many had unwisely signed long-term contracts with shippers before the war ended, at fixed prices. When peace came prices rose precipitously for a few years, so it was the merchants who reaped in profits. Several châteaux had to be sold and fell into mercantile hands. The Ginestet family purchased Cos d'Estournel and Pomys in Saint Estèphe, the Cruse took over Château d'Issan; both were old merchant families. New families, outsiders enriched by wine sales to the military, also bought in. For example, Désiré Cordier, who had started as a merchant in Toul in northern France in the 1880s, acquired Château Talbot with its huge vineyard of 100 hectares, as well as Gruaud-Larose in 1936. With these properties as a base in the vineyards, he established himself as a merchant in Bordeaux.[18]

Winegrowers in the Loire Valley did not benefit greatly from the war; certainly wartime sales did not reverse the decay of prices and persistent low yields that had begun before 1914. The whites of Nantes, Saumur, and Vouvray were not on the army's wine list in its search for *gros rouge*; no one believed that white wine was a masculine enough drink capable of inspiring bravery and élan. Like beaujolais, Loire wines were sold in cafés, cabarets, and in the lower-class bistros and restaurants in and just outside of Paris, Nantes, and other industrial cities. Neglect of vineyards during the war required reconstitution afterward, and there was an effort to enhance quality—too much, perhaps, for although yields remained modest, so did prices. The wines simply could not hold their own against cheap Mediterranean concoctions that flooded urban markets.[19]

THE INTERWAR: DEPRESSION

A period of general prosperity, long and anxiously awaited, came at last in the late 1920s. Wine sales profited from rising incomes within France and in other countries as old markets opened again in England, Germany, Switzerland, and the Low Countries. Producers of fine wines, however, seem to have profited less than those sending out ordinaries. Yet all growers could now convince themselves that their earlier investments in replanting and new equipment had indeed been wise and profitable. Inflation, at last brought under control by Raymond Poincaré, checked the rise of costs even while wine prices went up. Winegrowers began to move out of the red—financially, that is, not viniculturally.

These rising expectations were stunned in late 1929 by the world crisis that began on Wall Street in prohibitionist America. Little could growers divine that this financial depression would bring an end to Prohibition in the United States shortly after the presidential elections of 1932. This happy result, however, had little immediate effect. The North American market could not save exporters in Bordeaux, Burgundy, and Champagne from catastrophe because neither post-Prohibition Americans nor their whiskey-drinking neighbors, the Canadians, became wine buyers on a significant scale.

There was simply too much wine, good and bad, for buyers who lost their jobs or who feared losing them. Even the wealthy, when they were not jumping out of windows, suffered declining incomes and black moods that hardly encouraged them to buy wines. To forget their troubles they guzzled hard liquor. Although France was slow to feel the effects of the depression, her fine wines suffered early. In Médoc, for example, the directors of Château Latour stopped issuing dividends and distributed, instead, a double ration of wine in bottles that were piling up in the cellar. Other estates followed the same procedure, for now there was more wine than income.[20] Growers, if they did not leave the land, once more began to uproot vines in order to plant other crops, or they simply resorted to the age-old practice of cutting back on the care of vines in order to reduce costs to match seriously reduced incomes. They were all in debt to branches of the Crédit Agricole, yet they had to grub up money to buy chemical sprays lest their vines perish. They were equally indebted to the grocer, the butcher, and the artisans who built or repaired their buildings and implements. The small vignerons began to grow their own food, to fish in nearby rivers, to sell wood if they owned trees or uprooted their vines for firewood. Hope in the future, for creators of fine wines dependent on foreign markets, was utterly crushed by the revival of protective tariffs that followed the crisis as industrialists and general farmers clamored for barriers against cheap imports. Internal taxes shot up in every state to pay for public works and fell heavily on luxuries such as superior wine. Champagne producers were hit very hard, for sparkling beverages were especially vulnerable; most politicians and their electors did not take them seriously, saw them as symbols of a frivolous life, and felt all the more virtuous by increasing taxes on them.

Growers of ordinary wines were not as rapidly disadvantaged because they sold largely to the national market. But their turn came, especially after the excessive harvests that began in 1929: France pressed seventy million hectoliters of its own, and Algeria sent nearly thirteen million more, for a total of about eighty-three million hectoliters. This represented an excess of at least seventeen million hectoliters. Mildew reduced the crops of 1930 and 1932, but the wine from the harvested grapes was detestable and hard to sell. Another record crop came in 1933, thanks in part to a rapidly expanded Algerian vineyard that had more than doubled in size since 1920. As usual, an oversaturated market caused prices to fall below costs.[21]

Southern growers became desperate and looked for measures to encourage wine sales. Intense publicity campaigns were called for, but they were costly. The growers urged the education minister to abandon schoolbooks hostile to wine. They insisted that restaurants include wine in their fixed-price menus so diners would learn to consume the beverage simply because waiters placed it on the table.[22] What finally emerged was neither a mountain nor a molehill, but the Statut de la Viticulture, a wine code of laws consisting of a series of measures intended to bring production and consumption into equilibrium. The code ended the fairly free market in wine, a topic that I shall discuss in more detail later. It was not entirely successful, but it was still a factor in the salvation of small vignerons.[23] Their number declined as many gave up the struggle, but they did not disappear as a class as some economists predicted. In fact, the limited number who abandoned their small plots put land on the market at depressed prices, making it possible for growers with either cash or credit to enlarge their own vineyards. These were the ones who survived. The struggle was not always easy, but survive they did into the later 1930s, when a modest improvement in the economy helped to raise wine prices. This modest improvement is difficult to explain: was it the normal aftermath of an economic depression, or was it the result of military spending that created jobs? Perhaps a combination of both. At any rate, military spending rose dramatically in France during 1938–39. It had already risen portentously in Italy and Germany, two dictatorships determined to wage war, and in Great Britain, despite Neville Chamberlain's blind policy of appeasement.

WINE IN WORLD WAR II

In 1939 war broke out once more, with a kind of *douce violence* on the Western front, just before the grape harvest. And once more able-bodied men were called to the colors. As in 1914, women, children, and the elderly were left to harvest. Fruit was extremely plentiful and, despite the lack of harvesters, produced one of the largest crops of the century. Those who picked early, in September, were able to fill their vats with grapes replete of juice and sugar; those who had to wait until October were troubled by wet and cold weather, and vatted a sorry crop. There was at least one benefit: those who remained on the land were able to vinify in peace. After Poland fell into German hands, the so-called Phony War began; save for air raids, and a few unsuccessful attempts by the Germans to break through the Maginot line, the war seemed to be confined to the Balkans. But that was only a lull. In early summer of 1940 came the enemy breakthrough, the Blitzkrieg, and in a matter of weeks France fell to Hitler. This time the Champagne vineyard was spared, relatively. In fact, France's vineyards emerged almost unscathed, and the casualties among vignerons were too light to leave the great gap in manpower that the far more destructive First World War had produced.

In July the seventy-odd years of the French Third Republic came to an end. The Germans occupied the north and the Atlantic coast; they controlled the collaborationist government which set up its capital at the city of Vichy in south-central France. The major goal of this puppet state was to transform what remained of France's liberal or free economy into a corporatist economy, really a state-controlled system. The ordinary wine market was already regulated by the Statut de la Viticulture; but wines entitled to an appellation of origin were not included in the statute, and therefore had enjoyed a free market. Marshal Philippe Pétain's regime intended to fix prices and institute rationing for all wines and cautiously approached a notion of price leveling. The latter of course did not occur because such a policy seemed to revive the hated egalitarian ideals of the Jacobins. The hierarchy of prices remained firmly in place, a reflection of the hierarchy of social classes that was an integral element of conservative traditions.[24]

The Germans quickly arrogated the privilege of buying wine—the best—at artificially reduced prices. In addition, they simply confiscated their preferred beverages, as they did in Champagne. In Bordeaux they went well beyond confiscating wine; estates owned by Britons and Jews were taken over by the Vichy government. The Nazis would certainly have taken over the fine old vintages of these properties had they not been hidden away in the cellars of Clos-Fourtet, owned by Fernand Ginestet in Saint-Emilion.[25]

The Vichy regime was also frustrated, at least partially, in its policy to control the cost of living. Many rural products—especially bread, meats, oils, and wine, had ceilings placed on their prices. As was always true in wartime, both sellers and buyers devised schemes to circumvent these restrictions. Black market operations quickly appeared for essential items, and for the French, table wine fit nicely into this category. So, along with bread, meat, and butter, there arose an under-the-counter market for ordinary wine. As in the first war, appellation wines continued to enjoy a practically free market. Consequently prices steadily rose for fine wine, but not always as rapidly as costs, therefore creating a kind of scissors grip that seriously limited net revenue. And vines, as in the first war, were continuously at the mercy of insects and fungi. Chemical sprays were rationed; to acquire an adequate supply of copper sulfate, vignerons had to turn in copper products: one kilo of copper metal entitled the grower to a kilo of the chemical. So they went through their cellars in search of old pots, worn-out implements, wall ornaments, anything with a trace of copper. To complicate further the woes of growers, metal wire was badly galvanized. It rusted quickly and had to be replaced soon, raising costs even more.[26]

Due to deteriorating vineyards, the quantity of wine began to decline. The regime therefore allowed the sale of *piquettes*, that is, second wine made by pouring water over the grapes that had been pressed to make the first wine. These *piquettes* had always been used as a beverage for laborers, even for family use, and their sale was prohibited. Now they could be sold if labeled as such and if they measured at least 3 percent alcohol. They were, after all, a source of taxation just like authentic wine. Their sale was restricted to the local towns.[27] It was difficult enough for negotiants to transport real wine, since gasoline was in short supply and rationed. They usually refused to pick up wine in winter because if a truck broke down, there was no assurance that it could be repaired quickly, and the wine might freeze. Growers became increasingly self-sufficient, rooting up some vines to plant cereals or vegetables, pasture a cow, or raise chickens and rabbits. Life was hard, but at least most of the able-bodied men returned to cultivate their vines after they were demobilized following the armistice. Humiliated by defeat, yes, but alive all the same, the generation that reached manhood after 1900 was physically and mentally mature, ready to create a future as vignerons. Its accomplishments since 1918 were still present and ready for further development. It is these accomplishments and their postwar evolution that constitute the second phase of the wine revolution.

WINE SINCE 1945

The second phase of the wine revolution began after World War II or, to be more precise, during the 1950s. The five years that followed the end of hostilities made up a brief period of indecision, when the French were torn between rebuilding their homeland and recovering their rebellious colonies in the Far East. The decision to do both was made by the politicians who had successfully dissociated themselves from the 1940 defeat, by younger new politicians who now entered the chambers of power, and above all by the bureaucratic technicians who survived the German occupation. In the end they were more successful at rebuilding than at reconquering. At home rebuilding was not intended to become restoration, but as it turned out the best they could devise was a political clone of the defunct republic. As an affirmation to build anew, they called their creation the Fourth Republic, a gesture acknowledging France's continuity with her past.

And yet, there was not, after World War II, a deep longing to recover all of the past. In its odd way the new government, under the guidance of Jean Monnet, put in place an economy that combined a private and a public sector, that is, a mixed economy. Since by war's end even liberals accepted the notion of *dirigisme*, the state created a supreme planning commission to direct the economy. The aim was to modernize French productive power.

The wine industry, as an important provider of exports, held a prominent place in the commission's plans, and it was through the commission's efforts that the industry entered its second phase of change in the 1950s. The first phase had not been a mere preparation for its successor, but was characterized by several major innovations: the Code du Vin, which is still the legal foundation of wine production, was introduced; the cooperative movement achieved its greatest propulsion and preferential legal standing; and the appellation of origin, a step that encouraged a considerable improvement in the quality of wine was created. The first phase made its greatest achievement in the fields of law and organization.

The second phase was distinct from the first in that it made its entrance with the introduction of machines, both in the vineyard and in the winery. It was less a time of legal arrangements than one of mechanization and the frantic search to augment productivity without sacrificing quality. Such wizardry sounds comparable to the alchemist's search for the philosopher's stone, but it was somewhat more successful. Lead was not transformed into gold, but in certain markets wine became known as "red gold." Legislation to control production and achieve excellence did not diminish; on the contrary, viti-vinicultural regulation has become a growth activity, exacted by both winemen and politicians, a self-perpetuating process stimulated by two other factors in this phase: a planned economy which entailed a burgeoning bureaucracy, and the extension of the European Common Market to the wine sector of each member state. Wine statutes and rabbits seem to share a common destiny, that is, both reproduce prolifically. The legal basis laid down in the 1930s remains solid, and new codes tend more to repeat the old than to break new paths. What is novel about the codes is their recognition that the introduction of mechanized processes is reducing the number of persons active in the wine industry; therefore they offer monetary compensation to growers of ordinary wines who cannot afford to convert either to mass production entailing lower costs per unit of output, or to boutique production seeking both high quality and even higher prices. Besides joining a cooperative cellar, independent-minded growers have had these two main alternatives since the 1940s.

Given that a new generation of growers has entered the industry and that they are more highly trained, more open-minded, and more enterprising than many of their forebears, dramatic change was inevitable. Economic revolutions emerge not only from their pioneers, but also from entirely new social categories, disciples, and worshippers. There must be innovators who surpass the pioneers in imagination and foresight, as well as technicians who create and manage the infrastructure of revolution: all the mechanical devices, the large spatial arrangements that accommodate the original inventions and their successive improvements, and their transformation into systems of production unrecognizable to the pioneers.

The remainder of this book is devoted to discussions of the many facets of the wine industry. I want to show how each area became modernized, and how they are all interlocked so that change in one link stimulated change in the others.

A note about the organization of the following chapters is now in order. Unlike this one, each is devoted to a main subject and its wider ramifications. And though I try to deal with events in chronological order—the main objective of most historians—temporal sequence may take second place when the main subject matter demands.

❧ CHAPTER TWO

The Viticultural Revolution

CHARACTERISTICS OF VITICULTURAL CHANGE

The first great change in grape culture of the nineteenth century did not result from the rapid and planned application of new techniques by forward-looking growers. It issued, rather, from the immediate need to reconstitute the vineyards of France and of Europe after their complete destruction by the phylloxera. The phylloxera cleared the way. Within a generation after 1870 the deadly aphid had spread everywhere. The earliest experiments were aimed at saving the vines by protecting their roots through the use of chemicals injected into the soil. Being too costly, however, injection gave way to planting American rootstock that was resistant to the insect's deadly attack, and to grafting traditional vinifera vines to the new stock. Such massive replanting required an enormous study of vines, soils, training systems, entomology—a review, really, of all the old viticulture. Several important changes that had been tried earlier provided pioneer growers with some pragmatic knowledge. The new vineyards that emerged were the creations of highly imaginative, knowledgeable scientists and educated landowners. Government-subsidized laboratories and experimental vineyards provided most of the financial backing for research; the remainder came from well-to-do estate owners and merchant firms, such as the big champagne houses. Most of the government's subsidies, of course, came from taxes on land, as well as on shipments and on sales of wine. In the end, growers, merchants, and consumers financed most of the innovations, as well as the dissemination of information about them.

The stage was set for the first phase of the wine revolution during the interwar. It was a rather hit-and-miss undertaking, part of a national effort to recover from a devastating war. But recovery took place under a government still unwilling to take a leading role, save to partially subsidize wine-making cooperatives. Only reluctantly did it become involved in legislation, like the one creating the appellation of origin. It took action again with the Statut de la Viticulture only when wine prices collapsed during the depression of the 1930s.

The second phase of the wine revolution, beginning in the 1950s, emerged mostly from the desire to modernize the viti-vinicultural branch of the general national economy. Certainly the catastrophe of World War II and the setback it brought to France encouraged a broad dislike of tradition and produced a new generation eager to experiment, to innovate. This eagerness fitted well with official policy aimed at creating a broadly planified economy. The second phase, therefore, was a more organized, orderly process, emerging from the minds of theorists and bureaucrats, an integrated part of national recovery, even a national resurgence to lift France out of the morass of depression and defeat. Thus forcefully impelled, French winemen took the lead in this viticultural renewal, as in fact they had done in the innovations brought forth since the phylloxera devastation.

This second resurgence of change also differed from the prerevolutionary period in that its advocates sought not so much to reconstruct a destroyed vineyard as to create a truly new viticulture that would bring both well-being and security to growers. To achieve this goal the national planners sought to control vine culture as well as the wine market, an aspect the Statut de la Viticulture had neglected.

The cultivation of vines has always been, financially, a most hazardous enterprise, and it was a rare occurrence for farmers, even when they called themselves vignerons, to rely entirely on grapes for a livelihood. Not until the second half of the nineteenth century did growers, chiefly those along the Mediterranean coast, resort to a monoculture of vines. They left to their children and grandchildren an agricultural legacy that became a style of life, not easily or voluntarily abandoned when no longer profitable because work habits and human values became intimately commingled.

STRUGGLE AGAINST NATURAL DISASTERS

The history of viticulture is one of man's continuous struggle with nature. This of course is true of all agricultural pursuits. Winters that are too cold, springs that are too wet, summers too hot and dry—any of these can reduce, or even destroy, harvests of corn, cereals, legumes but only for a year. Soon after, if the farmer retains his land, he can plant again and usually recover his losses. But grape producers, like all fruit growers, have depended on plants that require years to mature if newly placed in the soil, and years to recover from attacks by hail and pests. Vines, although their longevity is phenomenal, are also very fragile, and the forces of nature can be menacing as well as helpful.

One of the most deadly forces is hail. There are numerous legends about hailstones as large as baseballs plunging from a dark gray sky and shattering entire vineyards. Hailstones are almost always rather small, yet even so I have witnessed them cut down flourishing vines, leaving a swath of mortally damaged vegetation a hundred or more meters wide and twenty times longer. These storms usually occur in late spring or very early summer after new bright green leaves have appeared and buds have opened. Leaves are ripped to shreds and buds are divested of their stamens, their means of pollenization. If the wood is not destroyed, the vines will recover in time, but they must be pruned drastically and their crop is lost. It is rare for this calamitous phenomenon to occur in late summer.[1]

Vineyards in the central and more northerly parts of France are especially subject to hail. So it was in the Champagne district that growers first turned their attention to means of protecting vines. During the later nineteenth century various kinds of horizontally revolving screens were set up on a small scale to form a protective roof over vine rows, but the experiment proved too costly for general use. At the turn of the century some imaginative men in Italy, Switzerland, and France built a device that resembled the wide-mouthed smokestack of an old railroad engine. An explosion inside a thick chamber at the narrow base was to send up a powerful current of air capable of breaking up thick clouds in which hail formed. Quite a few of these *canons paragrèles*, as the French called them, were put in place, but they were soon abandoned. The current of air was never strong enough to break up the clouds unless they were very close to the ground. Vignerons were really defenseless. Some, in despair, bought insurance against the damage caused by hail; but except for a few large growers, the price of a policy was too high, and compensation covered only a small fraction of possible damage.

Not until after World War II was a slightly more effective system made available: the launching of rockets that exploded at a given altitude to create a disturbance of air capable of dispersing clouds. The fellows who launched them, however, did not seem capable of provoking the rockets to explode at the proper altitude. More recently, rockets filled with silver iodide have been launched from airplanes. This chemical causes the clouds to form very small snowflakes that fall and melt before reaching the ground. This method is only effective for a large area and therefore the growers must organize and pool their resources to carry it out when weather threatens. Hence the importance of regional viticultural organizations, usually called *syndicats*.[2]

Spring frost is another natural phenomenon that has plagued vignerons since antiquity, and there is only one practice that has been found useful: the cultivation of vine species that bloom too late for the chill of frost to destroy budding flowers. Over centuries of time, practical experience taught growers to retain only the species most appropriate to the weather patterns of their geographic locale. Like nearly all viticultural knowledge, this too was pragmatic: the result of trial and error. So too was the gradual adaptation of favorable species to the colder climate of northern Europe, in Alsace, the Moselle Valley, and Champagne.[3] Modern methods of defense have also proven effective. In 1985 a vicious late-spring frost descended and reduced the grape crop in quantity, yet the quality was superb. Such is the caprice of nature. A more unfortunate caprice of nature came in 1987 when a wet, cold spring, and an equally wet fall, set the climatic conditions for one of the worst wine-producing years of the century.

Hearty vine stocks generally survive even very cold winters. But from time to time winters become so cold that large numbers of plants die. Such were the winters of 1929, 1933, and 1956–57. The latter was the most deadly and in some vineyards almost as destructive as the phylloxera. The worst of conditions, the nightmare of vignerons, occurred. The month of December 1956 and some days of January 1957 brought mild temperatures—so mild in Bordeaux, the Loire, and Burgundy that sap began to rise in the wood. Then, during the night of January 31 and February 1, the temperature fell in twenty-four hours from over plus four degrees celsius to nearly five degrees below zero. A cold air mass had moved in from the Arctic. It then stayed for four days, plunging thermometer levels to nearly eleven degrees below zero, or even more for shorter intervals. Such a record cold froze buds till they were black. It also froze sap, causing it to break or split the wood, killing the vine. Forty-five percent of the vineyard of Bordeaux was totally destroyed, 40 percent was wounded and weakened, and only around 10 percent was left unscathed. Early ripening varieties like the Merlot suffered the most, along with many of the oldest vines whose juice had enhanced the quality of wine.[4]

There was some possibility of salvation if the roots and trunk were not frozen. Where branches were long enough, growers could resort to layering, burying the ends of branches so they would put out new roots. This was an ancient practice that had almost disappeared in the nineteenth century, and now it was hardly feasible because of the widespread use of short pruning, which reduced the length of branches, and vine grafting. Regrafting could also help save a vine on sound roots, but the procedure was very complex and required a long time, so it was limited to the vineyards of great *crus*. More widely used was a technique called *récipage*,[5] by which a thick cane or branch was used as a trunk and pruned so that it would become the bearer of the vine's branches after a couple of years. In the end, however, a massive program of replanting was necessary nearly everywhere. Such an undertaking turned out to be too expensive for indebted producers, and the vine area of France shrank all the faster. Bordeaux, especially hard-hit, lost 11,200 hectares; Burgundy, having suffered far less, abandoned only 300 hectares. More northerly vineyards, where temperatures were more consistently frigid, also suffered losses except where early fallen snow had protected the roots and trunks of the vines by covering them and thereby insulating them. The large number of newly installed vines, once they were five years old, were very fruitful, and the quantity of grapes for wine rose steadily in the 1960s and 1970s.

Surviving vignerons, of course, were confronted with the possibility of future freezes and how best to safeguard their vines against them. Since the 1950s, as we shall see, they had been borrowing money and investing heavily in new equipment and machines. Now they had to protect their investments and pay their debts, but extensive hardships were evident: young people threatened to leave for the nearest city; revenues fell; food rations were skimpy; buildings remained in disrepair; and many gaps remained in vine rows due to the failure to replant. Traditionally, when a freeze threatened, growers lit portable, oil-burning stoves and placed them throughout the vineyard, or simply burned humid straw from stables to create a protective covering of smoke and a slight warming of surrounding air. This practice, even when successful, was laborious and costly. Straw burned too quickly, and smoke was shown to offer no significant protection. As for the stoves, depending on size, a grower needed 150 to 250 per hectare, and they consumed up to two liters of expensive fuel oil each hour. Happily, after 1945, a combination of practical and theoretical knowledge worked out a system of water outlets for creating an extremely fine spray over the vines. The humidity that slowly covered the vine stock and the heat of fusion released during ice formation served as bases of protection. As long as additional water was available to form more ice, the temperature of the ice and plant would not drop below the freezing point. If the plant could carry the weight of the ice, damage would be minimal. Fine spraying has proven especially useful against spring frosts, which are fairly common in northerly areas and even in areas such as Burgundy. Yet on April 30, 1974 a sudden freeze wiped out vines in the flatlands of Beaujolais: clusters of newly emerging berries and leaves turned black, and they pulverized like dried tobacco.[6] Even if fine spraying could not save the principal bud of a vine, and sprayers were not available at the time, it might have saved the two secondary buds that can replace the dead primary one. They are not as productive and are often sterile, but they can keep the vine alive. Once they also freeze, along with the soil, the vine dies. Fine spraying, alas, is not a perfect solution to an age-old problem; it works marvelously but only when the daytime temperature rises above the freezing point so that the fine spray itself does not turn to ice.

Northern vignerons face many adverse cold-weather conditions, but southern ones, close to the Mediterranean where winters are less menacing, face the sometimes excessive heat of summer. By July and August the sun may become intense enough to bake the maturing fruit, causing skin to shrivel in a raisinlike fashion. The juice becomes unbalanced because the sugar level is raised at the expense of acids. The resulting wine, if not blended, will have a faded, cooked taste. Salvation lies only in moderate irrigation to maintain adequate sap flow, and in preserving a heavy foliage to screen grapes from the heat.

Winter, spring, summer—all pose dangers. But autumn, if the vines and their clusters have fared well, has always been the season of rejoicing: it is harvest time. It is a time of levity, and yet it is the season when the grower has no protection against his greatest final enemy, rain. If rain threatens a plentiful, maturing harvest, the grower may, as has often happened in the past, begin to pray and call upon the priest to pronounce the holy—or magic—words that will dispel the clouds. Or, he may decide to pick before the grapes achieve full maturity and hope that the wine made of their acidic juice will be salable. Or, finally, he may harvest in the rain, crush grapes with rain drops on their skins, and risk getting a watery juice, low in both acidity and alcohol. Under these conditions, the main advantage of recently invented mechanical harvesters lies in their speed, and they offer the chance of saving a good crop menaced by rain. These harvesters were rare in France until the 1970s, because growers of fine grapes distrusted them, and they have been forbidden in Champagne. Fall is an unpredictable season: it can bring rain and ruin a beautiful crop, as in 1975 in eastern France; or it can bring sunshine and save grapes that had suffered from a cold, wet spring and summer, as in 1977 almost everywhere, though even then salvation was only partial and the harvest was mediocre.

STRUGGLE AGAINST PESTS

Since time immemorial vines have been attacked by myriads of insects and fungi. Until the nineteenth century, however, vineyards were rarely large in size. They were interspersed with other crops, often with considerable space between them, and were spread all over France. Devastation in one area therefore usually had no effect on other areas. This age-old viticultural geography came to an end in the nineteenth century. The phylloxera and the building of railroads led to the disappearance of commercial vineyards in unsuitable areas, and to the concentration of vines in more favorable locations. Replanting after the phylloxera, actively carried out from the 1880s to 1914, led to the wide distribution of rootstock that was often contaminated. Various insects were all the more easily spread by fast transport, by the concentration of vineyards in certain regions, and by the vineyards' considerable growth in size. By the late 1880s growers, after having planted native vines grafted onto American rootstock, were shocked to discover that their vineyards were under massive attack by various insects—moths, beetles, spiders—and that their only defense consisted of frequent spraying with high-priced insecticides. This increased their overall costs of production and added to the labor they had to expend during spring and summer. Many growers were unsophisticated vignerons, with little more than an inherited knowledge of viticulture. They often did not fully understand how properly to mix water with the chemical powders they purchased to make the insecticides. In a concoction called *bouillie bordelaise*, it was absolutely necessary to mix the correct amounts of copper sulfate, lime, and plain water. It was effective against mildew if applied early and frequently in wet years, yet harmless to the consumer because rain washed it off.[8] Sulphur powder was also sprayed onto vines; it was a complement to copper sulfate, yellow in color rather than blue. Both, of course, were dangerous to the health of the vigneron when he used a backpack tank. With this device he worked a lever to build up pressure, and he had a short hose with a nozzle to spray each vine separately. After a day's spraying he was colored either yellow from sulphur or blue, like a Druid, from sulfate.

During the interwar, large growers began acquiring bigger tanks that were placed on the backs of animals. Because the animals' backs swayed as they moved, these tanks were less effective than tanks attached to a wheeled cart drawn by an animal, with sprayer pipes extending from both sides and capable of reaching four to six rows of vines to right and left. Technologically, this was something of an interwar revolutionette.

The vineyard that was literally re-created after the phylloxera invasion was a far more vulnerable enterprise. It was more subject to attacks by insects, fungi, rots, and virus diseases such as fanleaf, which was carried from vine to vine by threadlike worms in the soil that were not visible to the naked eye. The virus itself dwelled in the cells of the wood, not on the exterior, and was also not readily visible. Practically nothing was known about virus infection until after World War II. The unrelenting attacks of entomological and biological enemies required an unrelenting defense for survival, munitioned chiefly by insecticides that, since the 1940s, became much more effective—and also more expensive. In consequence, the costs of vine culture have risen greatly since the 1880s. The financial malaise that had set in before 1914 and continued during most of the interwar resulted in part from the failure of wine prices to keep up with mounting costs. The technological innovations that formed the basis of the second revolution after 1945 raised costs even more, thereby also raising the question of survival for a mass of small growers with exiguous revenues.

Changing Technology in the Vineyard

Major technological changes in the vineyard came mainly after World War II. That is, they appeared with the rise of prosperity of the wine industry as a whole. The interwar years, save for the late 1920s, did not provide the constant inflow of capital that was needed for the application of new discoveries in vine culture. The interwar generation was also not quite prepared for the dynamic entrepreneurship and use of credit that were necessary elements in viticultural progress. The sons of the growers who fought in the 1914–18 war were still under the influence of their fathers who came back from the front; or they were orphans who relied on tradition, not knowing what to replace it with. It took another war and a planned economy to inaugurate a truly new vine culture.

Before the horrors of 1939–45, the chief sources of traction in the vine-

yard were either the horse, the mule, or the ox. Of the three, the ox proved
to be the most enduring; some estate vineyards in Médoc used them until
the 1960s. The ox moved slowly and required more time to plow, but it
was the heartiest of all the animals, less subject to sickness and the easiest
to feed, grazing mainly on grass. The horse was more widely used than the
mule; although it was more subject to disease and required a more expensive diet of cereals in addition to grass, it was easier to train to walk and
turn among the vine rows and twice as fast as an ox. There was often
affection between horse and grower. Louis Chapuis, for instance, recalls
that during his adolescence in the Beaujolais he believed that plowing with
a horse was a most honorable profession. A horse, especially a tall per-
cheron, was a sign of wealth, and cost four to six thousand francs in the
1930s. Its useful life was ten to fifteen years. Chapuis and his horse had to
pass between each two rows of vines three times in order to properly plow
the soil. This work required strength and skill; the shear had to be kept
in a straight line, with the point deep inside the hard rocky earth—but
not so deep that it cut through roots and endangered the vine's health. It
was solitary work demanding constant attention and the right horse was
often a good companion.[9]

Horses lasted until the 1950s because they were still much cheaper than
the earliest forms of mechanized traction. The first tractors appeared before
1914, but the few then in use on large estates declined in number even
more after the war. Despite a serious labor shortage, growers with properties large enough to profit from machines continued to use horses, partly
because of the lower costs of animal power, partly because the early models
of tractors were ill-adapted for use in vineyards, and partly because new
models of plows were even less well adapted, some of them uprooting too
many vines. Replanted vineyards had usually allowed for about one meter
between vine rows, and there were practically no tractors small enough to
move, or even fit, in such a narrow path, especially after the spring and
summer growth of branches. Throughout Burgundy vine rows were even
more closely spaced so that nine to ten thousand vines could be planted in
a hectare. Only one type of machine was adaptable to such a high population density; it was called a *tracteur à pont* in a test run of various types
in 1932, and was the forerunner of the *enjambeur*, or straddle tractor, which
did not make its appearance until the 1950s. It was a machine built on a
frame shaped like an inverted U, with the motor and driver placed high
above the vine row and the wheels moving along the two alleys on either
side of the row. All these tractors were large and intended for use on big

properties. The small vigneron used various models of small motorized, hand-guided rototillers, much less expensive to buy and use than tractors.[10]

The interwar also brought on the market spraying devices consisting of large reservoirs and sprayer pipes that extended over two or three vine rows on each side. A motor worked the sprayer pump, and the entire apparatus was mounted on a cart drawn by an animal. It greatly reduced the time required for spraying, yet these devices, although machine activated, still relied on horse power. And horses also continued to draw wagons carrying grapes to the fermentation cellar at harvest time, and to transport supplies and people. In addition, wagons hitched to animals carried plows and other equipment from one plot of vines to another, for it was a rare vigneron who owned a consolidated vineyard. Most family properties consisted of scattered plots of land purchased or inherited during several generations of time, with the result that moving equipment from plot to plot caused a loss of time and transportation problems. Machine traction did not solve all these problems. Among the early tractors, the most efficient for plowing were those mounted on treads instead of wheels, but they were very slow moving from plot to plot, and useless for rapid transport of grapes and equipment.[11]

The high cost of tractors was at first a basic cause of their limited market in France. The vast majority of agricultural properties were simply too small to use them efficiently, and the low incomes of farmers, including vignerons, who were still unwilling or unable to borrow precluded their purchase. High costs also were a consequence of the artisan techniques of manufacturing. In 1939 about seven hundred companies were making tractors, chiefly for general farmers, and nine out of ten employed fewer than fifty workers. The 1,700 tractors put on the market in 1938 represented 150 brands. About two thousand artisans built tractors with the same or similar skills their fathers had used to turn out horse-drawn coaches and the earliest automobiles before Henry Ford introduced the assembly line.

Not until the 1950s, as a result of extensive mechanization, did viticulture enter its second phase, the true take-off of the wine revolution. Many inefficient factories disappeared during this and the following decades. First, manufacturing techniques were modernized when International Harvester and Massey-Harris opened shop in France in 1951. At once they began to miniaturize machines for sale to small farmers. In 1954

Ferguson also built plants in France and soon merged with Massey. Happily there was sufficient competition to bring prices down.

Again, growers in the 1950s enjoyed higher prices and began to accumulate the surplus capital they needed to mechanize. Land, of course, was still cheap, so many growers expanded their properties and, given a growing labor shortage, simply had to acquire mechanical devices to achieve efficiency and reduce costs. Credit was still cheap and now more easily available, thanks to government economic planning that demanded increased mechanization and subsidies for agricultural credit societies. Older men, although conservatively set in their ways, nonetheless found themselves borrowing and mechanizing. They had to. If the pressure of planning commissions was not enough to encourage modernization, the sons threatened to leave the land if their parents refused to renovate. With the bluntness of the young, they blurted out that they did not intend to spend the rest of their lives "behind a horse's ass." The plow horse, once man's friend, fell from grace. In fact, now the tendency was to overmechanize.

Small growers began purchasing *enjambeurs*, sophisticated spraying equipment to attach to them, and other devices that they could not use efficiently on their small scattered parcels. The more realistic resorted to machine driven rototillers at less than half the cost. Some growers even hired the local blacksmith to attach a steering device and rear wheels that transformed their tillers into miniature tractors.[12]

For a real tractor to be profitable a grower needs at least ten hectares of vines, and, according to agricultural economists, must work it a minimum of six hundred hours each year. This is a rather high rate of use and probably includes tasks other than plowing. An efficient machine could draw more than a single plow, and in one passage turn all the soil between two vine rows, whereas a horse-drawn plow required three passes to till the same width. Especially efficient were the rigs that attached a left-hand and a right-hand shear to the same shaft, throwing soil to both sides of the space between rows. Equally useful for weeding were the new row plows, designed to turn the soil between vines in the same row rather than the soil between rows. The automatic type was supposed to swing away from each vine so as not to harm it, and then move back into the vine row to uproot weeds. Wise growers placed tall pegs in front of each vine to make sure that the row plow did not strike and possibly damage the vine trunk.[13] Before and after World War II, many estates in Médoc were large enough to use tractors effectively, yet most of them did not resort to tractorization until after the terrible freeze of 1956 destroyed much of the vineyard. Replanted vineyards allowed sufficient space between rows for the passage of *enjambeurs* or narrow-gauge tractors.

In the Entre-Deux-Mers vineyard in the Bordelais, and the Hautes-Côtes of the Côte d'Or, regular tractors appeared as a result of the decision to experiment with a new viticultural system tried out in central Europe: high vines and widely spaced rows. The advantage here was that these daring growers could buy tractors of normal width, mass produced for general farmers and therefore much cheaper. Where medium width prevailed, about a meter and a half, growers resorted to narrow-gauge tractors, even though they were more expensive per horsepower.

An official body, the Institut Technique de la Vigne et du Vin (ITV), with official backing and a budget, stimulated various local vine growers' societies, the *syndicats*, to organize trial demonstrations of tractors and other useful machines, to set up courses in tractor driving, and to give training in accounting so that vignerons could more accurately analyze the costs of their material and their own labor. French vignerons were remarkably ignorant of record keeping, and the planning bureaucrats decided that mass education of farmers was necessary, not only in modern cultural technology but also in bookkeeping. The modern farmer, to survive, had to cease being a peasant to become a businessman. As for the vigneron, a term usually implying peasant status, he was to become a *viticulteur*, a person with expert, up-to-date knowledge. Modernization had become a state of mind necessary for survival.

The tractor became the focal point of viticulture. Introduced first for dragging a plow, it became an all-purpose device as special attachments were designed and added to it. I have already mentioned the motorized spraying implements that were drawn by tractors of various sorts during the '50s. Indeed, tractors became more useful for spraying than for plowing. A suitable *enjambeur* could carry a sizable reservoir of sophisticated insecticides and moisten three to four rows on each side of it. Its value for plowing, of course, was limited in viticulture. Many of the best vineyards were on fairly steep hillsides, and contour plowing on such a slope was dangerous because an *enjambeur* or a narrow-gauge tractor could suddenly turn over.

To avoid such an accident, some machines came equipped with hydraulic pistons to raise the downhill side. This lessened the chance of overturn without removing it, and greatly increased the purchase price. On very steep slopes, say thirty degrees, no machines could be used except one consisting of a motor anchored at the summit and fixed with a winch or capstan, and a cable attached to a plow at the base. The motorized winch then wound the cable that pulled the plow in a line perpendicular to the contour. The resulting furrows had to be crisscrossed by drainage ditches to check the rush of rain water that would otherwise carry away both soil and vines. Such drainage systems have usually been of little help in times of heavy downpours, and their upkeep represents a considerable output of time, money, and labor. Small wonder that vineyards on steep slopes, as in the northern Côtes-du-Rhône, have almost completely disappeared.

On properties too small to benefit from mechanization, the owner must either become a part-time worker on someone else's domain and therefore a part-time grower on his own land, or he must find a job in another profession and trim his vines in his spare time. His tools are a rototiller and a backpack sprayer. Recent models of the latter have a small motor rather than the traditional hand lever to activate the pump. This style of artisanal culture is, of course, a world away from that of the larger grower who uses either a medium tractor to sulfate twelve to twenty thousand vines a day or a large tractor to cover up to thirty-five thousand vines. Insecticide coverage of this dimension has saved many a crop against various mildews and insects during normal years, when about ten sprayings are required, but above all in wet years when salvation requires up to twenty sprayings. In some areas small airplanes or helicopters do this job more quickly but less effectively because they cannot moisten the underside of leaves.[14] Recently, however, their revolving blades have served as horizontal fans to dry grape clusters moistened by rain before harvest.

Attachments devised for use on tractors have grown in number, especially those designed to facilitate the one task that has resisted mechanization: pruning. Pneumatic pruning shears have eased the job on large estates, where gangs of workers attack vine rows with a mobile compressor and move along rapidly, each trimming several hundred vines a day. But the human mind and the dexterous human hand have not been replaced and will not soon be replaced by a mechanical device, not for the final act of pruning that demands observation and judgment. As Louis Chapuis puts it, "Pruning is a dialogue between man and vine." And says "Papa" Bréchard, "In the pruning of vines there's a bit of instinct and there's a bit of reasoning."[15] Preliminary pruning, however, has become mechanized. Tractors with large rotary-blade attachments can cut away the heavy foliage—canes and leaves—that remains after the harvest, exposing the trunk and thicker branches. Thus the vigneron can quickly see the remaining canes and carry out the final hand pruning more rapidly. These blades can be adjusted to function vertically or horizontally and consequently can be used for the traditional task of *rognage* (topping) in July before the harvest—the cutting off of branch ends, useless wood, and leaves so sap will concentrate in the grape clusters and produce a desirable balance of sugar and acid in each grape; when that is achieved, the time to pick has arrived.

The mechanical grape harvester is the latest and most controversial machine to appear in the family of machines that constitutes this viticultural revolution. Every vigneron I have interviewed agrees with the utility, indeed the desirability, of an *enjambeur*, mechanical sprayer, pneumatic shears, and so on. But growers of fine grape—*cépages nobles* is the term they used—have looked upon this monstrously large machine with suspicion at best, and more usually with hostility. Watching it approach is really a frightening experience at first; the thing assumes the awesome appearance of a mastodon. Its foes argue that clusters must be picked by experienced, gentle hands so that the skin of berries is not broken. The issue is academic, however, for the classed vineyards, save in Bordeaux, are usually located on hillsides too steep for all except some lighter models of harvesters.

Their use, beginning seriously in the 1970s, is largely but by no means exclusively confined to the larger vineyards in the Bordelais (1,700 machines), Languedoc (1,500), the cognac region of the Atlantic coast (1,636), the lower and middle Loire Valley (382), the southern Côtes-du-Rhône (266), and the reemerging vineyards of the southwest (585). In the latter region harvest contractors purchase the machines and sell their services for a price. One may think it is odd that the machines have not spread more widely along the Mediterranean coast, but this oddity can be explained. According to Pierre Vagny, the fact that 75 percent of the vines there are raised in the *gobelet* (goblet) or head-pruning system, without wire trellises, makes them ill adapted to mechanical picking.[16] Special machines have been designed for this purpose, but they are still less cost-effective than cheap immigrant labor because of their high price and inefficiency. In Burgundy their use was limited until 1985, when growers became convinced that the machines did not harm grapes and bought them in large numbers. For the harvest of that year, 260 machines were sent into vineyards on flat or slightly inclined surfaces. They are only now making an appearance in Alsace and the Côtes-de-Provence. They will undoubtedly spread farther, perhaps even into Champagne where they have been prohibited since 1978 by the CIVC.

According to François Bonal, studies in Champagne revealed that wine

FIGURE 2.1. Terraced vineyards in the Banyuls appellation of Roussillon. Here, as in the upper Côtes-du-Rhône, vignerons must cultivate their vines by hand or with rototillers. Noticeable are the extensive bare patches behind supporting dry-stone walls, where growers have not replaced uprooted vines, and the full rows lower on the slopes where tractors can be put to use.

FIGURE 2.2. An *enjambeur*, or straddle tractor.

FIGURE 2.3. A horse-drawn sprayer in a vineyard south of Bordeaux.

FIGURE 2.4. Close view of a power sprayer with a nozzle that moves from side to side in order to cover several rows of vines.

FIGURE 2.5. A rototiller is used for cultivating the soil in small vineyards.

FIGURE 2.6. His majesty, King Grape. The clusters hang close to the rocky soil to benefit from heat reflected from the sun's rays.

FIGURE 2.7. Women and men harvesting the Corbières, Aude, about 1903. The low-pruned vines typical of this area required endless bending, which is still true today. Save for the clothing, little has changed in the methods of hand harvesting. The women pick and the men carry. (Photo in collection of Rémy Pech)

FIGURE 2.8. *Comportes* loaded on a wagon for the transport of grapes to the winery.

FIGURE 2.9. Traditional handpicking of grape bunches survives on small properties, and also in larger vineyards of the Midi, where the gobelet pruning system does not lend itself easily to machine harvesting.

FIGURE 2.10. A Carrier unloading grape clusters. At the bottom of the trailer is a stemmer-crusher and an outlet pipe that will be attached to a pumping system at the winery to send the skins and juice either directly to a press for the white fruit, or to a fermenting vat for the red. A tractor hooked to the trailer will attain a speed well above that of mules.

FIGURE 2.11. (*left*): Mechanical harvesters generally are equipped with stick beaters to strike each vine as they pass over it, causing grapes to fall onto conveyor belts that transport them to a container. The above is an American model sold in France.

FIGURE 2.12. (*below*): A small mechanical harvester pulled by a narrow-gauge tractor. Considerably lighter in weight, it proved its efficiency during the rain-drenched harvest of 1987 when many larger self-propelled machines became bogged down in the mud.

FIGURE 2.13. Vines awaiting the pruner. Mechanical prepruning will remove the ends of the long canes.

FIGURE 2.14. Mechanized perpendicular and horizontal hedging shears; they eliminate excess cane growth in order to facilitate spraying and hand pruning after the harvest. No machine has appeared that can replace the human hand.

FIGURE 2.15. Hand pruning is the traditional method of training vines. Monsieur André Brunet here demonstrates his technique with a long-bladed pair of shears. The canes were "prepruned" with a mechanical shearer.

made from mechanically picked grapes contained excesses of potassium, iron, and nitrates, all of which disturb the equilibrium of musts. Recent experiments have shown that the iron content of machine-harvested grapes is five to six times higher than those picked by hand. This rate increases the possibility that the resulting wine will be spoiled by *casse ferrique*, a malady causing a pronounced haze and metallic taste. On the other hand, according to Bourdier, the level of phenols diminishes, giving the wine more suppleness and deepening the color of reds. In addition, a slight rise in volatile components, especially alcohol, has been observed.[17] There are other serious drawbacks that must still be overcome. For instance, delicate berries suffer broken skin, which is why the machines are not used in Beaujolais and in southern wineries that ferment musts by means of carbonic maceration. A "satisfactory" machine can still break up to 50 percent of the crop! Even with less damage, juice will become oxidized when it seeps out if it is not protected from the surrounding air. The crop must immediately be sulfited or sent into air-free containers for conveyance to the winery. This is not a major difficulty but it raises costs.

More serious is the inability of mechanical harvesters to pick out rotten grapes that are indiscriminately mixed with good ones on the conveyor belts. Perhaps an acceptable solution will be found to this problem. Still in the experimental stage is a method devised by the shipping firm of Yvon Mau and the Enological Institute at the University of Bordeaux. Called "cryoextraction," it operates on the principle that berries that are less ripe freeze more rapidly than fully ripe ones. By using very low vat temperatures to freeze immature grapes, and pressing immediately, only the ripened fruit gives up its juice for vinification. This process would have been particularly valuable in a year like 1987 when grape maturation was uneven. Of course such an operation, if it proves to be successful, can be instituted only by very large firms and cooperatives able to bear the expense. That this problem exists at all undermines the assertion that mechanical harvesters detach only ripe grapes, leaving the unripe fruit on the stems. This selection sometimes happens, but not always.

Other problems remain. Mechanical harvesters leave about 65 percent of the stems on the vines, depriving wine makers of their use when the juice needs more tannin or, in the case of white grapes, when pressing, because stems facilitate this operation. Finally, leaves and other foreign matter are mixed in with the grapes, albeit not in great quantity, when the machine's beaters are shaking the vines. More sophisticated harvesters with air cleaning systems have partly eliminated this problem, but they remain enormously expensive and beyond the means of all but the largest growers. To compensate for these drawbacks, mechanical harvesters make it possible to gather quickly a higher proportion of clusters when grapes are ripe and conditions are optimum. Hand picking in a large vineyard takes two to three weeks, a length of time during which rain can fall and berries can lose acidity.

The disadvantages, however, are of concern. There is an approaching saturation of the machine market that has influenced the rate of purchase. Between 1971 and 1985 viticulturists acquired 7,360 machines of two types: 4,533 were self-propelled and 2,827 were drawn by tractors or attached to them. Total sales dropped off sharply in 1981–82, but for the self-propelled, sales leveled off rather than declined. It seems that the future lies with the thirteen largest manufacturers who are continuously seeking to lower costs and offer wider combinations of attachments capable of performing special operations. The increasing use of machines has resulted from the meeting of minds between growers and manufacturers. The former have often rooted up every other vine row to widen the space between them, trained their vines higher, and thus accommodated them to mechanical picking. In Médoc where the low trim is de rigueur, designers have adapted harvesters to collect grapes hanging close to the soil. Experiments at Château Loudenne in 1979 were successful enough to encourage owners of some classed growths to buy or to rent them. The 1987 crop has marked the definite victory of the machine: 75 percent was gathered by mechanical harvesters, whose number had grown from 1,500 in 1985 to 1,700. Although still disdained by most classed estates, they made their entry in the vineyards of Pontet-Canet, Grand-Puy-Ducasse, Brane-Cantenac, Camensac, and Lafon-Rochet. The Médoc peninsula, after all, is fairly level. To bear the immense weight of harvesters, the soil must be made hard and compact, and the growers have complied with the need to do so. It is precisely in areas resorting to new cultural practices that methods have been developed to facilitate the use of heavy machinery, including tractors that have become larger and more powerful. But oddly enough, tractors are now rarely used for plowing. The practice of turning the earth to uproot weeds and to pile soil around vines for winter protection has been steadily abandoned by progressive viticulturists in their search to lower costs.

THE COST OF INNOVATION

By far the most widespread innovation in grape growing has been *nonculture* (nontillage). This term simply means the abandonment of plowing as a means of weeding and the use instead of the tractor as an instrument to kill weeds with chemical sprays. The soil between rows remains compact and firmed by the binding of dead weeds and grasses. About half of France's vineyard in now under *nonculture* and, given the considerable saving in labor, growers of fine wines have not hesitated to practice it. Wherever tractors can be used, herbicides have been applied. Environmental concern about the noxious effect of weed-killing compounds has not spread among growers, nor, so far, among the public. Over the past decade or so, both official and unofficial reports have insisted that these chemicals leave no trace either in the soil or in the wine.[19]

The use of weed killers, insecticides, and chemical fertilizers has become a normal process in viticulture since the mid-nineteenth century, when new sprays were used effectively against powdery mildew. Vine growers have become large consumers of chemical products and they form a growing market. Contemporary viticulture could not continue to meet market demands for fine wines without the application of chemicals. The irony is that these same chemicals have so enhanced yields of ordinary wines that production far surpasses demand. Producers of *gros rouge*, whose troubles we shall investigate later, cannot give up chemicals even though their rising prices continuously push up the expense of vine culture.

In the hope of lowering outlays and thereby prices, vignerons in various vineyards have experimented with a new system of training vines. In Austria, a vineyardist named Lenz Moser has claimed that wide spacing of vine rows and pruning high is a more efficient method than the narrow spacing, low trim, and dense population of vines per hectare that has been widespread in France. High pruning means leaving four or more buds on the canes that will produce next year's crop. With far fewer vines and wide spacing there is better aeration and exposure to the sun, and therefore less cause for mildew. Frost damage can also be reduced by raising flowers and foliage higher above the soil, since temperatures are lower at ground level. Lenz Moser further found that fewer vines did not reduce yield because his method of training, leaving vine canes shoulder high, enhanced the yield per vine.[20]

His method, really dating back to the 1920s, was tried in the Hautes-Côtes of Beaune and Nuits, as well as at Volnay, in the department of Côte d'Or, in the Saône-et-Loire, and in the Gironde. The results varied. In Volnay and Saône-et-Loire, it did not produce the results predicted by the Austrian. Yields fell, as did natural sugar, leaving grapes with too high a level of acidity. This imbalance resulted from grape clusters hanging too high to receive reflected heat from a pebbly soil. After all, vines produce the finest grapes in soils unfit for other crops because of the large number of small rocks that absorb heat in the day, which they throw off at night, warming the air around grape clusters that traditionally hang just ten to fifteen centimeters above them. Comparative tastings of wines made from Aligoté and Chardonnay grapes have proven the old system of low training and dense population to be superior. To obtain a comparable wine of Pinot Noir grapes, tall vines must sacrifice a fourth to a third of their yield. This eliminates the benefits of wide spacing, which, because of the large space between rows, include the use of normal-sized, mass produced, cheaper tractors, plus the use of mechanical harvesters.

Experiments in the Premières Côtes de Bordeaux following the great freeze of 1956 seemed to offer more positive results. Growers there pulled up every other vine row, mechanized their equipment, and raised yields. Since the experiment seemed successful, growers in the Entre-Deux-Mers resorted to it as well, as did those in Cadillac. Indeed, the Centre d'Etudes et de Techniques Agricoles of Cadillac sent a delegation to Austria, met with Moser, and set out to translate the fourth edition of his text book, *Un Nouveau vignoble*, in 1960. Four years later a third of the vines of Gironde were wide-spaced and trained high. Moser's system was even more beneficial in the Hautes-Côtes of Beaune and Nuits. In fact, its use has placed these two areas, where vines had nearly disappeared, back on the viticultural map of France. Wines produced in these high hills overlooking the Golden Slopes have not only earned AOC status, they have won numerous medals during prestigious competitions in Paris and Mâcon. But here the experiment stopped. The new system was less cost-effective elsewhere, and it never tempted the men who administer the great châteaux of Médoc, Saint-Emilion, or the tiny but prestigious vineyards of Beaune and Nuits.[21] Vignerons in Champagne were too rich even to think about transforming their vineyards: why, they asked, tarnish gold?

In the cultivation of vines, the day-by-day processes that occupy the working hours of a vigneron, mechanization had a marked effect. There were only three major innovations in this area, and all really came after 1945. Where machine harvesters were introduced, exclusively on large estates, vine rows had to be rearranged to allow for the passage of the noisy monsters, and vines had to be trained so that clusters of grapes were raised higher above the ground to accommodate the machine. Later generations of harvesters were designed to remove low clusters, but the reorganization of large vineyards remained a major undertaking.

YIELDS, A MODERN MIRACLE

The highly innovative technology discussed above was introduced to improve the yields of vines and the quality of their fruit in the expectation of turning out better wine, and more of it. There is an old adage that affirms that the quality of wine results less from the cellar than from the vineyard. Good grapes make good wine. There has been a consistent inverse relation between the two: the higher the yield, the worse the wine. Modern researchers did not make this discovery; the ancients were fully aware of it through practical experience. Modern theory in viticulture, however, has challenged such old beliefs, not by artificially increasing yields through the use of chemical fertilizers and irrigation, but by safeguarding the plants from age-old and newer enemies, and, over the past three decades, by creating new varieties through hybridizing within the vinifera specie. So far, however, these hybrids have not attracted wide favor even though they are capable of yields well above one hundred hectoliters per hectare while maintaining high sugar—and therefore high alcohol—levels, along with the typical taste. If they do find favor, which is highly probable given their resistance to diseases, it will be in Languedoc and in the lesser vineyards of the southwest and east. Yields, however, have risen everywhere, in both the meanest and the finest vineyards.

The new hybrids are attractive because since time immemorial insects have been ravaging vines, and mildews or rots or both have been withering grapes, taking their share of man's fruit. In about three out of ten years they have taken more than their share. Given the helplessness and scientific ignorance of most growers before 1900, it is no surprise that yields were low. In the 1860s, after growers were able to overcome the powdery mildew—a major technical breakthrough—the national average yield was approximately eighteen hectoliters per hectare. Around the turn of the century, thanks to *bouillie bordelaise*, the yield rose to about twenty-four and then reached thirty on the eve of World War I.[22] The war, of course, deprived the vineyards both of men and of insecticides, and mildew in 1915 caused one of the lowest harvests of the century. However, recovery followed quickly, and the five years from 1915 to 1920 set an average yield of thirty hectoliters. Indeed, yields continued to climb: thirty-six in the next five years and between thirty-seven and forty during the 1930s.

National data obscure regional differences. Any mention of yields inevitably brings to mind the mass-production vineyards of the Mediterranean coast, Languedoc in particular and Roussillon. In the 1920s the average yield per hectare was over fifty-eight hectoliters, a level that declined slightly in the 1930s to fifty-six hectoliters. The largest quantity of juice per hectare was of course obtained by growers in the low coastal plains, where vines flourished in the rich alluvial soil that had, before the mid-nineteenth century, produced grain crops.

One would expect yields to be markedly inferior at the northern geographic extreme, where Alsatian growers tended much smaller vineyards. But in fact they attained quantities of juice varying from fifty-five to ninety-eight hectoliters per hectare, rivaling the Languedocians and far surpassing the fine growers of Roussillon. They achieved such extraordinary productivity by planting vines of lesser breed—even hybrids—and by adding sugar syrup, a mixture of sugar and water that augmented the volume of wine. The great increase came in the 1920s. In 1919 the average yield had been thirty-three hectoliters; by 1929 it was fifty-seven, and thereafter it rose steadily. The sugar also raised the alcohol content, a procedure that doting lawmakers willingly approved for the natives who, like lost children taken under German rule in 1871, had returned to France, their forgiving mother.

Yields rose everywhere, but with far less vigor in areas where old traditions of careful cultivation prevailed and where vines struggled to grow in the thin, pebbly soil of well-drained hillsides. Here vignerons pruned low, specifically to prevent excess production. This reserve notwithstanding, the viticultural revolution following World War II brought marked changes in cultural techniques, resulting in record yields in fine areas as well as in those engaged in mass production. In Champagne, for example, the numerous small vignerons were able to survive with twenty-four hectoliters per hectare through the 1930s. In the 1950s the level rose to thirty-three, in the 1960s to over fifty, and in the 1970s and '80s to over sixty. This latter figure, all growers insist, is not excessive. It is the result of several innovations: replantings with newer, healthier, specially selected plants; use of chemical fertilizers; renewal of the soil; fumigation of the soil to eliminate harmful viruses; improved chemical insecticides; and careful cultivation. Modern-day Champenois are far better educated and knowledgeable than their forefathers were, and they reinvest the money they earn in their own vineyards, hoping to achieve higher returns. A yield that in 1970 came to ninety-two hectoliters lowered neither the reputation of their vineyards, now almost priceless, nor of their wine, the most expensive sparkling beverage on the market.[23]

High yields and high prices are rarely a compatible couple. Yet the Alsatians, perhaps imitating the Champenois, have also succeeded in legitimizing this misalliance. It is noteworthy, however, that after years of neglect, the Alsatian vineyard has been renewed: lesser vines were replaced by Riesling and Gewürztraminer, hybrids have been uprooted, and modern scientific techniques are applied, at least by the major *négociants-éleveurs*.[24] In particular, careful clonal selection, which can lead to higher yields as well as to higher quality, according to some German specialists, is practiced. French officials of the Institut National des Appellations d'Origine are more skeptical, concerned as they are with limiting yields to improve quality. But they have not denied AO (Appellation d'Origine) status to most wines of Alsace. After all, they sell very well, providing the region with about one-third of its revenue, almost equaling the returns of champagne on a per capita basis.

The growers of the Golden Slopes in Burgundy have been less ambitious. Their average of about twenty hectoliters per hectare before 1850 has been raised to only a modest thirty. Oddly enough, they grow the same varieties of grapes used to make most champagne—the Pinot Noir and Chardonnay. Yet they are constrained by the rules of their local appellation from increasing yields. In some years their yields rise above AOC limits, but the excess cannot benefit from the appellation label. If the wine is truly exceptional in any year, ceilings are raised for the unique vintage. Such rigid restrictions have not been maintained for lesser districts of the large Burgundian vineyard; yields have risen to fifty or more hectoliters in Beaujolais and the Mâconnais, and even higher in areas producing ordinary burgundy.[25]

The Bordeaux region had as much variety as Burgundy. In the fine wine district of upper Médoc, where innovations were tested carefully before they were applied in the finest vineyards, yields were about fifteen hectoliters per hectare before 1961. Then they went up to around forty—quite a jump within a decade—and by the 1970s they ranged between fifty and sixty hectoliters. As in Champagne, the vineyard was largely replanted after the deadly freeze of 1955–56. Fertilizer, which had been added every twelve to fifteen years before 1963 and only every twenty years in the nineteenth century, was now plowed into the soil every seventh year. In lesser districts, yields rose more rapidly and were higher. This was especially true wherever growers specialized in white grapes. To escape the restrictions that controlled appellation rules imposed on them, they declassed their properties and expanded the production of ordinary beverages. Between 1964 and 1976 white VCC's (*vin de consommation courante*, also called table wine or *vin de table*) rose from 18 to 26 percent of Bordeaux's total production. This step affected the standing of the department of Gironde; in 1949 it had marketed half the classified wine of France, but by 1955 the figure had fallen to 34 percent. The result was a marked increase in the amount of wine, from just over three million hectoliters to nearly five million. Much of Bordeaux's vineyard was now in mass production, but it must also be noted that red VCC's fell from 15 percent in 1964 to 10 percent in 1976, and red AOC wine rose from 29 percent to over 44 percent.[26]

Yields in France's largest mass-production district, Languedoc, appear somewhat modest in the general context of rising production. Yields above two hundred hectoliters per hectare have been known, even in the interwar, though they have been limited to a few estates or parts of estates in the low plains of the departments of Hérault and Gard, and in the Salanque in Roussillon. In 1953 yields of over one hundred hectoliters represented only 5.7 percent of the district's wine and 2.7 percent of its vineyard. Average yield in 1979 came to seventy-five hectoliters, a desirable trend, as was the shrinking of the land area devoted to vines. However, higher yields have persisted and have been the main obstacle to bringing total production into balance with total consumption, the major goal of governmental wine policy since the 1930s.[27] That goal is also frustrated by the steady decline of consumption of ordinary wine, as distinct from appellation wine. Between 80 and 90 percent of wine on the market is ordinary, though it is not all *gros rouge*. Some of it is quite drinkable and well made by highly skilled professional cellar masters and enologists working for wholesale merchants or wine cooperatives. Over half of VCC has been grown in Languedoc-Roussillon, and production for all of France ranged from fifty to sixty million hectoliters from 1950 to 1975. Outside of Languedoc-Roussillon the area devoted to VCC has been declining since the 1800s, when, thanks to the railroad, cheap southern wine invaded and conquered northern and eastern markets that were once supplied by local producers. The shrinkage of vine area has been least noticeable in the Midi, where production has remained stable, albeit too high. Other regions with over 60 percent of their vineyards devoted to VCC are the Côtes-du-Rhône (70 percent); the Loire Valley (77 percent); and the southwest (62 percent).[28]

In 1964 the Midi produced just over 60 percent of France's ordinary table wine, the southwest 21 percent, the Loire Valley 9 percent, and the Rhône Valley 8 percent. Less than 2 percent came from other vineyards. Since the 1950s every area has sought to upgrade its vineyards in order to enhance the quality of its beverages, a topic to be discussed in more detail later.

PROPERTY: THE SMALL IS NOT THE LEAST

Yield and total production have always been related to the size of a vine-planted property. Yields tend to be highest on family-size plots. But the term "family size" is ambiguous and variable. In Champagne *viticole*, for an average family of four persons, the plot was traditionally about one hectare, depending on location and degree of mechanization. Since 1945 it has become somewhat larger, closer to two or even three hectares. Such a vineyard would occupy a grower full time, his wife part time, and at least one or two sons in their spare time while in school. In Languedoc before mechanization, a family could work full time and make a modest living on about four to five hectares with animal power; with the introduction of mechanical traction, and especially the practice of nontillage, a family of four needs seven to ten hectares to survive.

Vineyards have always differed considerably in size in every viticultural area. See table 2.1 for averages throughout France. These averages are useful in that they reveal that no one large viticultural region has had a monopoly on large, medium, or small properties. In fact, most vine areas functioned best where a mixture of sizes existed: large owners needed very small owners (those having less than one hectare) to work seasonally on their lands; and likewise, very small—even small owners with up to three hectares—could not survive without the wages they earned on large estates. They were owner-workers. See table 2.2 for the sizes of France's vine

Table 2.1. Average size of French vineyards

Department	Average Size (in hectares)
Gironde	3.3
Hérault	3.3
Indre et Loire	3.3
Rhône	3.1
Pyrénées—Orientales	2.8
Gard	2.7
Var	2.3
Côte d'Or	2.1
Haut-Rhin	1.1
Aude	0.9
Marne	0.9

SOURCE: Ministère de l'Agriculture. Statistique de la France, *Résultats généraux de l'enquête agricole de 1929*, 496.

Table 2.2.   Property sizes in areas of fine wines in France, 1929

Department	No. of Properties	0–1 ha	1–5 ha	5–10 ha	10–20 ha	20–50 ha	+50 ha
Marne	11,298	80%	18%	0.8%	0.3%	0.15%	0.04%
Maine-et-Loire	5,073	67	25	5.0	2.0	0.7	0.10
Côte d'Or	5,862	48	39	7.0	3.0	0.8	0.03
Gironde	23,780	37	43	13.0	5.0	2.0	0.50
Rhône	5,687	30	56	10.0	3.0	0.8	0.05

SOURCE: Same as table 2.1.

Table 2.3.   Hierarchy of prewar Mediterranean vineyards by size

Size (in hectares)	
− 1	Micro plots assuring supplementary income for worker-owners.
1–5	Small owners who need another source of income
5–10	Independent family vineyards
10–20	Family vineyards requiring hired labor
20–50	Large estates
+ 50	Very large estates run like a factory

NOTE: Terminology for vineyards was established by Rémy Pech.

properties in 1929, for comparable areas that produced most of the fine wines.

It is evident from the table that the Champagne vineyard was "pulverized," to use the word generally chosen to describe it. For over a century it has been in a class by itself, especially since one hectare of precious vines is needed to support a family. But in abnormal times like the 1930s, growers suffered miserably from low incomes; many of them survived only by making their grapes into sparkling champagne and selling it at a price well above that offered by shippers. The structures of most other vineyards tended to be more symmetrical than that of Champagne. In fact, they resemble the social structure of French society in general. See table 2.3 for a fairly well-defined hierarchy that prevailed in prewar Mediterranean vineyards.

As in any European hierarchy, the large lower class had far less wealth (land) than the smaller upper class. The department of the Var was an example of a type of structure characterized by the near absence of really large property, making it close to a rural democracy. Less egalitarian was the district of Saint-Emilion, which is typical of the Bordelais and of fine vineyards, other than Marne. See table 2.4 for a comparison of the two districts.

Throughout France small growers with fewer than five hectares produced not much wine individually, yet collectively they turned out more than half the annual total. See table 2.5 for the situation in 1937. The first two categories indicate very small and small producers. As Monsieur Morel put it, "From little streams great rivers grow." The little vignerons were never a negligible factor in cultivation and production. As a group they have survived all the ups and downs of the wine industry and have consistently fought against the pressures that would destroy them.

Their struggle, however, was not fully successful after World War II. The war itself was not a catastrophe: many small producers were able to

Table 2.4. Comparison of Var and St. Emilion by vineyard size

Size	Var		St. Emilion	
	% of Growers	% of Area	% of Growers	% of Area
− 1ha	50	12	25	3
− 5	40	35	28	12
5–10	7	21	25	24
10–20	2	15	15	28
+ 20	1	11	7	33

SOURCE: Jacques Girault, "Agriculture du Var en 1930," unpublished. G. Caumes, "Le Vignoble de Saint-Emilion," DES, University of Bordeaux, 1965, 69.

Table 2.5. Grower size and wine production

Production (in hectoliters)	% of Growers	% of Harvest
0–199	94.0	44.0
100–200	3.6	15.6
200–300	0.4	7.2
Total	98.0	66.8

SOURCE: L. Morel, *Economie dirigée* (1939), 22.

sell more easily on the black market than the large growers. And buyers in this market were not too particular about quality, an attitude of benefit to the little fellow, whose vinification was often less than perfect. Moreover, as many interviews with growers revealed, the wartime Vichy regime had an agricultural policy that sought to keep farmers down on the land. It was therefore blind to black market operations carried out on a small scale, and tolerant—permissive even—of the larger planting of Franco-American hybrid vines that needed less care and were highly suited to the mass of general farmers who had vineyards but little time to attend them. Hybrids that were disease resistant were welcomed; they could survive even the shortage of chemical sprays, which had become serious by 1942.

During several decades following the peace, the situation underwent some marked changes. The social structure of the interwar did not change drastically; it retained its large base of many petty owners and its apex of a few big owners. There are really two distinct structures in French viticulture: one consisting of owners classed by size and another based on the vine surface owned by each class. See table 2.6 for the numbers of each.

A factor that has somewhat distorted the larger picture of the social structure of vineyards has been the mass of very small properties whose owners cultivate vines only to make wine for home or family consumption; rarely, if ever, do they put their wine on the market. Theirs are really microholdings, usually under one-half hectare, dominated by hybrid plantings. Generally these growers have made up about half of all the persons who, by the law of 1907, must declare the size of their harvest to local authorities. Their inclusion in agricultural surveys and censuses swells the number of *déclarants*, as all growers are called, giving a false impression of the viticultural population. These numbers are used by vigneron pressure groups to influence politicians. In 1954 the total number

Table 2.6. Structure of growers and vine surface, 1960s

Size (in hectares)	% of Growers	% Vine Surface
−1	80.0	29.0
1–7	19.0	49.0
7–15	1.3	13.3
15–30	0.3	6.3
+30	0.1	5.9

SOURCE: EEC, *Conditions de commercialisation . . . des vins de consommation courante* (1969), 15.

of *déclarants* reached at least 1.6 million; in 1963 it fell to 1.3 million and has continued to decline until only 649,164 declared a harvest in 1984. In 1963 only 700,000, or about 54 percent of them, put their wine up for sale. About 500,000 were full-time, or nearly full-time, growers, true professionals. They are the ones who have tried to bring about a concentration of ownership by enlarging their properties and buying plots from old vignerons who have retired or died without leaving heirs willing to work in the vineyard. Their expansionist goals were not difficult to achieve after the war, when property was relatively inexpensive and heirs of retired or deceased owners, having taken to city life and nonagrarian professions, happily cashed in their inheritances. Mutual credit societies actively facilitated these sales with loans at low interest and aided in the purchase of modern equipment.[29] Today nearly all *déclarants* commercialize their wine or their grapes; most of those making wine for domestic consumption do not bother.

The 1960s constituted a transition in the ownership of land. Not only did cultural practices undergo a marked change, as noted above, but the cost of vineyards rose drastically in the fine wine areas. For vignerons actively buying land at moderate prices soon after the war, the change was both disconcerting and limiting. With an increase in the number of urban and larger buyers came an inflated price for land that gradually raised the cost beyond the means of the simple vigneron or the general farmer. His ascent was stopped, a most frustrating phenomenon. This situation was recognized by the governments of the Fourth Republic following World War II. Because both the wine and farm lobbies were powerful, laws were passed creating a bureaucratic entity, SAFER, to buy large available estates, break them up, and sell the plots to small growers. The SAFER, had it been adequately funded, could have brought about a veritable landed revolution, but its budget was too meager, and its land purchases were therefore limited, with the result that the basic structure of France's vineyard has remained unchanged. But the agency has made a contribution to several trends that began after the war, when all facets of agriculture were included in the new planned economy that was intended not only to modernize the highly traditional methods of farming but also the peasants' attitude. As we shall discover later, the SAFER was merely one link in a long chain of bureaucratic entities created to encourage—and even to finance—change.[30] Here indeed was a push from above, combined with the pull of the market that hastened the wine revolution.

The trend that appeared earliest was the decrease in number of the many small commercial grape growers who were incapable of adapting their old habits, or too old to do so. The sale of their properties has facilitated expansion of operations by other small and medium growers; the latter were now put in a stronger position in the highly competitive wine market. Vineyards from five to twenty hectares have been growing in number, with the ten to twenty hectare range expanding the most. Estates of fifty hectares have been reduced in size as plots are sold off to cut down on labor and social security costs and to enhance profitability. These tendencies were already apparent in the 1960s (table 2.6). Wine legislation, chiefly the Statut de la Viticulture, has always favored small producers by limiting the sales of large producers, as will be explained later. The former have many votes in legislative elections, the latter very few.

In some areas, such as Champagne, that specialize in fine wines and are not subject to the Statut de la Viticulture, expansion was facilitated by bringing more land, planted with other crops, into the controlled appellation area. It was cheaper than planted vineland, and its inclusion nearly doubled the surface from thirteen thousand hectares in 1958 to over twenty-one thousand in 1972. More recently, however, the cost of suitable land has risen so high that only very wealthy persons or companies can buy it. The egregious cost of land has therefore checked the ambitions of small and even medium growers in fine wine districts. This situation partly explains why small properties have remained dominant in Burgundy, Champagne, and Alsace, areas where the price of viticultural real estate has reached the sky.[31] Now, it is important to bear in mind that a vineyard of two to three hectares can support a family in these areas, whereas such a vineyard in the Midi or in the southwest or the southern Côtes-du-Rhône would offer only a supplementary income to someone with an outside job. By 1975 very small growers had declined in number, and so had their harvest (see table 2.7).

Even a superficial comparison with the situation of 1937 (table 2.5) shows that the number of producers of less than a hundred hectoliters had fallen by 25 percent and their contribution to the grape harvest fell by

Table 2.7.   Decline of small growers

Category	% of growers	% of harvest
0–100 hl.	75	16.5
100–300	16	21

SOURCE: Colin, "Vignoble . . . Champagne," 77–78.

16.7 percent. Those making a hundred to three hundred hectoliters held their own in numbers, as well as in their contribution to the market, until 1967. These producers, who proved to be remarkably resilient, owned the smaller family establishments that were so widespread. These wineries were saved by hard work and rising productivity, as well as by the wine cooperatives. The coops took over the task of combining their members' grapes to make a wine considerably superior to the thin beverages that small growers had sold to wine merchants, who buy either the grapes or young wine before it matures. However, since 1967 vineyards producing one hundred to three hundred hectoliters have dropped by at least 16 percent while those producing three hundred to one thousand hectoliters increased by 20 percent; and those producing one thousand to five thousand hectoliters rose 62 percent, while those producing over five thousand hectoliters increased only 20 percent. Vineyards of about fifteen to thirty hectares, medium size in VCC areas, have been most dynamic and continue to grow in number. [32]

There are, of course, regional variations, and decline has been more dramatic in areas devoted primarily to VCC. But even in regions turning out controlled appellation wines, there has been a decrease—not in hectares, but in the number of vineyards. In the Beaujolais, during the sixteen years between 1955 and 1971, they plunged 44 percent; the number has more or less stabilized since then. [33] Properties of four to seven hectares in size represented in 1972 only 23 percent of the total number, but they turned out 38 percent of the wine. Abandonment took place mainly in lower (*bas*) Beaujolais, where *vins de zinc*, that is, simple reds sold by the glass in local and Lyonnais cafes, were the mainstay. In the Côte d'Or, as well as in Champagne where a vineyard of two hectares is classed as a medium-to-large property, there has been a minimal of emigration or transformation from vines to other crops. On the contrary, vineyards have reappeared in the highland (Hautes Côtes) area where replanting had not taken place after the phylloxera. Apart from the Golden Slopes itself, with its myriad of world-famous properties, most of which are one hectare or less in size, the much larger department of Côtes d'Or did not differ from the norm: vineyards two hectares in size tumbled in number by just under 100 percent, those between two and five hectares fell by 18 percent. Only properties over five hectares rose in number, a result of an actively pursued policy of consolidation. [34]

Consolidation really indicated another trend. The key term here is *re-membrement*, that is, the policy seeking to encourage each grower to exchange scattered parcels of his land for those plots that are contiguous to his largest parcel but owned by someone else. The idea was to end up with a sizable property all of one piece. This made for more efficient culture, especially with the use of mechanized equipment. Even medium-sized properties (*exploitations*, as the French say) were often scattered over one or more communes, and these scattered plots were usually a hectare or less in size. The grower lost a good deal of time moving equipment from one plot to another, and their small size made mechanization too costly.

This trend of consolidation has moved more slowly than has the concentration of property in fewer hands, which resulted from land sales rather than from exchanges. Vignerons were often emotionally attached to their parcels and they were fearful of being cheated in a trade. Moreover, they looked upon scattering as a kind of insurance; if hail destroyed the vines in one parcel, the vines in more distant parcels could produce a crop and save the day.[35]

Yet *remembrement* has been taking place. It has not always resulted in the formation of a fully integrated vineyard, but rather in the enlargement of plots that remained dispersed over one or more communes, providing each one a larger surface for tillage, and giving protection from total destruction by a natural catastrophe.[36]

Another trend has been the uprooting of vines that produce wines of poor quality. The villainous vines were the hybrids that had spread across France since the 1890s and had replaced many old varieties during the lean years of the interwar, and even more so during the dark years of German occupation. Their presence was not limited to ordinary vineyards; they were often hidden among fine vines even in the best of properties. Quite simply, the postwar government outlawed them.[37] Decrees established a hierarchy of grape varieties, from the noblest to the most proletarian, and sought to upgrade quality by discouraging the continued planting of the latter. Many small growers, unable to find the capital to transform their plantings, simply gave up. Others, especially in Languedoc, argued that their high-yielding vines—the Aramon, the Bouchet—were "noble" when cultivated in their soil and therefore should be listed with the "recommended" varieties. Officialdom, however, listed them as "tolerable," and urged their reduction over a decade of time, to be replanted by varieties offering higher quality. In this case, the pull of the market had to be reinforced by the push of science, aided by the strong arm of bureaucracy. Part-time growers in particular have resisted this pressure, a resistance that has delayed but not prevented the transformation of the Mediterranean vineyard.

The concentration of property went on apace with the modernization of viticulture. In truth, the two phenomena were interlocked; modernization became feasible only where plots were of a size to allow the introduction of machines, to assure that heavy investments would enhance production and hence profits. In this respect, in the trend toward larger units of production, the viticultural revolution resembled the industrial revolutions of Western Europe. And yet there was at least one major difference: the family grower was not put out of business; his boundaries have simply expanded. And tending vines has increasingly become his main occupation. Wine making, formerly an activity normally associated with viticulture and a voracious absorber of time and money, has progressively disappeared from the small vineyard. It is doubtful that family producers could have carried out both a viticultural and vinicultural revolution.

CHAPTER THREE

Viniculture: The Marriage of Pragmatism and Theory

BIRTH OF ENOLOGY

Viniculture, the knowledge and process of transforming grape juice into wine, is the raison d'être of most viticultural activity. To be sure, many growers concentrate their energy on table grapes; but the great majority grow wine grapes that are rarely edible, almost useless for jams, and indeed are good for nothing but producing a rather acidic juice for making wine. Over millennia these two professions, viticulture and viniculture, have enjoyed a contrapuntal relation based on men's keen observation and accumulated knowledge. Through purely pragmatic methods, men learned to grow highly prized fruit and to transform its juices into various wines that were also highly prized by the taste standards of various epochs.

Methods to make wine improved over the nineteenth century without seriously altering the basic procedures. As always, the first step was the crushing of grapes to liberate the juice from the pulp. If the maker wanted red wine, as most did, he left grape skins and juice together in a large vat. The yeasts on the skins attacked the sugar of the juice (called "must" at this stage) to produce alcohol, carbonic acid and its gas, glycerin, tannic acid, color, and other chemical substances that within a week or so transformed the must into wine. This was the first, or alcoholic, fermentation, with the amount of alcohol depending on the level of sugar in the grape at harvest. Next, the maker drew off the red liquid, the "free-run" wine, and poured or pumped it into barrels for continued development. He then placed the wine-soaked skins in a press to squeeze out additional liquid called "press wine," of lesser quality, which he might or might not mix with the free-run. It was more often used to top off barrels, to keep them filled to the bung, since wine slowly evaporated through the pores in wooden staves, creating an open space that allowed air to enter and ruin the wine through oxidation. To make white wine, he sent the crushed or uncrushed grapes immediately to the press, avoiding skin contact for a longer time than required for pressing. Most red grape varieties will produce white juice, so they do need contact with the grape skins to extract coloring matter from them.

The gradual refining of taste over the last five hundred years has encouraged innovations in the cellar to satisfy a more discriminating market. Since about the mid-1700s some viniculturists sought to improve their methods to satisfy the expanding demand for better wines. Producers applied their knowledge to create better wine pragmatically, since there was a scarcity of literature on the subject, except for the treatises prepared by ancient Roman agronomists and preserved in monastic libraries. Much as the early literature on etiquette was of a practical nature, so were the early writings on wine making. Progress in the wine cellar was narrowly experimental, and, I suspect, often accidental, resulting from observation of cause and effect—the same procedure used by viticulturists to adapt vines to soil, climate, and topography over centuries of time. Achieving a higher level of quality was the aim of those with cultivated senses. Under their guidance viniculture became an art created by an elite that was well financed, literate, refined of taste, and often monastic. Its practitioners acted on the principle that wine is made in the vineyard, an aphorism meaning simply that the quality of the grape controls the merit of the wine.

The French Revolution, beginning in 1789, seriously disturbed this evolution. The revolutionaries killed or imprisoned a sizable segment of large landowners, confiscated their lands, and abolished the monasteries, which were the major centers of great wine making everywhere but in Bordeaux. In the course of the nineteenth century viniculture became laicized, that is, wine makers were no longer monks but lay professionals and either medium or large landowners; they were also cellar masters employed by nobles or upper bourgeois. Since about the 1850s they have also been academics and bureaucrats active in the Ministry of Agriculture or in newly established university research centers. In the latter case they bridged the gap between pragmatic viniculture and theoretical enology. The perfect representative of this coupling was that prolific, opinionated savant, Dr. Jules Guyot, whose nineteenth-century three-volume study of French vine and wine growing is still an indispensable source of information. His facts were not always accurate and his recommendations, given with dogmatic enthusiasm, were not always wise.

Since the 1840s viniculturists filled the local academies, vocational groups, *syndicats*, and regional councils that met in congresses from time to time and gave both amateur and professional growers the occasions to spread their ideas and learn from others. By no means did they all agree on the best processes to make wine; they were often as argumentative as they were assertive. These meetings were of great enjoyment to them. Here they were able to display the methods and results of their experiments with the oratorical skill and flourish so widely admired in France by men trained in the classics.

The emergence of a more disciplined science of wine making was supposed to bring proven theory and certainty into the field. To a large extent it did, though highly trained enologists have often proven to be as argumentative and assertive in their statements as their predecessors. They readily agreed on fundamentals; but it has been the refinement of fundamentals, especially in the use of certain instruments or machines, that has created divergent schools among them. Some consider Louis Pasteur to be their first authentic mentor, since it was his research in the biology of wine and its microbial enemies that laid the foundation of enology as a biological science. Utilizing both theory and experiment, he invented the technique of pasteurization, a method that can defend wine against microbial attack as well as save some of its value if spoilage is stopped early.[1] Others, while recognizing Pasteur's genius, consider the real pioneers to be the scientists who first began the study of fermentation as a chemical process, such as the chemist Joseph Guy-Lussac, whose formula gave a general explanation of the process.

The science of enology became more solidly based with the founding of the Station d'Oenologie in 1880 by Ulysse Gayon at the University of Bordeaux. His work has been carried on by his grandson, Jean Ribéreau-Gayon, the director of the institute and an active researcher until the 1970s, and Emile Peynaud, a teacher at the institute who also collaborated with Ribéreau-Gayon in writing major volumes on enology. Their enormous knowledge and influence have been carried on by Pascal, son of Jean, who is now director.[2] Peynaud on his own has exercised considerable influence in Bordeaux. He is a prime promoter of a "new style" wine—lighter, quicker to mature, and less astringent, thanks to the increased percentage of Merlot grapes and the decrease in Cabernet-Sauvignon which had dominated in the Médoc. Since the 1950s, a decade of enological breakthroughs, according to Peynaud, his advice has been widely sought and religiously followed, for it is the result of his wide experience as a consultant. His and his colleagues' work was both theoretical and practical from the beginning, in the tradition of Pasteur. They have passionately sought to discover the constituent elements of wine.

In the mid-1920s Lucien Sémichon had set out to summarize the enological state of the art—or rather, of the science. Although he is no longer recognized as having been a major enologist, it was his firm belief that little was yet known about grapes, and he complained that few industries were so ignorant of their raw material. He was particularly sensitive to the relationship between grape and wine, and maintained that more study was needed on the way grapes mature and how they determine the character of the resulting wine. Vine genetics was still in its infancy, as was the study of the influence of various yeasts on the characteristics of wine.[3]

Just after World War II Jean Ribéreau-Gayon put forward another call for action. He recognized that in the past the trial and error method had achieved wonders but took too long to obtain results that could be evaluated. More recently enologists, relying on an expanding knowledge of the chemical compounds of wine, have achieved far-reaching results more rapidly. They can, both theoretically and practically, predict certain results and prescribe how to make the best wine that the grape can offer. They improve on nature by guiding the wine-making process in the best direction. Through chemistry it is possible to discover all the constituent elements of wine, isolate them, study each separately and discover how they interact. This methodology is constantly expanding. In the early nineteenth century Jean Chaptal had found only six constituents: acid, alcohol, tartrate, various extractive solids, aroma, and coloring elements. By 1956 Jaulmes had estimated that there are 150 compounds. At present, it is known that there are over 500, and only a dozen have concentrations of over one gram per liter. Knowledge of the chemistry of wine has enabled scientists to follow the process of its aging, its reaction to various containers, and its state of health—and to take action when maladies appear. According to Peynaud, enology for too long limited itself to analytical and curative work. Only as it perfected its knowledge of wine over time was enology able to conquer the maladies. More recently it has become a preventive science, keeping maladies from developing, and sick wines are now rare. Indeed, the new style of wine is superior to the old, thanks to the changes that enologists have helped bring about. Before the 1950s bordeaux was lower in alcohol, higher in total acidity and tannin, and overly colored. Since then it has more alcohol, giving it a softer savor, lower acidity and tannin, and is less deeply colored. This means that wines are now drinkable at an earlier age, and they are more agreeable to the palate.[4]

Since the later nineteenth century, enology has not only sought to investigate the constituents of wine, but its laboratory-controlled experiments have come up with practical advice. For example, enologists have learned that keeping most white wines in wooden containers for more than a few months discourages the full development of their taste and aroma; therefore, these wines age better in bottle after a brief stay in oak, an assertion still rejected by some Burgundians. Science has also sought to improve on traditional knowledge. It has long been known that cold is of help in detartrating wine, chiefly white wine, a desirable procedure to stabilize it before bottling. Unstabilized wine will drop tartrate crystals when the bottle is chilled before serving or if it is stored in a cold cellar for aging. The enologists' contribution to traditional practice consists in the study of the most efficient means to refrigerate. They discovered that before the 1950s many refrigeration devices were too costly, cooled inadequately, or exposed wine to air. They also discovered that agitating wine provoked a more complete precipitation of tartrate.

In a similar way, scientists set out to investigate carbonic maceration, a way of fermenting must that was part of an old practice in certain districts of Beaujolais. Many growers had frequently dumped all their uncrushed Gamay berries into open tanks or vats that were relatively small in size, that is, not over sixty hectoliters. Others began hand crushing about half their crop while it was on the way to the winery; and in more recent times some mechanically crushed about 20 percent of their grapes. Finally, when the entire crop was piled into tanks, the weight of the bunches on top forced additional juice to ooze out of the fruit at the bottom. When this liquid came into contact with the natural yeasts on the skins, it began its alcoholic fermentation. Many growers did not bother to add the antioxidant, sulfur dioxide, while others put in five grams per hectoliter. None of them destemmed or mechanically crushed the entire crop. What distinguished this system was the intracellular fermentation that went on within the uncrushed berries.

Scientists at the Sicarex-Beaujolais, a government-backed research station, and teams of enologists headed by P. André have endorsed the traditional procedures when carried out under certain controls. Their experiments have been aimed at finding the ideal temperature for fermenting red must, between twenty-five and twenty-eight degrees Celsius in order to bring out the finest aroma. They have also experimented with the addition of sulfite. There is a difference of opinion, however, about the pumping of must over skins in an oxygen-free environment, a method used to extract additional color from pigments in the skins. André argues that it reduces the number of grapes going through intracellular fermentation. And yet this latter step, some vignerons maintain, is particularly necessary if the Gamay *à jus blanc* is used because the juice is colorless, yet it produces the finest wine. Pumping over is not really needed if the grower follows tradition and allows the fermentation to continue for ten to twelve days. André, comparing wine made in the traditional way with wine made from fully crushed berries, found the former slightly higher in alcohol and fixed acidity.[5]

Beaujolais growers believe that the best wine is not the free run, as elsewhere, but the wine resulting from a first light pressing of mainly uncrushed grapes, a liquid called *paradis* by the locals. The final product has always been a blend of free run, paradis, and the more astringent wine of the second pressing.

Carbonic maceration was particularly recommended because it produced a wine that was ready to drink within less than a year. The wine also faded quickly, and therefore this method has not recommended itself to those who produce fine wines. Since the 1940s it has spread from Beaujolais to other wine areas, especially the Rhône Valley and the Midi, precisely because it offers a kind of fermentation that prevents a too rapid rise in temperature in vats and avoids having to resort to expensive cooling systems. Its major defect is that it standardizes aroma and therefore destroys this form of distinction among wines. As far as I know, enologists have not denied the clear advantages of carbonic maceration for ordinary wines or even for some of the lesser appellation wines. In Narbonne, enologists under the direction of E. Flanzy clarified the technical parameters for the process during the 1950s–'60s. Early maturation is a major commercial advantage, given the rising costs of storage, and early decline has not been perceived as a weakness because most buyers of these wines intend to drink them at once.[6]

Other steps in wine making, however, have provoked debate. There are strong differences of opinion about the heating of must in order to extract more color from the skins and to destroy unwanted bacteria. This process, used by Pasteur to safeguard wine, was perfected by G. Marteau and C. Olivier, enologists at Montpellier, who studied it from 1955 through the 1970s. It has become a rather widely used process, but if carried out under less than ideal conditions it will give a burned or cooked taste to the finished product. Some of its early advocates continue to recognize its value but warn against its abuse. The problem here is that some techniques seem to work well in the laboratory but not in the winery. Often this failure is the result of faulty equipment. Early experiments before World War II were sometimes impractical because manufacturers of equipment did not make some of the devices specifically for wine. This was the case with the centrifuge used for clearing juice rapidly before fermentation; it did not protect the juice from oxygen while subjecting it to violent whirling action. Since the 1940s these machines have been redesigned to correct this weakness, and now they are widely used, but chiefly for lesser wines. Some enologists recommend them as a means of economizing on the long process of clarification; others see them merely as cost-saving devices that strip the must too early of chemical elements needed to produce the full character of a great beverage.[7]

There is a similar difference of opinion about yeasts, the living organisms that transform grape sugar into alcohol and carbon dioxide. Yeasts have been investigated carefully since the nineteenth century. Most viniculturists relied on the yeast that adhered naturally to grape skins, and many enologists agreed that these natural yeasts gave the resulting wine its natural character. After the First World War the word "natural" became increasingly a symbol of purity, honesty, quality. Particularly in the Languedoc-Roussillon region of mass production, the term *naturel* for wine became a watchword, making the supposedly nondoctored beverages of the Mediterranean coast more desirable than the highly doctored products of other regions.

Here we enter into a subject that is nebulous, emotional, and sectarian along regional lines, with science used as a weapon in a struggle that is decades, even centuries, old. The origins of this conflict are described in my book, *The Red and the White*, so here I shall deal only with its persistence after 1914. The source of the regional conflict has been sugar. Debate on the subject of sugaring wine, commonly called *chaptalisation*, came to the fore again in the 1920s with the early invention of concentrated must.[8] Concentration simply meant removing water from grape juice, leaving a jellylike substance with a high sugar content. It could serve two purposes: (1) By adding acid and water it could be reconstituted into grape juice suitable for fermenting into wine. This was not a practical use for commercial growers because the earliest methods of concentration consisted of boiling the original juice to eliminate water. Only recently have the techniques of concentration eliminated the burned taste caused by the heat. (2) By adding concentrate to natural juice deficient in grape sugar, it became possible to produce a wine with a higher alcoholic content, since fermentation produces alcohol in direct proportion to the sugar content. This process, then, was a form of doctoring, and in the eyes of some critics, a form of adulteration. Since warm, sunny climates like that of the Mediterranean increased the sugar content of grapes, the government in Paris prohibited southern growers from adding either sugar or concentrates. However, in 1931 it legalized the use of concentrates to enrich the musts of growers in cooler climates, allowing the addition of an amount sufficient to raise the alcoholic content by 2.5 degrees. These producers, however, were less concerned with concentrates, which were still very expensive, than with cane or beet sugar, which achieved the same enrichment at lower costs. The *Revue de viticulture*, however, urged growers to use concentrates to attain a better end product because concentrates had all the elements of real grapes and were therefore more *naturel*.[9] In this particular matter, however, the southerners did not give a hoot about being natural when demanding the right to use sugar like northern vintners.

The debate on chaptalization continued after the Second World War, and indeed is still current because excesses continue to plague the industry. Since the 1920s there have been four different wine interests (one could even say four different worlds of wine, for they are quite distinct and sometimes in conflict). There is, as noted earlier, the north and the south, and the VAOC (*vin d'appellation d'origine controlée*) and the VCC (the nonappellation or table wine). A 1929 law allowed chaptalization in all vineyards except those of Languedoc-Roussillon, Provence, Corsica, Bordeaux, Toulouse, and the Agennais, that is, those in the deep south and southwest. Sugaring of must was permitted in all other, more northerly vineyards on an annual basis, according to weather conditions and sugar content at harvest. The division was less clear-cut between VCC and VAOC because in 1929 Bordeaux produced over one-third of all appellation wine of France, as well as many ordinaries. Bordeaux producers, even in cold, wet years when the natural sugar level in grapes was low, were not given permission until 1938 to chaptalize. But since 1951 permission to do so has been granted with increasing frequency, even in good years.[10] And Burgundians, like other northerners, chaptalize almost routinely, above all in the lesser vine areas of Beaujolais and the Saône Valley.[11] In consequence, southerners have argued vociferously that this was gross discrimination. The privilege was not extended to southerners, because the government feared that it would lead to overproduction there. Weak wines were simply blended with those from Algeria, always high in alcohol, until the early 1960s, and then with southern Italian wines, which led to serious problems that have not yet been resolved. In 1979 a new law was passed to bring France into accord with the regulations of the European Economic Community regarding the enrichment of must. The EEC, with its power base concentrated in the north, was particularly indulgent toward northern producers.[12]

Southerners have become more convinced than ever that officialdom in Paris sold out to the German Federal Republic, to the Lowlanders, and to Italy, a major buyer of northern industrial goods. The enological aspect of whether sugaring is desirable has taken second place to national and regional economic interests. Although Germany and Italy have borrowed French AOC rules, neither has put in place the full range of the restricting wine regulations that have piled up in France since 1907. One must be a specialized lawyer to grasp all of them. Even when not fully enforced, legislation in France is far more limiting of certain harmful practices and more helpful in discovering and prosecuting practitioners of fraud. Particularly resented by southern French growers are the EEC regulations that set up five latitudinal zones descending from north to south.[13] In the far north lies zone A, the Rhineland and Luxembourg, where musts rarely attain more than the five-degree minimum required for a beverage to be legally designated as wine; so enrichment by sugar, saccharine, or concentrate has been permitted to raise the alcohol another five-degrees. The German Federal Republic allows the addition of grape sugar syrup, sugar dissolved either in heated must or water, or a mixture of liquids, which of course slightly increases the volume of wine on the market and is the quickest and cheapest way of expanding the salable product. Alsace, Champagne, the Jura, Savoy, and the Loire Valley are in zone B, where enrichment is limited to 3.5 degrees. Bordeaux and Burgundy are in zone CI. Producers in these zones used to rely more on blending than chaptalization, but recently they have tended to abuse the latter process; how else could the Rhineland and Alsace obtain such high yields with sufficient alcohol from sun-starved grapes? Growers of fine wine have, of course, found means to curtail the level of enrichment. Learned viticulturalists have invested more heavily in renewing their vineyards more frequently so that the average life of a vine is now twenty years, roughly half the useful life before the 1950s. Improved clones, carefully planted and tended, have produced grapes far richer in natural sugar than before, even while offering larger quantities of juice. For economic reasons, however, growers of lesser wines have found it more profitable to resort to enrichment, which keeps low the costs of production of the entire crop of wine because sugar is inexpensive when purchased in large quantities, and northern growers of VCC have been able to compete successfully with southern growers who had earlier applauded the EEC, seeing in the dismantling of national trade barriers a means of invading northern European markets. In the mid-nineteenth century their forebears had, thanks to the railroad, invaded central and northern French markets and nearly destroyed the local wine industries there. The progeny rubbed their hands in anticipation of doing the same to North European growers. Their lack of success embittered them grievously, as we shall see.

CENTERS OF ADVANCED VINICULTURE

It would be a mistake to imagine that wine making, apart from "adjusting" the must by adding sugar or concentrate, was carried out uniformly throughout France. Until the interwar there was no national press to spread new ideas everywhere. Viticultural journals were local or regional; even the *Revue de viticulture*, although widely read by professionals, was concerned chiefly with Languedoc and the producers of ordinary wines. Likewise, wine making manuals were written, for the most part, by men whose experience was regional. In consequence there was a good deal of variety in techniques, even among fine-wine makers, and astonishingly marked differences within regions. Of course, the transformation of grape juice into wine required several fundamental steps: the removal of juice from grapes, its fermentation in a container, its clarification and maturation. Bottling was not carried out by most small producers; they sold their new wine in bulk to *négociants-éleveurs*, the wholesale merchants who matured and bottled the wine in their own cellars. *Gros rouge*, also sold in bulk to retail outlets, never saw a bottle until the individual customer came bearing his own long-used containers, which the retailer filled from a large barrel. Since about 80 percent of wine was sold in this fashion until the 1950s, at a very low price, its producers were either the traditional wholesalers or, since the 1920s, cooperatives. The cellar masters of cooperatives and dealers were usually trained enologists or, if they were not, they in turn hired experts capable of analyzing the produce and advising on methods and the purchase of equipment. In these large wine factories, viniculture and enology worked hand in hand, not only in regard to procedures, but also in the blending of various types of wine to obtain a fairly consistent product year after year.

The better VCC, not sold in bulk, was bottled under the label of the company that had matured it. The cellars of these companies were best supplied with the implements necessary for large-scale production: enormous glass-lined or enameled cement vats, and machine-driven crushers, presses, pumps, and assembly-line bottling techniques which their cellar masters had learned from the early soft-drink manufacturers in the 1920s (see figures 3.12, 3.13). These companies played almost no role in the viticultural revolution; they rarely owned vineyards, finding it more convenient either to buy grapes or, more often, young wine from growers as well as from cooperatives. They were, instead, pioneers in the vinicultural revolution that demanded innovative mechanization, scientific analysis, and careful manipulation. Like large estates, these wine factories, whether private or cooperative, were few in number; yet they distributed the great bulk of wine put on the market, whether it was *gros rouge* or a better ordinary lacking in any particular character, or a lesser VAOC that the lower middle class served at Sunday lunches. These were mass-produced beverages for the urban population brought into existence by the industrial revolution. [14]

Far different was the world of wine making among men who were fully knowledgeable about processes and equipment and who proceeded in accord with traditions formed over generations of time. The old ways meant to them simplicity of apparatus and as little handling of the product as possible. Their output was small—a few thousand cases a year—and their prices were high. They grew their own grapes to meet their lofty desire for wine of distinctive character. Generally they were not enologists but vitiviniculturists: they read the wine press and the manuals written for their region; and they attended or sent their sons to attend specialized courses offered in the agricultural *lycées*, the secondary schools set up by the Ministry of Agriculture and Education to prepare young men—and women only recently—for advanced farming and wine making. Before World War I there were only a few institutions that offered advanced training in vine and wine growing: the universities of Bordeaux and Montpellier, where instruction was carried out as part of active research programs. Undoubtedly the crisis brought about by the phylloxera hastened the opening of other centers. It was the highly skilled and imaginative investigators of Montpellier who saved France's vineyards by grafting native vines onto American rootstock that was resistant to the phylloxera.

Around the turn of the century, collaboration between enlightened local growers and the Ministry of Agriculture led to the creation of *stations agronomiques et oenologiques*, such as the one at Beaune (1885), created first to fight against the phylloxera and subsequently made into a *lycée*. Louis Bréchard studied there, arriving as a young peasant and happy that none of the teachers ridiculed him or his fellow rurals.[15] Yet local vignerons, because the state required them to provide the buildings, had resisted its founding. Traditionalist and tightfisted, they had earlier refused to follow the experts' advice for fighting the dreaded aphid. But the numerous *négociants* of Beaune gave their support and benefited from the *lycée*'s programs, and they and larger growers hired its graduates as cellar masters. The hostile reaction of the peasant vignerons was not surprising, nor was their tardier realization that these *lycées* and experimental stations could provide useful services such as analyzing fresh must and subsequently the emerging wine during the course of its maturation. The classes offered were not concerned unduly with theory but with the practical knowledge required by commercial growers such as Monsieur Bréchard.

Less old was the Station d'Oenologie et de Viticulture at Colmar (1899), where competent faculty offered courses on viticulture and viniculture, gave public lectures that drew many growers, and carried out research.[16] The *lycée* at Blanqueford in the department of Gironde offered the same kind of program as did those in Champagne, Beaujolais, and the other major wine centers.[17] These secondary and university centers have turned out well-trained growers who either have taken over their families' vineyards or who have set themselves up as advisors to anyone able to pay their services. Many of them have been hired by the various branches of the agriculture ministry that investigate special problems, especially fraud in production and labeling.[18] They also work for companies that manufacture equipment and chemicals used by vignerons and cellar masters. In addition, they are prominent in the large number of semiofficial bodies such as the Institut National des Vins d'Appellation d'Origine (INAO) and the Institut Technique de la Vigne et du Vin (ITV). When EEC regulations were applied to wine in 1970 and created the huge market of the Community of Ten, Europe's wealthiest countries, the need for a large body of skilled vine growers and wine makers became increasingly evident.

EVOLUTION OF TECHNOLOGY

The young grower of today is a product not merely of professional education, but also of changing outlook. He has ceased to be a traditionalist; on the contrary, he feels old ways are suspect, and he has bent his parents to his will by threatening to leave the land if the family enterprise is not modernized. Like the vineyard, the wine cellar has been furnished with adequate equipment and power to facilitate the wine-making process from crushing to labeling. When a machine is too expensive to buy, such as an automatic bottle filler and corker, it is rented. Implements, whether owned or rented, need space, so growers have erected new structures or renovated old ones and brought in electrical power to run the motors. Many agreed to set up equipment cooperatives to provide stemmer-crushers and mobile presses. However, this type of setup has not been notably successful because generally all its members need the apparatus at the same time. Modernization, therefore, has required the purchase of expensive machines that are used only a few days out of the year, and which must be maintained until the next harvest.

Young vignerons in quality wine areas are proud of their excellent cellars (see figures 3.10, 3.11). They are not afraid of borrowing from banks, nor of spending on capital equipment, nor, for that matter, of acquiring more comfortable housing, furnishings, and food. In fact, they have discovered that they have to offer a decent standard of living to young women in order to marry. Women will no longer willingly look after animals, keep poultry and rabbits, wash clothes in the village laundry shed, or fetch water from the local well. The man who wants to attract a bride has to provide a satisfactory house, modern conveniences such as indoor plumbing, and a washing machine and vacuum sweeper. Most food and clothing are store-bought, and this requires an automobile for transport. These families, of course, are the owners of family-sized properties that have increased in size over two or more generations. Their forefathers, or their wives' forefathers, had bought plots when prices were moderate or they had "married land," as a spiteful saying goes, that is, land came as a dowry, with or without a woman's good looks. Their forebears, in areas of fine wine, had been full-time growers and had made wine, as in the Côte d'Or, that was sometimes light of body, fragrant, and tannic. They in turn sold it to merchants who, if they found it too light, blended it with the full wines of Châteauneuf-du-Pape or of Gigondas in the Rhône Valley. For these merchants, storage costs were low, so they matured the blend in wood for a year or more and sold it in bottle or cask to well-to-do buyers who resided in buildings with cool cellars and with patience enough to let it soften over ten or more years. Like the vineyards, these private wine collections were passed on to the next generation. As for the hard-working vignerons making their own wine, they did not follow the eighteenth-century method of short fermentation. On the contrary, they seem not to have separated the stems from the grapes. In open wooden vats they carried on a long fermentation of two weeks or more, daily pushing down the mass of skins into the bubbling liquid with their naked bodies (see figure 3.1); or else, if they had already obtained the color and fullness they wanted, they drew the must off the skins and let the fermentation continue in barrels. [19]

Around the turn of the century, enologists such as Paul Jamain began to question the merits of this process. In the Côte d'Or they pointed out that stems contained water that weakened the must during fermentation, and they also absorbed some color. [20] As this knowledge spread, producers began to buy the newly invented stemmer-crushers. But tradition was often deeply rooted, so they kept some of the stems in the vats, a practice that some enologists recommend for grapes low in tannin. It was during the interwar that they began experimenting with a shorter fermentation, five or six days only, in order to obtain a lighter wine that was quicker to mature and offered more finesse in place of fullness of body. Since World War II the tendency toward short fermentation and complete destemming has accelerated, as has the abandonment of wooden vats in favor of closed vessels of glass-lined masonry or stainless steel, complete with heat control. Defenders of quicker processing recognize that wines of recent vintages are lighter in color and body, reach maturity earlier, and are commercially successful because few families demand wines that must age over many years, and modern dwellings rarely have the cellars to store many bottles. Life-styles have changed and wine makers have hastened to respond to the taste of new generations. This argument works nicely for growers and shippers who are spared the increasingly heavy costs of storage, but there is some opposition to quicker processing. Whether the customer has benefited from this cost cutting is a subject I shall take up later.

Another tendency, and this one has turned to the advantage of some progressive wine makers, has been the use of selected yeasts. Until the 1960s many, perhaps most, viniculturists relied chiefly on the natural yeasts growing on the skins of grapes. And by no means has this practice been abandoned. But on the skins there are "good" yeasts that will produce a natural fermentation, turning juice into wine; there are, however, "bad" yeasts that can harm wine by destroying its alcohol, or that can turn alcohol into vinegar in a short time. Makers have long inoculated their juice with sulfur dioxide to kill harmful ferments and other dangerous organisms, and hoped that good yeasts would do their job. Pasteur taught them that heating juice or wine also killed bacteria, especially those that combined with some wild yeasts, and caused the growth of acetic acid or provoked excess volatile acidity, above all during the fermentation of botrytized grapes. Pasteurization, however, has become an expensive process, with the result that wine makers lacking the necessary equipment still rely fully on sulfur dioxide to kill harmful yeasts. There are still many growers, especially in the Bordelais, who rely on natural yeasts. France's two leading enologists, Ribéreau-Gayon and Peynaud, have not been able to discover a positive correlation between a wine's quality and the yeasts employed in making it. They have not found that a classed beverage could be improved by ferments prepared outside the wine's area of production. And yet more and more viniculturists who use stainless steel or vitrified concrete vats are using selected yeasts created in specialized laboratories and sold commercially throughout France.[21] Setting aside some fresh juice, they add sugar and special yeasts to prepare a "starter" (*pied de cuve*), juice that has begun to ferment, to the contents of their vats. This method assures a quick-starting fermentation and, according to the yeasts chosen, can impose a particular quality to the finished nectar, influencing above all its aroma. Much of the scientific information about the nature and effects of selected yeasts has emerged from the researches of Pierre Barre, presently director of the microbiology laboratory at the Institut des Produits de la Vigne, a part the INRA of Montpellier.

When red wine of quality was stored in barrels for two or more years, viniculturists concerned themselves chiefly with the first, or the alcoholic, fermentation. If it went well, the wine took care of its own biological evolution. This evolution, enologists learned, involved a second microbial action called the "malo-lactic fermentation" because most of the malic acid, characterized by a very harsh taste, was transformed into lactic acid with a milder taste. As the maturation time in vats or casks grew shorter, makers had to be certain that the malo-lactic process took place before bottling. If it occurred in bottle, it would disturb the wine's clarity. Inducement of the step has, as a result, become just about universal wherever high acidity challenged the wine makers' art.

It is important to emphasize here that growers of fine wines have moved far more slowly to change than growers of ordinaries. The latter, after all, have to compete in a volatile and difficult market—indeed, in a market that has been declining. Their prime need has been to hasten the necessary steps of vinification and eliminate the unnecessary steps, such as frequent racking of wine that evaporates in wooden containers. The family and es-

FIGURE 3.1. An "artisanal" method of forcing the "cap" (compacted grape skins) back into the fermenting must below in the vat. It was not uncommon among small producers in Burgundy before 1939.

Les Vendanges — PRESSURAGE - Le Foulôir
Se compose d'un coffre généralement cylindrique, ouvert en haut pour introduire la vendange et traversé dans son ax
par une vis à l'extrémité de laquelle se trouve un treuil, muni de chevilles actionné par la palière.

FIGURE 3.2. This photograph looks like a scene from a Charlie Chaplin silent movie. The instrument on the left must be the grandfather of the horizontal press. (Photo in collection of Yves Rinaudo)

FIGURE 3.3. Early steps toward mechanization shortly before and after World War I. A round basket on tracks was loaded with macerated grapes removed from vats. The basket was then rolled on tracks and positioned under a hydraulic press, visible on the left in the next photo. The press juice was then pumped to barrels or to a closed maturing vat. The pumps were activated by a series of conveyor belts ultimately attached to the flywheel of a motor, seen at the upper right of the next illustration. (Photo from collection of Yves Rinaudo)

FIGURE 3.4. This illustration complements the preceding one, showing the hydraulic presses in the lower left, cement vats, and an electric motor with conveyor belts at upper left. (Photo in collection of Yves Rinaudo)

FIGURE 3.5. Workers breaking the "cake" of pressed grape skins in a perpendicular basket press, an expensive operation. (Photo François Bonal)

FIGURE 3.6. A battery of concrete vats with glazed interiors. They are closed except for air locks at the top to allow gas to escape during fermentation. (Photo Jean Poitrasson)

FIGURE 3.7. A horizontal press used widely in most wine areas.

MARAUSSAN (Hérault). - La Cave Coopérative Commune des « Vignerons Libres »
Vue intérieure, montrant dans le fond : les filtres, les pressoirs et les cuves de vinification

FIGURE 3.8. Interior view of the cooperative, Vignerons Libres. Located in Maraussan in the Midi, it initiated socialist penetration of wine production in 1901–1903.

FIGURE 3.9. Large stainless steel fermenting tanks with temperature control and automatic computer-operated racking. These containers, with a capacity of several hundred hectoliters, are also used for storing wine, especially white wine, to retain freshness and fruity aromas that would be lost in wooden storage.

FIGURE 3.10. An authentic Burgundian underground cellar of a small winery, at least several centuries old, with the original arches that are pleasing to the eye, but which make it difficult to move and top barrels with mechanical equipment.

FIGURE 3.11. Monsieur Gualco taking barrel samples of his wine. The true wine maker watches over the contents of his barrels with the same care that a doting parent watches over the rearing of children. (Photo Henri Gualco, Château Etang des Colombes)

FIGURE 3.12. Bottle filler with five outlets. This type is still used in small wineries, but is becoming a museum piece.

FIGURE 3.13. State-of-the-art assembly line to fill and cork bottles that have just been sterilized. (Photo Jean Poitrasson)

FIGURE 3.14. The evolution of bottle shapes toward the tall, slender type that can be laid on its side in order to keep the cork moist and swollen in the neck.

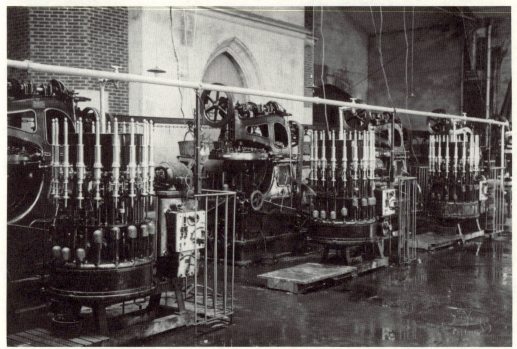

FIGURE 3.15. Mechanized *tirage*, filling bottles with still wine, sugar syrup, and yeast to begin the bottle fermentation, at Pommery. (Photo Grilliat-Jaeger Co.)

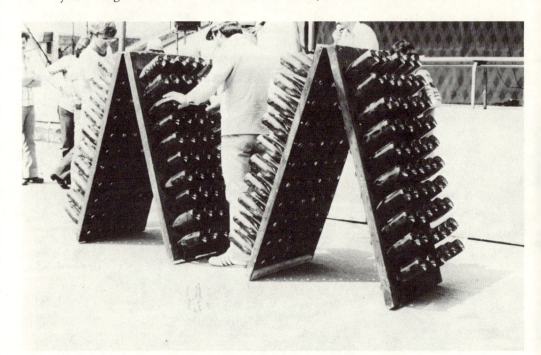

FIGURE 3.16. A riddling competition attracts professionals and amateurs who believe that the dexterity of their wrists is sufficient to joggle each bottle in a fraction of a second.

FIGURE 3.17. Mechanized riddlers, *gyropalettes*, are less romantic but far more cost-effective. The firm Taittinger treats 3.5 million bottles a year using 210 of these machines. Their whirling speed is controlled by a computer, and they function continuously. According to the firm Piper Heidsieck, the machines improve the quality of champagne by a finer control of the riddling process.

FIGURE 3.18. The *déboucheur* (uncorker and disgorger) who, when pulling the cork, released some wine and dead yeasts in the upper neck of the bottle. Before it became possible to freeze the upper neck to form a small block of ice containing the dead yeast, this worker had to be very skillful to avoid losing too much wine when the gas shot out with considerable force. He checked for clarity against the candle. Note the bottles standing neck down in the basket, waiting to be disgorged. (Photo François Bonal)

FIGURE 3.19. Assembly line for disgorging (second from right), dosing, corking, and muzzling champagne bottles. Still in use in the interwar. (Photo Grillat-Jaeger Co.)

tate producers in fine-wine areas have accepted change pragmatically. Their market is far less competitive: there is, after all, only one wine labeled château latour, or lafite, or margaux or mouton or haut-brion, just as the production of a montrachet, or a corton-charlemagne, or a vosne-romanée, and so on is extremely rare and commands fabulous prices. These wines, like fine champagne, have always been luxuries, seriously harmed when the rich cut back purchases, as in the 1930s, but exceedingly prosperous since the 1950s.

This hesitancy to change, a reluctance to be identified with any kind of revolution, can be discerned in the transition to modern presses. The old basket-type perpendicular press remained standard equipment in Côte d'Or, Médoc, and Champagne long after the general shift to horizontal presses had occurred elsewhere (see figures 3.2–3.5). The first change occurred when electricity, late to come to remote rural areas like Médoc, was used to replace human power with hydraulic power. After all, fine wine resulted first from free-run juice, then from press juice, provided the skins were not squeezed too hard. The powerful presses used in the Midi, capable of wringing out the last drop of fermented must from the "cake" of packed skins, gave an execrable liquid that profit-minded growers and merchants mixed with wines from Algeria and Spain in order to render it palatable. Fine-wine makers raised their grape-stained hands in horror at such practices. They clung to the perpendicular basket press until the 1950s, more often the 1960s or '70s. They knew, as competent enologists knew, that the basket press gives a wine that is easier to clear simply by racking.[22]

And yet certain types of horizontal presses that challenged the superiority of older models appeared on the market (see figure 3.7). This has not been true of the continuous-screw device, which is not recommended for fine wine and is even prohibited in some VAOC areas. Other types of horizontal pneumatic presses, particularly the bladder type, which presses inward from the circumference, treat skins with such tender pressure that press wine is almost of the same quality as free-run, with the result that the two are more frequently blended. Equally important is the greater ease of breaking up the cake of pressed skins, either for a second and third pressing to obtain a lower quality beverage or for removal. With a large perpendicular basket press it took a team of workers using wooden shovels hours to break and rearrange the cake after each pressing—time-consuming labor that added to costs.

Horizontal presses are particularly useful for white grapes. Modern equipment in the vineyard and wine cellar has undoubtedly speeded not only the removal of white grapes from vineyards to the cellar, but also the processes of destemming, crushing, and pressing. White grapes and must are now more delicately manipulated than in the past. The wider use of centrifuges has obviated the need to keep must for a day or two in a vat for *débourbage*, that is, to let solid matter such as bits of skin, stems, seeds, and dust drift to the bottom, before the cleaner juice is pumped into a vat or into barrels for fermentation. Small producers with limited equipment had often neglected this step, claiming that these solids *nourissaient*, or fed, the fermenting must. In the Loire Valley enologists often complained before and after World War I that local wines were amber in color, even brownish, rather than pale gold or white. The deeper color resulted from oxidation during the slow movement of grapes from vineyard to cellar, where they were crushed and pressed, or from leaving the crushed skins, loaded with pigments, too long in contact with the must.[23]

Experimentation has confirmed a theory held for decades by some thoughtful producers, that is, that a long, cool—even a cold—fermentation of white must in a closed vat preserved aroma and fruitiness (see figures 3.6–3.9). Before 1914 enologists in Champagne had recommended fermenting at fifteen to twenty degrees Celsius, as well as using selected yeasts to encourage the fuller development of aroma (*parfum*). At these temperatures it was still possible to use natural yeasts in especially good years, on condition that producers added a starter. However, since natural yeast ceases to function in a must that is either too hot or too cold, specialists had to create yeasts adapted to a colder fluid. With the introduction of effective cooling devices, advanced wine makers have been able to reduce vat temperatures to ten degrees Celsius to obtain an aromatic, fruity wine.[24]

By no means is cold fermentation the only method to obtain a mellow product. And by no means are all enologists and wine makers in agreement about the several procedures described above. In Champagne the big firms tend to hold to basket presses, and cooperatives to various horizontal devices. In Côtes-du-Rhône, especially in Hermitage, crushing with naked feet was still customary in several large cellars until the 1950s.[25] Some growers destem and others do not; some practice carbonic maceration for only a few days, which shortens a wine's life, while others do it for up to ten days to give a longer life to the final product; or they blend wines made by both types of fermentation with wine that has fermented for weeks, to create a beverage that will improve over the years.

Blending is of course also a widely used step in viniculture. There are very few commercial wines that are made from one type of grape: Alsatian AO wines that are labeled according to the grape, and the finest wine from the Golden Slopes, made from the Pinot Noir or the Chardonnay. In the literature I have found no suggestion that blending has evolved from an art into a science. Some enologists have devised schematic diagrams that look impressive, but merchants, who do most of the blending, do not seem to use them. For these men, blending is a highly personal task, requiring, first, a keen ability to taste and evaluate differences and, second, an equally good memory of flavors and aromas. These innate abilities also require years of training to hone them. The methods used today do not appear to have changed since Dom Pérignon, in the late seventeenth century, began mixing ingredients from various vineyards to obtain a *cuvée*, except that he blended *grapes* he tasted, whereas champagne makers today evaluate the *wines* derived from various grape varieties and vineyards, not the grapes themselves, and continue their tasting routine over a month or two, evaluating many mixtures before one is chosen.

It is at this point that the elaboration of champagne becomes unique. In the spring after one or several *cuvées* are created, the wine is induced to go through a second fermentation by the addition of sugar and selected yeasts. It is bottled and stoppered with a cork wired down or, given the high price of cork in today's market, with a metal crown cap. During this fermentation, dead yeasts and assorted matter build up in the bottle, which can create enormous problems for producers seeking a sparkling, brilliantly clear liquid. This problem was somewhat minimized with the invention, in the 1820s, of tables with holes for riddling and, in 1840, of upright triangular racks (*pupitres*), also with holes that enable the *remueur* to twist, joggle, and slightly lift the bottom of each bottle to move the sediment onto the closure (see figures 3.15–3.19). In four to six weeks, another worker snapped off the cap and, under the pressure that had built up in the bottle, the solids shot out with a small quantity of wine. Another worker topped the bottle with wine and sugar syrup in quantities measured according to the level of sweetness desired. Then another corked the bottle, and another placed a wire basket over the cork to hold it in place, and still others dressed the bottle with a label and other decorative material. This was truly a rather specific division of labor and assembly-line setup. Needless to say, it was very costly. After World War I, as workers demanded higher wages, managing engineers began to adapt the mechanized bottling processes devised for the soft-drink industry, adjusting them to the more complicated steps of champagnization.[26] Hand riddling, however, remained sacrosanct, the one necessary human intervention in the winery, comparable to pruning in the vineyard. It is still widely used, even in large firms such as Lanson. But within the past decade, machines called *gyropalettes* or *pupimetrics* have appeared on the market. They are capable of whirling a large number of bottles that lie in a metal basket, a procedure that gives the same results as hand riddling, but much more rapidly. There are now about nine thousand such machines in operation, and local manufacturers have sold three thousand more to French and foreign producers of sparkling wine. Undoubtedly their use will spread. Their efficiency goes beyond accelerated riddling; one million bottles in stationary *pupitres* take up 1,500 square meters, in *gyropalettes* only 400. The latter's introduction into the cellar has added one more link to a long chain of automated processes that has markedly reduced the need for manpower. In 1950 at least one cellar worker was required to manipulate every six thousand bottles; in the early 1980s, only one was needed for forty to fifty thousand.[27]

It is evident that champagne blending was merely an early step in a long, complicated assembly line from which human hands have nearly disappeared. In comparison, the elaboration of still wine is simplicity itself. This is true even among producers who have raised blending to the level of an art. Those in Châteauneuf-du-Pape put together twelve or more different varieties of grape, each selected to add some desirable characteristic: body, color, smoothness, aroma, and so on. No machine has been invented that can do this.

Careful blending can make good wines great; but it is also a means of perpetrating fraud.

Fake Wine

In order to understand what a fraudulent wine is, we must first understand the nature of an authentic wine. In a law of 1907 governmental experts and politicians tried to define authentic wine as a beverage made exclusively from the fermentation of fresh grapes or the juice of fresh grapes; its ingredients are water (85–90 percent), alcohol, and dry extracts. This is also the definition of the OIV, the Office International de Vin.[28] Given this definition, a beverage made of raisins or of concentrates would not be considered wine. The progress made in chemical analysis techniques has made it very easy for antifraud inspectors to detect such wine—indeed, even to detect wine made from the fresh grapes of Franco-American hybrid varieties, a product now banned in France.

During the phylloxera crisis and until vineyards were more or less replanted, the shortage of grapes had induced many merchants to concoct wine from raisins or other dried fruit and to add all kinds of chemicals either to render the product palatable, or to disguise its origins, or both. But even before 1900 this practice was on the wane because of a surplus of grapes and therefore there was little inducement to resort to other sources. During the interwar, most of the wine on the market was almost certainly authentic in that it was derived from fresh grapes. By this time, fraudulent methods consisted more in undesirable additions to fresh must or fermented wine. As Professor Branas put it during a wine symposium, two enologies arose: one that sought to grow wine as a pure natural product, the other that sought to distort the natural product by recourse to artificial additives.[29] To combat the latter, French legislators have passed more laws than the average vigneron can read in a lifetime. And yet illegal practices continue. Probably about one-third of wine sold since the 1920s has been fraudulent due to illegal additives, and it is highly unlikely that it is ever detected. There are still too many growers and merchants speaking with a forked tongue: they denounce falsification, yet they practice it, either through ignorance of the complex wine codes or out of financial necessity in a cold, wet year. This fraudulence occurs especially in areas of restricted production, where demand exceeds supply, as in Beaujolais, located in zone CI of the EEC's zoning area. Many growers, to stretch their produce, add an excess of sugar. By law, those in this zone may, in poor years, add enough sugar to raise the alcohol in the must by 2 degrees but they often pour in enough to obtain 2.5 or 3 degrees. They can then add water to augment the volume. For purists like Constantin Bourquin, chaptalization is "legalized fraud," deforming a natural product. This view is extreme, a bit like asserting that marriage is legalized prostitution. What he is really condemning, of course, is the long-accepted custom of pricing wine according to its alcoholic content—an inducement to cheat, especially among growers of ordinary wine. Since the early years of the century, as noted already, the French government has prohibited the addition of sugar to grapes from the deep south and North Africa, two areas listed in zone CIII of the EEC, where chaptalization remains prohibited. But this position runs counter to the big beet-sugar producers of northern France. In 1907 southern vignerons rose in riotous actions against the use of sugar, seeing it as the chief cause of overproduction and falling prices. Since then many politicians have been torn between these two highly organized pressure groups, and indeed, many southerners are less than sincere; when large shipments of sugar appear in local markets, the happy event is announced over loudspeakers: "Sugar has arrived."[30] Southerners, however, have long had trouble selling their ordinaries at a good price. In Beaujolais, the thirsty market absorbs whatever is labeled as coming from there. In his inquiry Doutrelant suggested that only one-third of the region's wine on the market is *honnête*, one-third is *impéccable*, and the other third is a common wine not worthy of the appellation. He also argued that in France 95 percent of shippers have adulterated their wine at one time or another. Piat, a negotiant, replied that excess sugaring has been carried out by growers, not by the merchants, who can do it only if they too own vineyards. He is, nonetheless, indulgent toward chaptalization; it improves the final product and so consumers benefit.[31] Even Bourquin admits that adding sugar is acceptable, "mais à un dégré modéré," and only in very poor years. One must be "raisonable."[32] It is probably true that the least "raisonable" are the producers of Alsace. In that cold northeasterly area, the most northern of French vineyards, sugaring is as normal a process as pressing grapes. As noted already, only a few privileged vineyards, facing south or east and sheltered by hills, can reduce chaptalization to a minimum. But appellation rules are so tolerant that considerable sugaring has never been looked upon as a fraudulent practice, even by the purest of the pure. This tolerance, it must be noted, pertains only to whites, but then, the northeast turns out whites almost exclusively.

It is now certain that growers will find that excessive chaptalization is a far more dangerous practice than in the past, when its detection was scarcely possible and certain. With the invention of a device producing nuclear magnetic resonance, the technicians of fraud squads can easily discover whether a must has been sugared beyond legal limits. During a recent visit to a viticultural village in the south I was informed that the local cooperative had been heavily fined for excessively enriching its must. However, a native son, highly placed in the administration, succeeded in having the fine removed. I mention this incident simply to point out that today it is possible to discover fraudulent practices by the use of science. The extent of illegal vinicultural methods depends more on the will of government agents to act. This is particularly true of fraud involving the laws on labeling.

Far more serious is the crime of false labeling. Here in particular, the issue of blending has arisen on numerous occasions over decades of time.

And however innocent merchants might proclaim themselves to be about sugaring, false labeling is an illegal act practiced almost exclusively by them.

Mendacious labeling has to do chiefly with the origin of a wine. That is, if a wine has a label stating that it is a beaujolais or a bordeaux or a côtes-du-rhône, the buyer assumes that the contents of the bottle come from grapes cultivated in those areas. This assumption is probably correct most of the time, especially for wines with a place appellation. Even when French law allows a blend, usually all of the wine must come from the place named on the label, such as "bordeaux." If not the blend will be degraded to the level of a simple table wine. For common beverages both French and EEC rules are simple in the extreme, since any of the ordinaries of the ten countries can be mixed at will and sold under the blender's label, provided no geographic location is printed on the label. The amount of wine sold on the market that comes exclusively from one vineyard, from one commune, from one limited region, such as Médoc, is but a very small quantity of France's total production, around 15 percent to be generous. Unfortunately, I cannot give fully precise figures because, over centuries of time, merchants selling wine with a geographic appellation have insisted on blending outside wines in order to correct local deficiencies, or to turn out a concoction whose taste is consistent year in, year out. No local vineyard can offer that guarantee, hence the mixing. In the past, *négociants* of Bordeaux had added Spanish or Algerian or both wines during years when the local product lacked body, color, aroma.[33] Today EEC legislation prohibits mixing of EEC and non-EEC wines, a measure enacted to protect Community producers. Burgundian and Beaujolais merchants bought Côtes-du-Rhône wines to add strength to the ruby musts that were sometimes too pale, or too weak new wines that local growers offered them. In many cases the blend was superior to any of the wines tasted separately. That is not the issue. The issue—a legal one, of course—is that the label on the bottle did not state or even suggest that the bottle's contents were a blend. A bottle labeled beaujolais might—and often did— have 80–90 percent of its contents from Beaujolais, and the rest from the Côtes-du-Rhône or from the better reds of the lower Midi. This practice has diminished considerably in recent times. Community regulations require that such a beaujolais lose its appellation.

To counter this prohibition, merchants have sometimes resorted to labeling by grape variety, thereby profiting from more lenient EEC rules. Instead of "beaujolais" a label can display "gamay" or "pinot noir" or "chardonnay." A bottle bearing this label, if not produced in France, need contain only 85 percent of the named grape, the remainder consisting of a variety determined by the merchant's sense of his market's demand. French laws, however, are more demanding, and a bottle labeled for a particular variety must contain 100 percent of it. Exporters, intensely driven by market analyses, do not turn out many varietal wines for the home market. Rather, they poll shoppers and blend accordingly. The printing of a varietal name on their label, a procedure they employ mainly for exported wine selling at modest prices, can easily convince buyers that they are procuring the great wines of denominated regions renowned for a grape variety. The name Pinot Noir suggests a great burgundy; Cabernet Sauvignon symbolizes a fine bordeaux; Gamay brings to mind an appellation, beaujolais. Bordeaux merchants using the label "claret" were the happiest of all; every Englishman knew claret, but had no idea of what it consisted. Their ignorance left knowledgeable shippers considerable leeway, which they used for concocting all sorts of beverages. Some of them were fairly good, "une sauce réussie," as Bourquin put it; others were scarcely drinkable.

Shippers had an old and tried method of evading strict labeling regulations. With the expansion of estate or domain bottling, which meant that all of the wine in a bottle had to be made from grapes cultivated by the grower in a given vineyard, merchants printed on their labels the words "Produced and bottled by. . . ." This little supplement allowed them to add 25 percent of wine not grown in the vineyard mentioned on the label. Merchants looked upon this practice as necessary to maintain consistency from year to year; it had been part of the vinification process for too many decades for merchants to look upon it as fraud. When informed that technically it was, they reacted with feelings of astonishment and distrust.

Dishonesty did not arise from the rather complicated procedure of blending wines of different origins. It resulted from the deliberate act of putting one kind of wine in a bottle and applying a label that said it contained another. M. Doutrelant has explained how this form of "magic transformation" takes place. A negotiant buys, for example, two hundred hectoliters of weak, pale pommard. He knows the wine is not salable in its pure condition; what he bought, in fact, was the official document that declared that he now has two hundred hectoliters of pommard in his cellar. He blends about half the pommard with full-bodied wine he brought in from Roussillon or Côtes-du-Rhône and sells it as pommard for a high price. The remainder he combines in varying quantities with ordinaries, devises a name—"Cuvée du Pape" or any such title that looks impressive to the uninitiated—and sells them for a lower but still profitable price. He has managed to boost his income from two sources, the fake pommard and the ordinaries with the impressive labels.[34]

Of course the legality of mixing wines can and has facilitated false labeling. Since the nineteenth century Bordeaux and Burgundian shippers have studied the English market. Here they discovered that the English, when not drinking beer and whiskey, preferred the stronger, doctored wines to the weaker authentic ones. So they blended to suit the market. If they did not, the English importers did. Since the 1940s this practice is largely a historical relic, if only because Algerian and even Spanish wine is less available and taste has changed. Besides, it is illegal.

Growers, easily forgetful of their own sins committed by excessive yields and sugaring, have been full of praise for "pure" wine. In Burgundy, they were attracted to domain bottling as a defense against shippers who sent out fake burgundy and ruined the reputation of the pure product; so the honest producers resorted to putting their wine in glass on a small scale before 1914 and on an increasingly larger scale since.[35] Bottling is a long, drawn-out task that usually fell to the womenfolk. Before the 1950s, however, not many could afford to do their own bottling because it meant buying equipment and financing the high costs of storage until their wines were ready. This required making loans, and even though branches of the Crédit Agricole existed, borrowing other people's money was still frowned upon. So they tried to survive for two or three years with no steady influx of money. Given this undesirable alternative, it was too tempting to sell their newly fermented wine to merchants who made a first payment soon after delivery and subsequent payments at agreed times. These payments helped finance the cultivation of vines, which is what most growers did best. Only after World War II did domain bottling take on significant dimensions, mainly because prices for burgundy rose impressively after 1960. In 1969 as much as 25 percent of the crop was bottled by growers. The huge jump in prices of the early 1970s raised that figure to 45 percent by 1976.

In Bordeaux, steps against fakery began earlier in the century, but with the English market in mind. Growers accepted the fact that some blending was desirable; after all, they mixed several varieties of vines in their properties to make a particular style of beverage that the English called "claret." So in 1911 their leaders reached an agreement that allowed the addition of Rioja or other alcoholic wine of Spain, or even some strong

Algerian wine, for the active market across the Channel. This so-called Bordeaux agreement limited to about 10 percent the amount of outside wine, which meant that the remainder was authentic.[36]

This does not mean that all growers in Bordeaux were tolerant of the practice. The major estate owners, who had obtained inclusion in the 1855 classification, set up in 1910 a Syndicate of Defense against Fraud. It survived the two wars, and from 1934 to 1954 it successfully prosecuted 565 practitioners of falsification, sending some to jail, forcing all of them to pay fines.[37] On a more limited scale, some of the first-growth châteaux began estate bottling in 1924, a practice they did not invent but which they made customary and eventually mandatory. Philippe de Rothschild of Mouton seems to have been the initiator, immediately followed by Yquem, and by the others the next year. All came together to create a set of rules to govern their actions. Dealers, as was customary, bought a part or all of the new wine; but the rules stated that the growers would decide when to bottle, and even when not to bottle if a wine of a poor year did not meet their standards. In the latter case shippers could sell the wine, but not with the château label nor with its name branded on the cork, another practice that was now used to identify the place of origin of the beverage. Eventually all the 1855 classified châteaux joined the group, and in 1972 in Médoc château bottling became compulsory for all classed appellations.[38]

When domain bottling first occurred on a large scale, the *négociants-éleveurs* were strongly opposed to it. They saw it, rightly, as a menace to their control over the vinicultural process of the fine médocs, graves, and sauternes. It also meant an end to their practice of blending to satisfy the demands of various markets. Perhaps it was this new and menacing reduction of the vinicultural role of merchants that was partly responsible for the decision by the firm of Cruse and Sons to perpetrate fraud on a sizable scale. The motivation was the incredible rise of prices for fine Bordeaux in the early 1970s, when the Japanese and Americans began speculating in fine wine, buying anything and everything at unprecedented prices. Little else was needed to tip the scales of honesty. And that little else was the limited harvest of 1971 and of 1972, when demand surpassed supply, and the temptation to miraculously augment supply was too great for some merchants to resist. In this situation lie the origins of "winegate," a term derived, of course, from the American political scandal called Watergate.[39]

Involved was the firm of Cruse et fils, an old and respected merchant company dating back to the nineteenth century. Incredibly its directors clandestinely and knowingly entered into an agreement with Paul Bert, a local merchant with a public record for fraudulent practice. In 1972 he had bought AOC white wine and sold it at a slight loss as VCC in order to obtain an *acquit vert*, a receipt showing the purchase of appellation wine that was required as part of the dossier when selling it. Only, Bert used the *acquit* to sell as AOC bordeaux a cargo of red wine he had purchased in Roussillon and Languedoc. In this deal he made a handsome profit, amply covering his small loss on the white wine, because the prices of fine bordeaux white were rather depressed in the early seventies, while those of all red bordeaux, even ordinaries, were shooting skyward like rockets.

Given this inflation, the owners of Cruse, short of red wine because of the smaller harvests of 1971 and 1972 and the massive selling that had depleted stocks, joined with Bert to blend Midi reds with appellation bordeaux and sell them as pure bordeaux, with the brand label of Cruse. Bert brought good-quality wine of the current vintage from Roussillon, counting on the serious difficulty of identifying young wine by place of origin in the hope of concealing his illegal commerce. An informer notified local authorities, and a team of inspectors of the fraud corps of the tax bureau became aware of Bert's activities. Finally, without prior warning (almost unheard of), they arrived at the Cruse warehouse on the Quai des Chartrons in June 1973. They wanted samples of all the wine stored there for tasting and analysis. The house of Cruse of course did not buy directly from Bert; two of its owners, Lionel and Yvan, were aware of his reputation and his convictions; they dealt rather with Bert's quickly assembled front company and his front men. They were surely aware of his scheme and decided to take advantage of it. They probably would have succeeded had not Bert carried out his illicit activities so openly, as though he were thumbing his nose at both the AOC laws and the inspectors who enforced them. When the tax inspectors demanded entry, the Cruses refused for at least half an hour to let them in, and then hid their record books. After the agents departed, they set about erasing and writing over several entries in their dossiers. After a series of similar searches, the justice ministry became convinced that it had ample evidence to prosecute. The trial took place in late 1974. By this time eighteen persons were included in the accusations, but after lengthy hearings only eight were found guilty. The only person who paid dearly for the affair was Hermann Cruse, who, although not connected with the scandal, leaped to his death from a bridge into the Gironde River. Bert received a two-year jail sentence, the others were given suspended sentences. On appeal, in May 1975, all the sentences were greatly reduced, and with the new presidential election they were canceled; even Bert was released from prison. And if all these reprieves did not neutralize the laws on false labeling, the termination of the surveillance imposed on the house of Cruse was sufficient evidence that AOC legislation was, like rubber, malleable. What remained were the fines, settlements owed to suitors who were victims of the fraud, and back taxes, a matter more important to the state than the indictments.

The sums demanded from the company were sizable but, like the jail sentences, were moderated by the pickup in wine sales in 1974–75. The economic crisis resulting from the sudden leap in oil prices and the fall of the dollar began to ease. Wine prices soon fell to a reasonable level, ending the mad speculation that had encouraged fraudulent labeling. During the trial there was widespread fear that the reputation of Bordeaux and indeed of all French wine had been seriously impaired. Apparently wine drinkers have short memories and ask no questions about the origins of their drink. Cruse did not go out of business; it simply sold its wine under another label until it was taken over in 1979 by the Société des Vins de France, a huge concern. Perhaps Bert was right: his wine was fake bordeaux but it was good. He, in turn, was condemning the vast array of AOC legislation on two grounds: first, it inhibited the kind of blending he carried out to "improve" wine; second, it was flouted by all merchants who were aware that it was not vigorously enforced. These, I believe, were self-serving arguments—not entirely false, but still far from the truth. The trial resulted in a tightening of AOC laws in the hope of saving viniculture from culprits like Bert.

The temptation to commit fraud was abated by the above scandal, but not eliminated. Recently a negotiant, Pierre Coste, and an estate grower, Pierre Ségéric of Château Gandoy-Perrinat, were convicted by the Tribunal Correctionel of Bordeaux for selling simple table wine as a vintage, château bordeaux. Like the Cruse, they were each given a six-month suspended sentence and fined the equivalent of $310,000.[40] What is most ironic is that Coste published a book in 1987, *Les Révolutions du palais ou l'histoire sensible des vins de 1855 à nos jours*, with a preface by Emile Peynaud, in which he extolled the progress of wine making and the need to maintain high quality and honest merchandising! Evidently the fraud squad was not taken in by his rhetoric.

❧ CHAPTER FOUR

The Attack on Fraud: Classification and Appellation

STRUGGLE FOR THE APPELLATION OF ORIGIN

Although the French government may at times seem lax in the enforcement of wine laws, and may even appear ever ready to create rules and regulations in numbers that make them unenforceable, the appearance belies much of the reality. The vast wine code that is the subject of this chapter was not created by bored politicians looking for something to do; rather, they were the midwives. The real progenitors of the code were the myriad grape and winegrowers who pressured the highest powers to bring forth the laws they believed would facilitate their fight against fraud. The very old pure food legislation was not, to their minds, sufficient. Wine production and trade, they argued, involved problems not covered in food laws, in particular the problem of varying quality masking itself under the same label, an operation that differed from the preservation of purity. Above all, adulteration was to be punished, and quality preserved.

The wine code was not the product of one sudden birth, but has emerged over several generations. It is a living body of laws in that it has changed and will continue to change. In the process the French brought forth their greatest legal contribution to the world of wine: the *vin d'appellation d'origine* (VAO), that is, wine designated as having been made from specified grapes cultivated in a given geographic space, in accord with acceptable, time-honored methods. The effort to identify wine with a distinctive viticultural area is very old—indeed, it goes back to the Greeks and Romans. Since the Middle Ages and early Modern period, producers in places such as Bordeaux, Burgundy, and Champagne, along with the wholesale merchants who distributed their wines, sought to spread the idea that wines from these vineyards were naturally good, that these vineyards in a particular setting turned out a superior product that should command higher prices. The connection between geography and quality had become a widely accepted belief, if not to say myth, by the nineteenth century, and is still the gospel of enophiles. It was precisely because these geographically identified wines had acquired a reputation through costly publicity that dishonest merchants, both in France and out, resorted to the practice of false labeling, as I have already explained. Since imitations of them were most often of petty quality, the reputation of the authentic product was at risk: the unknowledgeable buyer, paying a high price for wine sold as clos vougeot or médoc, was disappointed with its insipidity and not only did he stop buying, he also felt tricked by deceptive marketing.

To combat fraud, growers and shippers began a campaign after 1900 to induce legislators to help them set up a series of laws prohibiting the sale of beverages sold under misrepresentative labels. Their early focus was on geographic location, that is, to prohibit wine that had never seen the Golden Slopes from being sold under the label of a côte d'or, the name of the department in which the famous slopes are located. Their first success came in 1905 with a law on appellations of origin. This matter of geographic origin went beyond wine; it was equally relevant to mustard from Dijon, cheese from Roquefort, cider from Normandy, beer from Alsace, and so on. However, legislators were still thinking in terms of fake labeling rather than of a type of wine connected to a location, because their attention was focused on the rising anger of Languedocian vignerons who began a series of terribly destructive riots in 1907.

Hoping to avoid the spread of violence to other areas, the government, guided by experts in parliament, took the first steps in August 1908 toward creating areas named or delimited as the source of specified wines: it decreed that only wines originating in these areas and made according to "local usage" and custom would henceforth be entitled to bear the area's name on their labels.[1] This legislation was applied first to Champagne, and when a commission of experts made public the boundaries of the delimited area, growers who were not included were furious. Yet a geographic site called "Champagne viticole" retained exclusive right to the word "Champagne" on its bottles. Producers in excluded communes, even though they grew vines within the confines of the old province of Champagne, were urged to find a different designation. Similar procedures were used for delimiting Cognac, Armagnac, Banyuls, Clairette de Die, and Bordeaux. In all of these regions, except one, the process created some tension between the included and the excluded, but no violence. The exception was Champagne, where rioting broke out in 1911.[2]

Wartime damages suffered by all Champenois dissipated much of the bitter feeling engendered by the decree of 1908. In 1927 a large number of communal commissions of "experts" began the process of redrawing boundaries. Its members were very generous, including 407 communes, most of them in the departments of Marne and Aisne, with a few in Aube. The new zone covered forty-six thousand hectares—far too extensive—and included many vineyards that had always grown ordinary wine. Yet, this delimitation remained intact until 1951, when a law reduced it to thirty-four thousand hectares and 302 communes. Apart from the boundaries, the conditions set out in 1927 remained in effect, even though more than half of the land was not planted in vines. Grape varieties were limited to the Pinot Noir, Pinot Meunier, and Chardonnay. Other varieties, such as the Gamay, widely used in Aube, were condemned to be uprooted in eighteen years, but the date for the elimination of Gamay has been continuously postponed. Other varieties, the Arbanne and Petit Mastier, have disappeared.[3]

In Champagne various decrees imposed fairly strict limitations on cultural practices; only approved systems of pruning were allowed, irrigation was forbidden, as were ringing (*incision annulaire*) and mixing in grapes from vines less than three years old. Mechanical harvesters were prohibited in 1979. Yields, as already noted, have been a touchy issue. At first they were limited to fifty hectoliters or 7,500 kilograms of grapes per hectare. That was the basic yield, a maximum, however, that could be raised in good years, and in 1982 and 1983 it went up to 13,000 kilos! Endlessscrew horizontal presses were banned, and the amount of press wine that could be added to the free-run was set at one hectoliter for 150 kilos of grapes. Press wine over this amount must be declassed and used for making wine for employees, or for distilling into alcohol.

All of these restrictions were contained in a series of decree-laws that resulted from compromises between the experts and the vignerons who sat on various commissions set up to study soils, climate, grape types, exposure—indeed, all the conditions that have given a particular area its originality and character for making superior wines. Often the experts—enologists and ampelographers, agronomists, engineers, economists—opted for stricter controls than the vignerons. For example, in 1935 the experts demanded that yields over fifty hectoliters and those low in sugar be declassed. The vignerons rejected this recommendation, hence the tolerance of higher yields in good years and chaptalization. There has not been a tendency toward communal delimitations in Champagne because the larger firms combine wine from a variety of vineyards in different locations in order to create a *cuvée*.

Large merchants used the same procedure in every wine region. The designation "Bordeaux" was officially promulgated in 1911 and reserved only for vineyard districts, communes, or parts of communes that met established criteria—very broad, easy-to-meet criteria, to be sure. But wines produced in outlying areas of the Gironde department such as Arcachon and Lesparre in the west and north, and others in the east or upper country, were no longer to be labeled "Bordeaux." As in Champagne, a committee had been set up in 1907 by the minister of agriculture. It was loaded with politicians who argued and shouted for several years, heedful of special interests and resolving nothing. Growers in the departments of Dordogne and Lot-et-Garonne wanted to be part of the delimitation, insisting rightly that their wines had been used to improve those of Bordeaux since the Middle Ages. Finally, another minister dismissed the first committee; in its place he formed one of technicians, archivists, and professors of agriculture in the Gironde. They drew up a report in a few months and a decree established the AO Bordeaux. From this regional appellation emerged during the interwar a large number of local appellations. Some of them covered several communes, such as Médoc, or Saint-Emilion, while others were confined to one commune, such as Saint-Julien or Margaux.[4]

In Burgundy the move to appellations of origin began at the local level, usually communal. Along the Golden Slopes, communes had begun affixing the name of their most prestigious vineyard in order to enhance the sales value of their communal wines. There emerged, as a result, a host of hyphenated names: Gevrey-Chambertin, Chambolle-Musigny, Morey-Saint-Denis, Vosne-Romanée, Aloxe-Corton, to list but a few. This practice had its origins in the nineteenth century and now acquired greater importance with the emergence of geographic appellation. In fact, since the denomination process was all but taken over by viticulturists, it led to an explosion of minute appellations, much against the wishes of *négociants* who readily understood the confusion that would result. For instance, not only was there to be a communal chambertin (200 hectoliters), there soon appeared chambertin-clos-de-bèze (322 hectoliters), chapelle-chambertin (120 hectoliters), charmes-chambertin (700 hectoliters), ruchottes-chambertin (66 hectoliters), and griotte-chambertin (52 hectoliters). The same minute denominations appeared in Montrachet, the smallest of which was criots-bâtard-montrachet, producing an average of merely 35 hectoliters. This was, and still is, absurd. Almost all other denominations in France produced several hundred and, for most, several thousands of hectoliters for the market, a quantity that a merchant was more ready to publicize at a considerable cost. Merchants complained that this fragmentation presented serious problems of identification and marketing; but they did nothing to prevent it, and indeed, even worsened the situation by inventing some fake *clos* or châteaux.[5]

In regions where several townships sought to exploit a well-known name, such as Saint-Emilion in Bordeaux and Chablis in Burgundy, officially appointed commissions usually, after much discussion and wrangling, come up with acceptable compromises. In the Chablis district a three-level appellation of descending values was agreed on in 1920:

1. Grands Vins de Chablis, at the top, covering eight communes;
2. Chablis Village Supérieur, covering other villages within the canton of Chablis and seven outside; and
3. Chablis Village, granted to any of the local wines not made from the Chardonnay grape.[6]

In Saint-Emilion the issue was finally resolved by allowing outlying communes to attach the regional name to their own; thus Saint-Georges, which meant little on its own, became Saint-Georges Saint-Emilion. These attached appellations have become known as the "satellites."

A regional appellation for Burgundy, in gestation and vaguely used for years, was finally created by the civil tribunal of Dijon in 1930. In territory it was far more restricted than the AO that had been created at Bordeaux. It was 200 kilometers long, since it included the Beaujolais to the south, but it was only 650 meters wide in the Golden Slope and only several kilometers wide in Beaujolais.[7]

Beaujolais, although included in Burgundy, has long enjoyed a distinction of its own, like Saint-Emilion in the Bordelais. The name covered a variety of soils and topography and the main grape has been the Gamay. The best vineyards were in the hilly section to the north, Haut-Beaujolais, and merchants recognized a hierarchy of growths since the nineteenth century. As in Bordeaux and the Côte d'Or, communal syndicates of growers drew up the report that was part of the process of acquiring an appellation, and between 1935 and 1938 the communes of Chénas, Chiroubles, Fleurie, Morgon, Moulin-à-Vent, and some others each won an independent

AOC status. As in other areas, vignerons in neighboring communes resented that they were excluded. Responding to their complaints in 1943, the INAO accorded thirty-one of them the right to add their village name to that of Beaujolais, and in 1950 thirty-nine won the AOC "Beaujolais Villages," one notch up in the hierarchy, with simple Beaujolais at the bottom. Until the 1950s most of the region's wine was the product of the plains area near the city of Lyon, and none of it was bottled; rather, merchants sold it in bulk to the cafés of surrounding industrial cities of Lyon and St. Etienne, where workers bought it by the glass or pitcher in the company of comrades. It was—and still is—a *vin de zinc*.

The same was true of most wine of the mid- and lower Loire Valley, chiefly light whites and some reds that were scarcely known outside of their immediate areas. They were the *petits blancs* so enjoyed by river fishermen and Parisian artisans during their morning and afternoon breaks from work. They had no identifying label; they did not even have a bottle. Only the wines of Saumur and Vouvray enjoyed a wider reputation.[8] A similar area of nondistinction was the Rhône Valley south of Tain. In large quantities that varied with the years, these wines, including châteauneuf-du-pape, were sold in bulk to Burgundian merchants who blended them with the fine wines of upper Burgundy to obtain color and alcohol. AOC rules put an end to this very old practice.[9]

During the interwar the growers of these anonymous beverages were terribly hard-hit by the depression. The prices they received hardly covered their costs, and yet their wines were often good, fairly well made; but merchants were not interested in promoting them. Merchants preferred quantity over quality for their *vins de zinc*. Farsighted growers, therefore, began organizing syndicates, whose main functions were to encourage discipline among the members to achieve quality, resist fraud, and obtain an appellation. For these vignerons, an appellation was seen as a kind of passport into the light of public recognition, a light they hoped would glitter with the color of gold. They also began to organize cooperative wineries (to be discussed later) in order to achieve better quality. In truth, it was worthless to advertise a wine without an appellation. What could one call it?[10]

These steps toward quality during the interwar constituted the most advantageous strategy for growers. Even if they did not bring immediate benefits, they laid the groundwork for a postwar regeneration. A successful example is Châteauneuf-du-Pape. Long a provider of *vins médecin* of high-class burgundies, growers obtained low prices for their bulk wine; they lacked public recognition and were without bargaining power. Vignerons knew that they could, and did, produce a wine of high quality. Why then sell it in wood to enrich a merchant class whom they did not respect anyway? After World War I, fairly young viticulturists became aware of the true value of their beverages. To enhance them further they began replanting with quality stock, and those with some capital began to retain some of their wine in order to age it in wood, bottle it, and sell it by mail order under the Châteauneuf label. But the label did not yet have wide recognition, and vignerons had no control over their wine's commercialization. Local merchants bought a barrel of their good local wine, blended it with one or two barrels of lesser wines, and sold it as authentic Châteauneuf. To combat this practice, growers like Joseph Sabon and Paul Avril had two aims in mind: first, to obtain an official local appellation as a means of identifying and promoting their authentic wines; and second, to terminate the false labeling that hurt their reputation. They began by reorganizing the local syndicate of growers, not an easy job because dues would have to be collected to enable the syndicate to take action. They also chose as head of the syndicate a young lawyer, Baron P. Le Roy de Boiseaumarie, who accepted the job after studying the problem in 1926–27. They drew up the necessary report and presented it to the court in the city of Nîmes. Local merchants and some growers sought to block the process, as did those in communes that were not included in the project. As usual a committee of experts was appointed by the Ministry of Agriculture to draw up a recommendation based on their own investigation of the area and on the syndicate's report. The trial dragged on, but the court finally approved the delimitation and Châteauneuf-du-Pape now became a recognized *appellation d'origine* as a result of a judicial decision. That judges who could claim no expertise in matters of vine and wine growing made such important decisions was an odd element of the various methods resorted to in the history of the AO.[11]

The first phase began with the 1905 law, designed to end mislabeling, and the appellation of origin grew out of the efforts to end fraudulent wine sales. It recognized as a geographic entity a delimited area with a long tradition of viticulture, and, as it turned out, the task of fixing boundaries fell to the Ministry of Agriculture, that is, to the bureaucracy. Hence these initial steps are referred to as the administrative phase. Agents of the national government reviewed the documents prepared by vigneron syndicates that requested an AO and handed down their decision. As already noted, their first decree sought to create an appellation for Champagne, and it indicated the concept of AO in the bureaucratic mind: the focus was on a geographically defined territory, and any kind of wine produced in that territory could claim the appellation. Quality was not an element that appeared relevant to bureaucrats, nor to a great majority of wine growers. At a congress organized by the Société des Viticulteurs de France in 1906, representatives from major wine regions sought to describe the salient characteristics of their wines. The term *appellation d'origine* was not yet in wide usage. Joseph Capus spoke for the Gironde growers and used the occasion to emphasize the need for quality control as an integral part of the AO, thereby adding the *controlée*, creating the AOC. He denied that the present system, by limiting its concerns to geographic considerations, could eliminate fraudulent labeling: the administration could not identify the origin of a wine without tasting and chemical analysis, and these, in turn, required that AO wines meet certain standards resulting from acceptable grapes, limited yields, alcoholic content, and purity.[12]

Apparently the representatives, all well-to-do producers, were horrified at the thought of so much bureaucratic interference. Only the delegate from Mâcon approved; the remainder were more tolerant of fraud than of the kind of police control proposed by Capus. Moreover, producers were not above adulterating their wines. And the government in Paris was not eager to undertake serious assessment of wine; in fact, given the ill-will of growers and the riots of Champenois in 1911, the Ministry of Agriculture, by a decree of the same year, shifted responsibility for deciding on AO applications to the regional courts. Judges were called upon, when defining products with the name of origin attached to them, to take into account the nature, composition and *qualités substantielles* of the products. This last consideration was again included in the law of May 6, 1919. But it did next to nothing to discipline vignerons or merchants into making superior wines. Local growers, with vineyards in the river flats of Barsac, turned out a sweet wine and labeled it "barsac" even though it was not at all comparable to the fine products made from noble grapes grown in more suitable locations. In lower Médoc, where René Pijassou discovered that nearly half the polycultural farmers grew hybrids, their mediocre wine carried the label "médoc."[13] People drinking these unpalatable concoctions would inevitably conclude that all barsacs and all médocs were of the same low quality and grossly overpriced. Quality growers complained of this abuse of the AO which, after all, did include the words "substantial quality." Since AO's were defined in courts, local syndicates brought suits against the most flagrant abusers and often won a conviction from an understanding judge, who might be a vineyard owner. But the offenders, usually merchants, then appealed, and higher courts, not always located in judicial districts marked by viticulture, doggedly held to the view that an AO was strictly a matter of geographic origin, not a type of wine, and overturned the lower court's judgment.

The struggle to put teeth into AO legislation went on for years. Its leaders were Joseph Capus, elected to the Chamber of Deputies in 1919, and some local syndicate leaders like Le Roy de Boiseaumarie of Châteauneuf-du-Pape. Men like Capus were bent upon safeguarding the already established reputation of a wine area, and men like Le Roy de Boiseaumarie were bent on creating the conditions for the emergence of a great vineyard. Both sought to enhance quality by the production of wines typical of their respective zones and to eliminate the abusive use of these wine's identification, their labels. The label must come to indicate not only geographic origin, but also a type of wine, and Capus equated type with high quality.

His bill to achieve these ends was debated in 1925, when it encountered a good deal of opposition from commercial interests. Its final version became law two years later, but in greatly modified, or rather emasculated, form. Its provisions were not obligatory and only the elite of grower syndicates favored it. In fact, the mass of vignerons exploited it simply because wine, when classed by appellation, was not as limited in the use of sugar for fermentation. In the end, Capus and his cobelievers could not breach the fortress of laissez faire until a serious crisis hit in the 1930s. Then, and only then, would the two worlds of wine come to an understanding and batter beyond repair the fortress of resistance. The growers of ordinary wine, as we noted already, encountered an increasing imbalance of production and consumption. Their leader was Edouard Barthe, deputy of the department of Hérault in Languedoc. As president of the powerful wine pressure group in the Chamber, he united with the deputies of fine wine areas and together they managed to push through legislation that brought public authorities directly into the economy. I shall deal shortly with the Statut de la Viticulture as it affected ordinary wine; for the moment I shall focus on the 1930s legislation that finally gave meaning to an AO. In both cases, state control of production and sales came about because the mass of vine and winegrowers called for state controls in the hope of economic salvation during a time of depressed prices and declining consumption.

This flight from laissez faire was by no means limited to French vignerons, or even to France. In a time of world depression, industrialists demanded and got high protective tariffs, that is, higher than usual tariffs because French commercial policy had been protectionist since the 1880s. In addition, farmers and cattlemen obtained subsidies and various forms of price support. Viticulture was not alone in its evolution toward a form of economic *dirigisme* by the state. As it turned out, the central powers acquired far greater controls over the production and distribution of ordinary wine than over those protected by an appellation. In fact, the legislation that came into effect in July 1935 created a system that encouraged growers of finer wine to police themselves and excluded them from the rather severe controls set up earlier for ordinaries.

The law of July 30, 1935, was almost revolutionary in its import. It is still the basis of French wine policy and has been adapted by all the major viticultural areas of Europe. It has not eliminated fraud, as we discovered in the previous chapter, but it created the forces of control, supervision, and investigation that have undoubtedly curbed false labeling of wines.

As regards fine beverages, the law set aside the courts as determining bodies in the creation of AO districts. In their place it set up a special organ, the Comité National des Appellations d'Origine (CNAO), with members, at first, selected from the presidents of viticultural syndicates of AO regions with at least ten years existence. In addition, delegates of the agriculture, finance, and justice ministries were included, men whose experience with grape growing was extensive. In this way, the profession and the state combined their knowledge and powers to improve quality. The Committee, later called the Institut, was financed by a fee of two francs per hectoliter on AO producers. One-fourth of this total income went to the government to finance its participation; one-fourth formed a special budget to pay for publicity in favor of AO wine; and the remaining half filled the coffer of the CNAO to carry out its mission: to study the soil, climate, topography, history, and grapes of syndicates applying for AO status, and to supervise the growing practices of already recognized appellation districts.

Since it enjoyed extensive powers, the CNAO could and did do a sweeping job by tightening standards for grape types and yields. In 1934 there were 15,720,700 hectoliters of AO wine, about 20 percent of total production. Over several years the CNAO brought that down to 10 percent by declassifying roughly half of it. For a while, though, both large and medium growers of VCC, adversely affected by the Statut de la Viticulture, as we shall see, had won from the courts a fanciful AO recognition. Armed with it they escaped the limits the Statut imposed on their production, but in no other way improved their wine. However, the growers who could not meet the new standards were either reduced to VCC status or given the title of AO Simple, a less rigorous category than the now stricter AO Controlée (AOC), that is, controlled by the CNAO. The *simple* appellation came to an end in 1942, and although it was later revived, by 1944 the new total of AOC wine came to only 5,720,000 hectoliters. By the next year the Committee's experts had achieved an astounding record: they had examined about one million parcels of vines and created a vineyard survey based on quality, soil, cultural usages—in fact, all the phenomena associated with viti-viniculture. Parcels with hybrids were rejected without appeal. For example, the Côtes de Blaye in the Gironde produced 51,000 hectoliters of AO wine in 1943; two years later this sum fell to 7,500 hectoliters. The AO Simple was once and for all abolished in 1974.[14]

The INAO, as the CNAO became known in 1947, continued to function in the traditions laid down by Capus. An AOC wine was the product of a recognized area or vineyard, displayed its own originality of type, with its personality consecrated by age-old usages and a constant renown. These qualities resulted from

1. natural factors, such as climate, soil, exposure, and grapes, in a defined area; and
2. human factors, such as methods of training vines and of making and maturing wine.

An AOC acquired a collective character and required constant discipline among growers to maintain standards. The INAO, with a membership enlarged from twenty-four to forty-six members by 1954, remained a private organization with a public mission. But since the 1950s, because of insufficient income for its vast goals, the agriculture ministry has maintained it by subsidies, which has transformed its private status into a more decidedly public one. Because of this, many growers feel that it is closer to the state than to their syndicates and that it is overly bureaucratic. Its power to issue and enforce decrees has certainly increased the paperwork of both growers and sellers. Red tape can be overwhelming and alienating, and during interviews some growers complained of this. Chapuis went into more detail in his book, *Vigneron en Bourgogne*, and his views are shared by many independent vignerons who would like to have more freedom in the selection of grapes. Chapuis explained that he used to produce an excellent white wine from Pinot-Beurrot, a scarcely known variety, yet the wine sold very well. When the vines became too old he applied for permission to plant anew. The local technical counselor of the INAO refused and insisted that he plant only recommended varieties of his AO; if Chapuis resorted to Pinot-Beurrot, the INAO would force him to uproot. The INAO now decides when to harvest and will declass grapes if they are picked earlier. There are now so many regulations that not even the experts can agree on how to interpret them. The grower would be better off studying law rather than viticulture. Resentment has also been directed against a perceived overbearing arrogance among the hoard of inspectors who investigate wine cellars, whose image is that of grand inquisitors for whom all vignerons are capable of falsification and must be watched at all times. In short, growers are all guilty until they can prove themselves innocent. Alas, these same growers, a kind of collective sorcerer's apprentice, brought this system upon themselves.[15]

And yet, all quality growers recognize the need for discipline. They would prefer that it come from within, from vignerons acting through their syndicates and in control of the INAO, rather than from without. A great many vignerons seek to resist the expansion of control. In the AO Côtes-de-Provence, the Institut hoped to reduce the percentage of Carignane grapes in the traditional blend. In response, the president of the wine cooperative of Cuers stated that he, as well as other presidents or heads of local organizations, had no influence or power over the mass of growers who favored this grape because of its high yield. Moreover, the AO Côtes-de-Provence covered a large and diverse geographic territory, thus conditions differed and varying blends must be expected. The problem of legalizing certain varieties of grapes was a thorny one. The first decree of August 1951 setting up the AO Côtes-de-Provence did not recognize the Sémillon—in fact, refused to admit to its existence and did not provide data of the land it covered. Yet experienced growers continued to blend it in their *cuvées*, from 30 to 50 percent, and they made highly reputed whites that they exported. The response of the INAO was odd indeed; its technicians feared that some growers did not know how to vinify the grape and made faulty wines. The result: growers who used it to advantage were in violation of the law![16]

With the increase of consumption of AO wines, both technicians and growers agreed on the need to focus on excellence. This meant even more stringent controls and the declassification of wines that failed to meet accepted standards. In the 1950s many growers were enjoying AO status who clearly did not adhere to the limits on yields; in Gironde, for example, AO vineyards achieved yields that hardly differed from those producing ordinary grapes. The result was the inundation of several markets with large quantities of mediocre wine that hardly differed from the local VCC. To counter this tendency, local syndicates began the practice of tasting new wines to evaluate them. The Entre-Deux-Mers started this in 1953, Saint-Emilion in 1954, and Médoc in 1959. Growers brought their own bottles, and panels of judges carried out blind tastings. Their verdict was: acceptable, rejected, or set aside for a second trial several months later. At first the rejections were significant, as were the adjournments, and a lot of vignerons were quite angry.[17] However, the practice became accepted in a large number of regions and is the basis of a more effectively controlled AO. Since its appearance growers have seriously striven to improve their product. Given the expanding sales of AOC wines, customers now see in the label a form of guarantee, not only of origin but also of quality. The dream of Capus has come true, at least as an ideal put into practice.

Unfortunately, testing by a panel has not always guaranteed excellence; these panels are composed of a number of local growers whose palates have not always proven trustworthy, nor are they sufficiently detached and objective in their evaluations. But then, human institutions have never been perfect. It is abundantly clear that after the temporary termination of AO Simple in 1942 the amount of appellation wine dropped precipitously, as noted above. Since 1944 the percentage of AOC wine has continued to rise. In 1970 it represented 15 percent of the total metropolitan harvest. By the mid-1980s AOC's made up 44 percent.

Now in this latter figure are included two new appellations that have replaced AO Simple: *vin de pays* (country or regional wine) and VDQS (Vin Délimité de Qualité Supérieur), which I shall discuss shortly. They stand between AOC and VCC. Table 4.1 reveals the percentage of each category in 1985. Not included in the total are 10,723,000 hectoliters of wine pro-

Table 4.1.   Percentage and quantity of wine by appellation

Appellation	Percentage	Quantity (in hectoliters)
Vin de table (VCC)	52.2	30,562,000
Vin de pays	14.9	8,710,000
VDQS	3.4	2,016,000
AOC	29.5	17,238,000
Total	100.0	58,526,000

SOURCE: INSEE, *Annuaire statistique* (1986).

duced and distilled to make brandies, and therefore neither classed nor consumed as wine. It is notable that the volume of AOC rose 100 percent in fifteen years. If we put table and *vin de pays* or regional wine together, as they often are, their share of total production has fallen from 72 percent in 1965–69 to 61 percent in 1980–84, and to 57 percent in 1985.

Producers of better ordinaries, unable to obtain an AO label, had begun to lay plans for some kind of identity after World War II, following the discontinuance of AO Simple. This desire spread chiefly among Mediterranean vignerons. In Languedoc in 1952, just under 2 percent of the mass production enjoyed an AO, and most of these were the sweet wines of Lunel, Frontignan, and Roussillon, called *vin doux naturel* (VDN). These wines had old, well-established reputations. Table wines, however, were mostly *gros rouge*, with a small production of superior beverages. To give some indication as to which were better, a ministerial decree in December 1944 created the label of VDQS. This appellation, the creation of Philippe Lamour, has spread rapidly throughout the lower south. Languedoc and Roussillon turned out 77 percent of the VDQS of France in 1952 and 81 percent in 1979. If Provence is added, the lower south produces 86 percent of the total, a figure that has scarcely varied since.[18] This was a delimitation really made to order for the cooperative wineries of Languedoc. These producers in general make over 60 percent of VDQS. This label has greatly enhanced the product of areas like the Minervois and Corbières, whose wines can in good years surpass in quality many lesser AOC's. Growers in the latter district finally obtained an AOC classification in late 1984–85, after two years of struggle to win this superior status. Meanwhile Lamour persuaded the EEC to include the VDQS in its VQPRD, a special classification I shall discuss later.

This victory signals an almost revolutionary change in the classification of wine, indeed, a leveling comparable to that accomplished by republican revolutions of the past. Formerly a badge of high degree, of nobility after the rabble of simple AO's had been eliminated, an appellation has now been attained by wines that were once of low status, enabling them to acquire a new standing and the serious consideration that accompanies it. Wines, too, can enjoy upward mobility. Of course an AOC margaux and an AOC corbières remain a world apart, but the title "appellation" is to the lesser one the equivalent of the title "citizen" to the lower-class Frenchman. There is the element of equality, even if only in the title.

Equality, however, although it existed for a long time in some growers' minds, does at last exist in Languedoc, the main region of jug wine. The prestigious *Revue du vin de France* had, in its issue of May 1988, gone beyond the mere title of VDQS and advocated a full-scale classification of wines from the seven appellations of Languedoc-Roussillon: Côtes-du-Roussillon, Collioure, Fitou, Corbières, Minervois, Côteaux-du-Langue-doc, and Costières-du-Gard. The jury consisted of some ten highly recognized enologists in the region and several sommeliers and restaurant owners. No merchants were included. The experts set up three categories: *bons crus* at the bottom, then *grands crus*, and at the top, *crus exceptionnels*. Fourteen estates entered the lowest level, nine the next highest, and none the top level. This classification has recently become "official" and has the force of law behind it. It is as yet only a beginning, an effort long overdue, a belated recognition of a kind of mini wine revolution quietly underway in the lower Midi and which continues as other regions improve their wines.

An appellation-of-origin label, even when controlled by tasting, has never become a perfect guarantee of quality. This weakness has been especially true of the largest regional appellations—Bordeaux, Burgundy-Beaujolais, and Côtes-du-Rhône—as well as those of the lesser in size, such as Côtes-de-Provence, Champagne, Touraine, and so on. The village appellations cover wines that range from superb to those no better than ordinaries, save that they have been fancied up in seventy-five centiliter bottles. The exigencies of the INAO and its repeated attempts to upgrade the quality of AO wine has undoubtedly led to a gradual, more selective choice of varieties of grapes and to more efficient viti-viniculture. If the best appellation wines still come from areas that produced the finest beverages in the nineteenth century, and even earlier, the availability of an AOC label has helped the emergence of relatively new, or improved, viticultural areas in the Côtes-du-Rhône, the Loire Valley, the lower south, and the southwest around Cahors. The expansion of appellation vineyards was significant. Today nearly 33 percent of the wines elaborated in France carry some kind of special label that indicate their ranking in the hierarchy of VAOC. This is well over three times the volume of quality wines grown on the eve of World War I.

From Laissez Faire to *Dirigisme*

Unlike the producers of fine wines, the growers of *gros rouge* were not concerned with labeling but with the increase of false ordinary wine that competed with their product in the national market. After 1900 they were convinced that the root cause of their lack of sales and low prices was an increase in the amount of bogus wine not made from fresh grapes, and stored in the cellars of wholesale and retail merchants. They set up the Confédération Générale des Vignerons (CGV) after their riots of 1907, and it rapidly spread to include all of the lower south. Before and after World War I, it actively pursued frauders and was remarkably successful, being more active than the few agents the government employed in this enterprise, and obtained numerous convictions. In the course of the 1930s, however, the CGV fragmented into several sections and fell increasingly under the control of large landowners.[19] In 1930 it was further weakened by the founding of the Ligue des Petits et Moyens Viticulteurs, inspired by Edouard Barthe, deputy of Hérault. In the interwar, Barthe was to producers of ordinary wines what Capus was to growers of VAO's. Barthe was the kind of socialist who defended small family property, seeing in large capitalist estates the true perpetrators of fraud. Through his journal, *Le Vigneron du Midi*, and his activity in parliament he sought to check the expansion of large property and set up a kind of state-planned viticultural economy that would safeguard the artisan vigneron, the family grower. If Capus can rightly be called the father of *appellation controlée*, Barthe has equal parental claims to the Statut de la Viticulture of the early 1930s. Like Capus, he worked through the powerful wine lobby in the Chamber and Senate, a pressure group broad enough to include republican conservatives like Capus and pale-pink socialists like Barthe. It also brought together anti-Masonic monarchists and Catholics, as well as anti-clerical radicals.[20]

The so-called Statut de la Viticulture, also called Statut du Vin, consists of a series of acts, promulgated by the government, between 1931 and 1935 and modified by various decrees since.[21] It was the product of politicians, at least of a majority of them, who believed that small is beautiful; it had a definite bias against large property, an aspect that aroused the anger of some members of the wine lobby who sensed in it a menace to the right of private ownership. Yet the majority, who also voted for laws that prevented the building of supermarkets, seeing them as a general threat to small merchants or the family store, saw in the Statut the salvation of the family vineyard and therefore the salvation of the family. Even conservative deputies and senators, although worried by the Statut's threat to large property, accepted its main provisions. As nationalists they felt the need to keep farmers on the land; what would happen to France's army if there were too few peasant conscripts? Conservative admirers of corporatist ideals viewed it as a step away from republican laissez faire policy and more disposed toward economic control by semi-autonomous professional bodies, the basis of traditional corporatist philosophy.[22] Socialists and radicals favored it because it would lessen the distress of small vignerons in the lower Midi who voted massively for the republican left. Finally, it was interpreted as a necessary measure in a world suddenly struck by deep depression. Liberal policies had failed.

As a means to end the crisis of small vignerons, the Statut had three objectives:

1. To avoid surplus production by cutting back the size of the national VCC vineyard;
2. To stabilize the market by controlling supply; and
3. To provide growers with a *prix social*, that is, a price that brought in a net profit sufficient to retain a family on the land.[23]

Achievement of the first objective would require time. As an immediate step the Statut prohibited new vine planting in the major viticultural departments. Exceptions were allowed for small vignerons; if they owned ten hectares or less, they could plant ten hectares more. They could also replace vines removed since October 1931. This right was seriously reduced for owners of thirty hectares or more. Steps were also taken to reduce the national vineyard by about 150,000 hectares, because this space represented around ten million hectoliters of wine, the estimated excess. A law of July 30, 1935, provided for a very complex process of subsidies for voluntary uprooting. Increasingly, legislation for ordinary wine became as complex as that for AOC wine, and a growing body of regulations, fattened by more and more decrees, became the peasant vigneron's nightmare and the lawyer-politician's and the technocrat's paradise: only those two could understand the highly detailed and complex codes phrased in French legalese.

To stabilize the market (*assainir le marché* is the commonly used terminology), several measures were provided. One sought to reduce excessively high yields by imposing extra taxes on producers with a harvest of over two hundred hectoliters and whose yields exceeded one hundred hectoliters per hectare. Since the tax structure was graduated, growers of over two thousand hectoliters paid extra taxes if their yield exceeded eighty-one hectoliters per hectare, and a harvest of over fifty thousand hectoliters must not surpass fifty-one hectoliters per hectare. The tax in all cases was five francs per hectoliter. Yields were also controlled by fixing minimum percentages of alcohol, which varied between 8.5 degrees and 9 degrees for the Midi, and 6 to 7 degrees for the north. These requisite alcohol levels were not rigidly fixed but varied annually, depending on the harvest. In warm years they went up, and in cold years they went down.

Apart from yields, the Statut allowed for forced distillation of excess wine. And if wine was so abundant that distillation was not sufficient to balance supply and demand, then the government could resort to blocking a part of the wine in cellars; that is, the excess could not legally be sold, except for its gradual, spaced-out removal to the market by local officials as the need arose. Growers of under two hundred hectoliters were exempt from these proscriptions unless the harvest was so large that even their crops became a menace to stabilization. About half of the 1.66 million small vignerons grew wine for home consumption only and were not a factor in the market. As already noted, the other half turned out a lot of wine, roughly 40 percent of the total, and could sell it at once, which they usually did at a low price, because of their limited storage capacity and need for cash. That so much wine was not regulated constituted a serious weakness of the Statut. On the other hand, compulsory distillation had, as was intended, a beneficial effect on quality: it discouraged growers from excessive pressing of grape skins to get more juice. Since the prices paid for alcohol were below those paid for wine, growers had no reason to seek a surplus of wine that would have to be distilled. Large growers, if their yields surpassed eighty hectoliters per hectare, had to distill a larger percentage of their wine, and they often ended up losing money.[24]

Keeping wine off the market was intended to achieve the second aim of the Statut, and it was also intended to achieve the third aim, a prix social. In fact, the official decision to hold or release wine was based on price, and on advice from each local syndicate. Maximum and minimum prices were determined for regions and types of ordinary wine. If prices fell below the minimum, wine was blocked in the cellars in order to raise its monetary value; and if price surpassed the maximum, wine was released to bring down the price by increasing supply. A very mechanistic approach.

During the depression of the 1930s all the capitalist governments resorted to some form of state intervention, from the New Deal of President Franklin Roosevelt to the corporatism of Mussolini. The Statut de la Viticulture was the first step for French intervention and, on paper, it seemed a marked reversal of tradition, save for tariff protection. Perhaps what was lacking was experience with an *économie dirigée* in the 1930s. Whatever the cause, the Statut was hardly a success. As Bardissa put it, the Statut staved off the immediate ruin of small growers, but not their slow pauperization.[25] The channels of rapid communication did not exist for hasty decision making. Prices of ordinaries did not cover costs in the early 1930s because of sizable harvests that the Statut was unable to hold down. When prices rose after 1935, they were responding partly to blockage and distillation, but more definitely to lower production resulting from frost and mildew. Neither blockage nor distillation was sufficient to handle the massive harvest of North Africa—Algeria in particular—used by merchants to blend into the common reds of the Midi to enhance alcoholic content. There were simply too many variables for a sophisticated but overly mechanistic approach that was, in the end, too sparing of small growers, as well as of ordinary wine grown in other vineyards outside of the lower south. The Statut was really tailor-made for the Midi but the red tide that inundated the market swept in from other areas of France too. In fact, a large amount of mediocre wine obtained an appellation just to escape the Statut's restrictions and it competed for the same clients as ordinaries. AOC wines, even prestigious *grand cru* wines, were losing money. Inevitably the world depression belatedly hit France by 1933 and not even the wide-reaching Popular Front government of 1936–37 could ring up prosperity. Conditions stagnated until rearmament began in preparation for war.

Since I have already described the vicissitudes of the wine industry during the war, I shall not repeat them, except to emphasize that the Vichy regime, committed by its own ideology to a corporatist economy, encouraged further steps leading toward the organization of the market. In Champagne, the first Comité Interprofessionel appeared, set up along corporatist lines with representatives of growers, shippers, and the government. It was able to survive after hostilities came to an end.

The postwar temperament in France was highly critical of the laissez faire ideals of the Third Republic, but mindful enough of history to designate the new government as the Fourth Republic. And as it turned out, the political activity of the new regime, even without the archly conservative senate, resembled that of its predecessor. The major innovation was in its economic policy, which was fully committed to planification without the abolition of private property. The various plans for economic reform, nationalization, and recovery included the modernization of agriculture, and therefore of viticulture.

Beginning in 1951 a continual stream of laws and decrees came out of the ever-pregnant planning committees and the wine pressure group. We have already noted their effect on AO growers; as for producers of ordinaries, most of the acts resembled the old Statut de la Viticulture. The one major innovation was the creation of a new bureaucracy, the Institut des Vins de Consommation Courante (IVCC), the equivalent for ordinary wine of the INAO for appellation wine. That bureaucrats are very creative—of more bureaucracy—was as true in France as elsewhere.

The tasks assigned to the IVCC were important. It undertook a national survey of vineyards, completed it in several years, and published it in a volume-per-department collection, full of useful data. The purpose was to classify vineyards according to soils and grape types. Areas not suited to profitable vine culture, particularly the flatlands—low-lying areas subject to excess humidity, areas of heavy clay soil—were to be converted to other, more suitable crops. Vignerons with these lands were to be encouraged, by means of subsidies for uprooting, either to move away or convert. The ultimate goal was the migration of vines from plains to hillsides, a decline in total vine area, and a decrease in the viticultural population. These prescriptions were aimed particularly at the mass-production vineyards of lower Languedoc and Roussillon, most of which were located in the vast coastal plain.[26]

The IVCC also drew up a list of grapes, classed as "recommended" (the best), "authorized" (all right), "tolerated" (acceptable but to be replaced in a given number of years), and "prohibited" (chiefly hybrids). As in the 1930s, the interdiction to blend hybrids into commercial wine was maintained.[27]

The old system of maximum and minimum prices was preserved for wine classed in the *quantum*, that is, the amount of wine needed to supply the national market; the surplus was the *hors quantum* and to be distilled. In 1961–62 the latter came to fully one-third of total VCC production. The old system of blockage continued, and financial aid was offered to growers of blocked wine, with their stock serving as guarantee for low-interest loans. Stoppage occurred when prices fell below the minimum, the *prix de plancher*. If the price rose above the maximum (*prix de plafond*) the IVCC allowed the massive release or even the importation of wine to hold down prices. This occurred after the killing freeze of 1956–57, when a shortage of VCC pushed prices from 3 francs per degree of alcohol and per hectoliter to 7.50 francs in 1958. The government, guided by the IVCC, not only allowed sizable imports but also doubled taxes on wine. The growers of the Midi were furious, but the government remained adamant; its entire planned economy depended on controlling inflation, hence its efforts to control prices.

The practice of setting prices according to alcoholic content and per hectoliter was also intended to discourage excessive production: the higher the yield, the lower the alcohol content. Unfortunately this created a fixation on alcohol. A minimum of seven degrees was required of a beverage for it to meet the state's definition of wine. Any wine falling below this strength was distilled, not blocked. Blockage eventually created a trade in *droits* among growers. A producer who chose not to release his ration of wine at the date fixed for its release obtained a right for a given quantity, a right he could sell to a grower in need of immediate release of this quantity. The seller then held the remainder of his crop for later release at, he hoped, a higher price.[28] This was truly a gamble because the planners in Paris were determined to keep the prices of VCC at a modest level, within plus or minus 8 percent of what they called a *prix directeur* or *prix d'objectif*, an abstract ideal price. They were therefore ready to release a large volume of wine on the market even before prices might surpass the *prix de plafond*. The *prix d'objectif*, the *quantum*, and the *hors quantum* lasted only five years, from 1959 to 1962. The remainder of the system stayed in effect until 1970, when wine was included as a product to be treated by the European Economic Community. Two years before this entry the wine planners, doggedly determined on raising quality, created a new wine category, *vin de pays*, a higher level VCC originating in a named area, such as *vin de pays de l'Aude* or of Hérault. Unlike the true VCC it was wine grown from recommended or authorized grapes in the denominated area and registering ten degrees alcohol. Like other appellation wine it was free of blockage; it also enjoyed preferred financing and priority entry into the market.[29]

The advertising campaigns in favor of *vin de pays* have enjoyed a modest success, encouraging many meridional growers to create new vineyards on the hillsides of the Garrigues, a rather wild land of scrub bushes and rocky soil where vines had once thrived. However, the vignerons adventurous enough to replant upland have complained that negotiants would not pay them prices higher than for ordinary wine from the plains, yet their yields were lower and their costs higher. Wholesale merchants simply could make bigger profits by buying very low-alcohol, cheap jug wine and blending it with very cheap alcoholic wine from Algeria. *Vin de pays*, offering smaller profits, hardly interested them.

Continuous rioting and violence among southern vignerons is demonstrable evidence that the serious problems of low quality and excess supply

still await resolution. The enormous increase in legislation, often dupli-
cating prewar models, has simply given more jobs to bureaucrats without
raising the basic income of vignerons, even during the period of great
prosperity that followed the end of colonial wars in Indo-China and Algeria.[30] The rising costs of administration and of these wars had led to higher
taxes on wine. The loss of North African territories steadily lessened the
huge inflow of cheap wine grown with native labor. In the 1950s one could
read the plea "Stop the flood of Algerian wine" everywhere in Languedoc.
By the late 1960s, that flood was reduced to a trickle as liberated Algerians
uprooted vines to plant cereals. Algerian imports fell from 9.463 million
hectoliters in 1961 to about one million in 1985. But this reduction did
not embarrass the merchant-blenders. They rapidly arranged to import a
nearly equivalent supply from southern Italy, a member of the EEC and
whose produce enters freely in accordance with EEC rules on interstate
commerce. Neither the EEC, which became operative for wine in 1970,
nor the great expansion of cooperative wineries, as we shall see, offered
solutions. Each may even have worsened conditions, the cooperatives by
making it possible for inefficient, even marginal growers, to remain productive on the land, and the EEC by enacting legislation that was more
favorable to northern than to southern growers.

The inclusion of wine in the EEC free trade agreements in 1970 was
hailed with great expectations by vignerons in France. And indeed, growers of AOC wines have benefited considerably by the removal of most barriers to interstate trade. Languedocian growers believed that the great decline of Algerian wine and their own easy access to the rich industrial
population of North Europe would bring back the prosperity of the 1860s,
before the phylloxera destroyed their vines. Given that their expectations
rose so high, their disappointment was the more intense. First the hoped-
for buyers did not appear. The two major markets, Britain and West Germany, were disappointing. In Britain extremely heavy excise taxes on alcohol raised prices well above middle-class budgets, already hard hit by
income taxes; and the lower classes obstinately drank beer. Most Germans
also drank beer, as did Netherlanders, but the German middle class was
rich enough to buy AOC wines as well as beer. German representatives in
the EEC policy-making councils also defended their national wine interest
by pressuring their colleagues in nonproducing countries to liberalize the
more strict controls on viniculture previously imposed in France. German
growers, along with those of northern France, especially Alsatians, were
allowed to chaptalize profusely, which, as noted earlier, raised their yields.

As we have also noted, alcoholic wines from southern Italy, where labor costs were low, now gained access to France, enabling merchants to blend them with wine needing their strength and color. Simply put, southern Italian wines replaced those of Algeria, albeit on a somewhat smaller scale. Before long the entire lower Midi was up in arms against Italian imports and the merchants buying them, and literally in arms as gangs of vigneron action committees resorted to tactics ranging from roadblocks and dumping of Italian wine to the destruction of merchant wine cellars. Under pressure like this, with southern vignerons moving close to a rebellion of the 1907 type, the government in Paris tried to block the entry of Italian imports in 1976. But it was called to order by the EEC and forced to back down lest Italy block the import of French industrial goods—lest, indeed, the whole EEC structure collapse, which would seriously harm France's new, modern economy. On another occasion the French imposed unilaterally a tax of 1.13 francs per degree per hectoliter on Italian wine crossing the border. To appease the EEC they turned the proceeds over to the Community's agency that subsidized the farmers in EEC countries, and this body used the money to aid Italian grape growers!

Policy toward the Midi remained unchanged, save that the IVCC was abolished in mid-1976 and another agency took its place, the Office National Interprofessionnel des Vins de Table (ONIVIT). And since the term "wine of current consumption" was unattractive, in its place appeared "table wine," meaning dry wine to be consumed with meals. Interprofessional meant that growers and traders were to work in harmony to promote table wine, and to ameliorate it. The wine commission of the EEC created its own appellation for finer wines, calling them, to use the French term, Vins de Qualité Produits dans des Régions Déterminées, or VQPRD for short. Both AOC and VDQS growers, if approved by the specialists of the EEC, enjoy the right to display this appellation on their labels.

The hierarchy then has grown in complexity. For growers of Languedocian table wine, however, the EEC has become the enemy. The government in Paris, they firmly believe, has sacrificed the interests of the deep south to aid the northern industrial economy, and the various EEC viticultural agencies are dominated by more northerly winemen who arrogate to themselves many privileges—sugaring must, for one—that they deny to southerners, arguably for their own good. Worse, the entry of the wine industry into the EEC in 1970 has simply meant the addition of another monstrous bureaucracy in France.

It has become evident, however, that burgeoning bureaucracies cannot eliminate adulteration of wine, but perhaps the more rigorous enforcement of laws intended to prevent it can have some effect. Fraudulent practices are probably more widespread among merchants than among growers. Estate bottling is one way by which vignerons have sought to prevent merchants from "cooking" their new wines, that is, using good wine to give a little more character to mediocre wine. Another defense has also arisen— the vinicultural cooperative, which had its origins in the deep-seated, ancient desire of vineyardists to bypass the merchant in order to sell directly to the consumer.

CHAPTER FIVE

Cooperatives among Individualists

ORIGINS OF COOPERATIVE WINERIES

The creation of cooperative wineries (*caves coopératives*) is a factor in the wine revolution that is as important as the new technology. It contributed enormously to the modernizing process. In fact, it is really difficult to avoid the idea that without these collective enterprises the vinicultural revolution would have turned most small vineyardists into a rural serving class, if not a landless proletariat. Modernizing would have certainly taken place, but almost exclusively to the advantage of large landowners and *négociants-éleveurs* who would have used the small growers to trim vines and provide them with fresh grapes. Given the sizable costs the new viticulture entailed, and the steeply rising price of suitable land, the great majority of family growers simply could not have found the capital to buy all or even a part of the equipment required by a state-of-the-art winery. The cooperative cellar, therefore, became the small growers' salvation. By pooling their savings, and with loans and small state subsidies, they could hire an enologist to make their wine after procuring the latest machines. That these highly self-centered vignerons managed to join forces was itself an indication of a marked change in outlook, a change that resulted from their willingness to strike a balance between their traditional individualism and modern collective action.

Here I must distinguish between viticulture and viniculture. This distinction was often less clear before the rise of cooperatives because many grape growers, even small ones, either made and matured their own wine, or they pressed their own grapes and carried the process of wine making only through the first fermentation. Within a few weeks of the harvest most of them sold their new wine to a *négociant-éleveur* who matured it in his own cellars, blended it with other wines, and shipped it under his firm's label. Champenois were the main exception in that they usually sold grapes to champagne houses that maintained presses scattered throughout the vineyards in order to press at once the grapes they bought and to carry out the fermentation in their immense vats.

Cooperation brought with it an ever-sharpening division between grape and wine growing because so many vignerons looked upon the land and the vines growing in it as their personal property, an extension of their persons, a means of self-identification. Wine, with which so few of them had anything to do after fermentation, was more impersonal, the product of someone else. Vignerons were merely the providers of raw materials, and the final product had little if anything to do with each grower's contribution, since his grapes or new wine were lost in the mass. The shift to mutual wine making, therefore, was rendered easier by this vinicultural tradition long profitable to wholesale shippers. The transition was a rapid one if placed in the historical context of wine making; less so if viewed only in that of the wine revolution.

Cooperation as it first appeared in 1902–1903, was conceived of as an association of producers pooling their resources and efforts to turn out a product that belonged to them in one form or another. Since the idea of cooperatives had appeared in the nineteenth century as an aspect of socialist ideology, it was sometimes the case that an effort was made among growers of a commune to treat their plots as mutual property, to set up a cooperative, and to sell their wine collectively. But this was rare—very rare—with the result that in most villages where cooperatives appeared, vigneron members preserved the private ownership of their vineyards. At most they brought their grapes to the winery, where hired personnel made wine. That is, all the members' grapes, regardless of condition, were crushed, fermented, pressed, and vatted together indiscriminately. Once the wine was ready for sale, collective activity came to an end. In the early years of the movement each vigneron collected his share of the finished product and sold it at his own initiative. And the amount of wine each member received was prorated according to the weight of the grapes he delivered in the fall. The cooperative movement, its socialist origins notwithstanding, did not become a basis of truly socialist organization; it had almost no appeal as such. As it spread, it assumed the form of a public convenience; it performed a process, wine making, that was more and more onerous if not impossible for its members to undertake individually.

Even in this mitigated form it did not spread like wildfire in dry grass, but rather like one in a wet field. In 1908 there were thirteen cooperative cellars, most in the Var department where small growers, who were motivated by a half century of left-wing traditions, dominated. The Mediterranean south was the cradle of cooperation on a large scale. In 1920 the number grew to ninety-two, and storage capacity from 120,000 hectoliters to one million. On the eve of World War II their number had risen to 838 and their capacity to twelve million hectoliters. Most of them were still located in the Mediterranean south. Their rate of growth was about as rapid in the prosperous years of the 1920s as in the depression years of the 1930s, for the goal of the thousands of little vignerons who joined them was independence—that is, independence from the burden and increasing costs of viniculture, and independence from the *négociants-éleveurs*.[1]

These same reasons motivated small growers in fine wine areas to follow the example of southerners, but they were unable to attract a sizable membership and reach the size of southern enterprises such as those in Languedoc, which became veritable wine factories managed by highly skilled enologists and technicians. Vignerons in fine wine areas were too individualistic to adapt themselves to mutual action and many, perhaps most, made their own wine. They readily joined viticultural syndicates set up to defend their interests, above all to inform them about market conditions, especially prices, and to influence politicians. But, as was typical in Burgundy and Bordeaux, each was convinced that his wine was superior to his neighbor's, and no force could induce him to mix his grapes with others. But when the 1930s depression struck and champagne firms bought grapes at only absolutely minimal prices, some of them came together to create a cooperative. Others, as in the lower Côtes-du-Rhône, hoped to end the exploitation of the negotiants who bought their grapes strictly by weight, ignoring the various qualities of fruit and waiting for several days before making an offer until the water in each grape underwent some evaporation, reducing the weight. Like so many simple growers, they were ignorant of the procedures to follow to form a cooperative. So they made a pilgrimage to the lower south, especially to the Var, where the cooperative experience was old and solid.[2]

ORGANIZATION

Fortunately the Ministry of Agriculture was filled with technicians sympathetic to the vignerons' cause, as were many local agricultural agents.

The ministry distributed a model constitution as well as pamphlets on the procedures to follow to set up a cooperative. Following in this wake, politicians voted sums to be used to subsidize newly planned cellars, the Left seeing them as experiments in socialism, the Right as a way of preserving private property in land and the rural family. Usually the founders managed to raise about 50 to 70 percent of the capital required, the government provided 10 to 20 percent, and the Crédit Agricole the rest as a fifteen-year loan at low interest rates of 2 percent at first, 3 percent after 1930. Most mutual enterprises were organized along similar lines. Membership was limited to vineyard owners, whether they worked the vines or not. Each member subscribed to shares and had to bring in the quantity of grapes he agreed to upon joining, but his contribution did not necessarily include all his grapes. Governance was based on precedents set by petty vignerons before 1914; it was highly democratic and fully egalitarian. The principal was, and largely still is, "one man, one vote," regardless of the size and production of each adherent's property. The membership, ranging in size from less than a hundred in the earliest phase to several hundred and even thousands recently, belonged to a general assembly that met infrequently. This large body elected an administrative council of a dozen or more members that was usually renewed by one-third every year. The council in turn chose the president, one or more vice presidents, a secretary, and a treasurer. It also hired the permanent staff: a director, a cellar master, and technicians and secretaries as required.[3]

Relations between the cooperative and its membership varied from close to tenuous. For example, in Var the contract required that members bring all their grapes to be vinified; elsewhere, especially outside the lower Midi, members subscribed for only that part of their harvest they could not vinify themselves for lack of storage space.[4] And in the early years, members brought back the finished wine and sold it themselves, either directly to customers or to merchants. Once more it was mainly in the lower Midi that members allowed the cooperative to sell their wines because it was in a better bargaining position vis-à-vis the shippers and almost always won a higher price. Most merchants were by no means reluctant to do business with well-run cooperatives. They recognized the advantage of getting a better product and, just as important, a consistent one. These benefits reduced their costs of searching for suitable wines among many small vintners and having to deal with so many different qualities. From the vigneron's point of view, he was relieved of the costs and labor of wine making, could devote himself fully to vine training, and concentrate his investments on improving his vineyard or enlarging it. In addition and of great comfort, he received a dividend at specified periods. Even if the cooperative's director chose not to sell the wine at once or to sell it in spaced-out lots, he could pledge it, while in storage, as security to borrow the sums he periodically needed for distribution to members. Operating costs were not cheap, running to about 20 percent of gross income for salaries, for maintenance, and for renewal of equipment and structures. The director met these costs by subtracting a given amount of wine from the total and using income derived from its sale for managerial ends.

In the interwar the sizes of cooperatives varied considerably. Small ones producing merely a few thousand hectoliters of ordinary wine rarely survived one or more poor harvests. Those that continued to produce found it necessary to grow and, in the Midi, to grow rapidly. The Cave Coopérative des Vignerons de Marsillarques in Hérault expanded from 10,000 hectoliters capacity and 70 members in 1910 to 100,000 hectoliters and 397 members in 1924. It became the largest in the world. It covered its expenses by deducting 20,000 hectoliters of wine from the total vintage it sold for its members.[5] The average volume in ordinary wine coops was about 15,000 hectoliters. Compared to these were the smaller establishments in Beaujolais, Côte d'Or, Champagne, and Bordeaux, where vigneron leaders sought to capitalize on the well-established reputations of their regions, emphasized quality, and even sought to acquire AOC status. In the smallest, membership consisted of a few dozen vignerons who contributed their own equipment to the common cause, and who managed to get the free use or a lease on a local cellar. It was in these fine wine areas that vigneron individualism was most deep-rooted, and any owner of a hectare or more took egregious pride in making his own wine. As M. Chapuis put it, "The symbiosis between man and product . . . results in the vigneron becoming conscious of his personality through the quality of his wine."[6] Vignerons of this mentality were hardly attracted to any kind of collective action and ignored it until the hard times of the 1920s and 1930s. Even then they joined cooperatives that put emphasis on quality, penalizing members who brought in faulty grapes during harvest while offering a supplement to those growing the finest. An excellent example was the village of Vosne-Romanée, where a cooperative was set up under the leadership of the mayor who offered vats, a cellar, and five hundred francs. Little growers there had exhausted their financial resources replanting vines after the phylloxera. By 1918 their cellar equipment had been sold or had decayed, so they could not transform their grapes into wine, and, to bring down the price of grapes, local merchants had nearly stopped buying them. The coop paid thirty-three francs for one hundred kilograms of grapes; merchants paid only fifteen to eighteen francs when they bought at all. Compelled by similar conditions, growers elsewhere created associations in the early 1920s, but these remained small and precarious. In Musigny the crop came to only 100 hectoliters, while at Gevrey-Chambertin it averaged 1,300. With an average harvest of only 300 to 400 hectoliters, the organizations remained limited; yet in 1929 there were seventeen, most of them in areas known chiefly for lesser wines. The majority sought to sell directly to merchants, to restaurants, and to individuals, chiefly in barrels. Only two had bottling equipment. But in 1925 appeared the Cave Générale des Grands Vins de Bourgogne, a bottling and sales cooperative. This was a unique inspiration and eight small units joined, each providing one-fifth of its wine.[7] This form of centralization was not widespread, and I have not found any additional information about the Cave Générale. At best, coops joined in federations within each department, but until recently, carried on their business independently. Their penchant to be unique, combined with prosperity since the 1950s, has weakened the cooperative impulse. The coop at Vosne has disappeared, and so have others.

In Burgundy, Bordeaux, and Champagne cooperative cellars were able to benefit from the names of communes and wines already well known through massive publicity campaigns usually organized by large shipping firms. In areas without this fame, cooperative cellars were sometimes able to improve the quality of wine and contribute to the locality's reputation. This was especially true in the Côtes-du-Rhône, in the northern sector at Tain, which specialized in reds, and in the southern sector at Tavel, where rosés dominated. Tavel won an AO rating in 1928, thanks to the efforts of some knowledgeable grape growers. The cooperators recognized, however, that Tavel's reputation was still to be made, since other producers were slow to replace moldy vats that turned out faulty wine. They therefore began to construct a building for a communal cellar and had just completed furnishing it with up-to-date equipment when the 1937 harvest arrived. Using this crop as a warranty to borrow money to pay the 75 members, they were in a position to mature the crop longer and to sell it in selected lots at steadily rising prices from 1938 on. The next year they sold it wholesale and even found a market in the United States, unfortunately just as the war broke out. This success before the tragedy of conflict induced other vignerons to join before and even during the war, so mem-

FIGURE 5.1. The cooperative winery L'Espérance in Coursan, Aude, in the late 1930s, with horse-drawn carts for carrying grapes to the loading dock. The capacity of the dock was already inadequate for the growing membership.

FIGURE 5.2. Use of Archimedean screws to hasten the flow of fresh grapes from the loading area to stemmer-crushers inside the winery, and then to fermenting vats by means of electrical pumps.

FIGURE 5.3. A large bottling cooperative, the Cellier des Dauphins, in the Rhône area. It bottles the wine of five smaller cooperatives nearby. The enormous tanks are temperature controlled, and bottling is highly automated by a computer network.

bership rose to 103 by 1945. By this time Tavel had already won its reputation as the best—and most expensive—rosé.[8]

Such a role was hardly possible in Champagne. Petty growers actively
reconstituted their vineyards after the first war, and the impulse toward
collective action came from the Syndicat des Vignerons, which was laic
and radical or left-of-center in politics. It helped create a Société Coopérative Civile, which pressed the grapes of its 181 members and amassed a
small capital of 20,800 francs in 1921. Ten years later it had 2,500 members and a capital of 344,600 francs. With such a sizable group, the coop
was able to obtain various grapes from many different vineyards, blend
them in its *cuvée*, and turn out superior sparkling and still wines. In 1922
it had shipped 2,800 bottles; in 1935 its shipments attained 56,000 bottles, as yet a minuscule total compared to the millions sent out by the
major firms. It finally set up shop in Aÿ in 1935 and is still there.

Local branches of the Syndicat set up coops in other villages with recognized vineyards. For example, in Mailly villagers were also unable to
sell their grapes and turned to collective action in a desperate effort to
survive. A renewed impulse came in the 1930s when firms, also suffering
from the depression, bought few grapes and reduced prices drastically,
following the same policy as their Burgundian colleagues. As for the vignerons, the value of a collective cellar was that it pressed, fermented, and
stored members' wine, which, unlike delicate grapes, they could sell later
at higher prices to firms in need of an extra supply or type to complete a
cuvée. Almost unique was the formation of a Coopérative des Grands Crus
in 1923. It accepted only growers with vineyards rated at the quotient of
80 or above. A rating of 80 on a 100-point scale represented good but not
superior quality. In 1927, a prosperous year, its membership reached 260,
with 360 hectares of great and first-growth vineyards. Just before the war
it shipped thirty thousand bottles. The vast majority of growers, however,
still sold fresh and quickly perishable grapes to shippers who were also
affected by falling exports, and who did not buy except to round out a *cuvée*
in short years. As everywhere, the 1930s remained the "years of poverty."[9]

POSTWAR EXPANSION

World War II brought serious setbacks to viticulture, but it was not as
catastrophic as World War I. French armies were not engaged in battle
after the defeat of 1940, and most of the vignerons who survived were
demobilized and returned to their homes. The Vichy regime, with its al-

most fanatical cult of peasant and rural virtues, was well disposed toward cooperatives of all sorts, finding in them a form of peasant organization compatible with the corporate state. Their number, therefore, did not decline; their production, sales, and prices were simply brought under the control of the ministries of corporations and of agriculture. Wine, like everything else, was rationed, which, of course, augmented its value on the extensive black market. Even *gros rouge* found its way into elegant glasses. Sales of wines made by cooperatives were not yet extensive because so many members picked up a portion of their share and sold it themselves, an old practice facilitating the flow of wine into black market channels. With the money they earned, vignerons, like most farmers, purchased land. Luckily for them, land had fallen in value in the 1930s and prices remained accessible during the German occupation.

The purchase of parcels of land continued after the war—parcels that were, in most cases, minuscule. Yet their agglomeration modified the structure of the national vineyard. Whereas the average land size of cooperators was just under one hectare before the war, it has steadily increased in dimension, although slowly, rising to only 1.56 hectares in 1950 and 1.61 hectares by 1964, 1.68 in 1970, 1.90 in 1980, and 2.05 in 1985.[10] This was a rise of 31.4 percent over thirty-five years. The present figure seems meager; yet given the rapid rise of vineyard prices since the 1950s, it represents considerable privation, a very painful sacrifice of comforts and amusements in order to raise capital.

The war, the defeat, and the liberation from German occupation probably engendered a new sense of comradery, of Gallic fellowship, and this seems to have encouraged a new spurt of cooperative organization that began to moderate only after 1980 (see table 5.1).

This second leap forward in the wine cooperative movement is less notable for the increase in the number of establishments than in that of membership, capacity, and hectares belonging to members. More vignerons with larger vineyards joined mainly because they could not mechanize both their vineyards and their cellars. As we already noted, they put their liquid capital into land purchases, tractors, sprayers, and replanting, all of which rose seriously in prices. They bought into cooperative cellars in order to benefit from the modern equipment that was being installed in them, thanks to government subsidies that covered over 30 percent of the costs of cellar expansion and modernization. There were other advantages: cooperatives were practically immune from taxes. They did not pay the land tax for their buildings, nor the taxes on equipment, nor the license

Table 5.1. Rise of cooperative wineries

Year	Number of Coops	Members	Capacity (in hectoliters)	Area of Vines (in hectoliters)	% of Total Wine
1945	858	154,672	14,853,176	229,464	25
1951	997	207,386	19,868,402	336,572	27
1959	1,128	252,565	27,955,800	395,102	35
1969	1,202	289,970	44,813,012	495,819	42
1980	1,158	263,646	55,042,567	501,722	49
1983	1,163	251,200	57,088,877	494,860	44
1985	1,158	273,711	56,945,414	486,547	47
% rise	35	77	283	112	88

SOURCE: *Annuaire des caves coopératives de France*, 1st–6th eds.

fee (*patente*) on agricultural, industrial, and commercial activity, and so on. Private wineries were therefore at a disadvantage when competing against mutual cellars in the marketplace, and by the 1960s coops were selling most of the wine of their members, even in reputable areas. By 1986 they sold nearly all of it, save in Champagne. As we shall discover later, wine commerce underwent a change disadvantageous to small growers, hence their entry into cooperatives and their greater reliance on the cellars to commercialize their wine. Moreover, the larger shippers, actively putting their smaller competitors out of business, were not even interested in small lots of ordinary wine except at extremely low prices; the costs of collecting it were too high. This explains why, by 1975, 45 percent of French wine was made in cooperative cellars, and in 1985, 47 percent— figures very close to the aim of the government's planning commission. In addition to the annual yield, they brought out older wines that had matured in their cellars. In 1985 they marketed slightly more than half the national production (50.7 percent).[11]

During the 1970s cooperatives, like private negotiants, began either to fuse or to centralize certain of their processes, such as bottling, labeling, and packaging, in one plant. This concentration was far less evident in areas where cooperatives concentrated on ordinary wine, because it was shipped in bulk to wholesale houses for blending before being retailed either in glass or plastic liter and multi-liter containers. Growers in Languedoc-Roussillon were the most active joiners of coops that used to turn out from 50 to 63 percent of total regional wine production (and reached

71 percent in 1985), but most of it was VCC. Quality wine, the VDQS that appeared chiefly in the Midi, increased by 82 percent in volume between 1950 and 1964, but really declined by 13 percent of the total national production. This type of beverage, although made chiefly in coops, never quite lived up to expectations, and as more and more of its growers acquired AOC status, its production dropped behind that of VAOC: 725,725 hectoliters in a total of 7,386,448 hectoliters in 1985.

The trend everywhere was toward wines with an appellation; they were easier to sell and more profitable for growers. Even in other Midi departments, such as the Var, where coops made 75 percent of the department's total, the large coastal cellars managed to induce members to plant better grape vines. Therefore they were able to increase the proportion of VDQS and VAOC, especially the Côtes-de-Provence type of rosé that the growing tourist and vacation trade encouraged. The huge improvement of motor, railway, and air transport brought throngs of vacationers to the south, where they learned to enjoy chilled local wine during the summer and then ordered cases of it the rest of the year to remind them of their sun and fun. Demand grew at such a pace that cooperative managers decided to centralize shipments. Fourteen cellars formed the Coopérative pour la Commercialisation des Vins du Var (COVIVAR), which simply bypassed merchants and sold directly to retailers, such as supermarkets and chain stores.

The same trend became evident in the Rhône Valley. Villages that had produced olives, fruit, and grapes before 1939 rather rapidly abandoned the first two, utilizing the space to concentrate on the third. Some of them became highly if not completely viticultural after the terrible freeze of the mid-1950s that left their olive groves looking like a sparse forest of gnarled ghosts. Most of them tried combining fruit trees and vineyards and were satisfied with the ordinary wine they sold to merchants. However, those on the slopes well away from the river prospered after they had turned principally to grapes, and acquired either regional or special village appellations such as Gigondas, Cairanne, Vacqueras, and so on. Nearly all the cooperative wineries appeared in the southern section of the *côtes*; the department of Vaucluse alone, where most of them were concentrated, turned out over 76 percent of the valley's total during the 1970s, and 77 percent in 1985. In fact, all such enterprises accounted for over 79 percent of both VCC and VAO. These wineries contributed to a steady improvement of quality, so more wine acquired the general appellation of Côtes-du-Rhône. Cooperatives vinified about 65 percent of AOC wine, if we include the one big cooperative at Tain in the northern sector. The lengthy narrow vineyard of the Rhône Valley, given its smaller dimensions, rivaled the lower Midi for its intensity of mutual enterprise.[12] There remained, on the other hand, a larger number of independent growers scattered over the area. Those of Châteauneuf-du-Pape have stubbornly refused to put aside their independence; only one cooperative was recently set up, small in size. Having acquired their appellation before the Second World War, the growers perfected their skills and followed the brilliant, aggressive leadership of the men who had first taught them that an AO confirmed not only a geographic space, but high quality as well. Châteauneuf lies in the extreme southern tip of the valley. At the northern extreme, growers also resisted the lure of cooperation, with the exception of those cultivating vineyards near the small town of Tain, where one large cooperative serves hundreds of small full- and part-time vignerons.

In the extensive vineyard of Burgundy, cooperatives spread rather widely, but unevenly. They produced in the 1970–75 quinquennial about 35 percent of AOC beaujolais, 17 percent of beaujolais village, and a small quantity of the *crus*, such as morgan, fleury, juliénas. In southern Burgundy, chiefly in the vineyards around Mâcon and the Saône-et-Loire department generally, they vinified about 35 to 40 percent of the total in the 1970s, and 42 percent in 1985; for all of Burgundy they made 30 percent of VAOC. The early ones were set up mainly to produce white Mâcon, and they greatly improved its quality. Hired enologists have abandoned the practice of mixing all the grapes, but as in Viré, they now vinify separately grapes from the plains, those from the slopes, and those from higher localities, referred to as the *montagne*. The results have been impressive. In 1971 AOC wines won eleven gold, eight silver, and eight bronze medals in various tasting competitions. Yet vinicultural cooperation has never spread widely; in 1985 membership came to only 16 percent of the zone's *déclarants*.[13]

In regions with an old tradition and reputation for excellent wines, individualism has resisted cooperative viniculture. This has been the case in the Golden Slopes, except in the Hautes-Côtes of Nuits and Beaune. It is equally the case in the Bordelais. In 1979, only 32 percent of growers there had joined cooperative ventures. In 1985, for all of Aquitania, there was a decrease to 23 percent. These were chiefly small growers, each averaging about three hundred hectoliters. Their firms produced VCC, AOC Bordeaux, and AOC Bordeaux Supérieur, the lowest levels of AOC classifications.[14] Throughout the southwest, cooperatives limited their efforts to ordinaries, and their production of appellation wine actually declined as a percentage of total production by 49 percent between 1950 and 1964. Since then, at least in the Gironde department, more stringent controls of grape culture have led to improved ordinaries, especially whites from Entre-Deux-Mers, turned out in massive quantity at low prices. For a brief period in the 1960s, white wine became fashionable, but French consumers have always shown a preference for reds. The well-established communal cooperatives in Médoc, therefore, enjoyed a less fragile market, given that they specialized in red wine and profited from the renown of their communal names. Yet membership steadily declined as small owners sold their land and departed. But this was not a phenomenon limited to Médoc.

More solid were the coops of Alsace and Champagne. In the former AO area, half the growers were cooperators and they turned out about half the wine. Even more prosperous were those of Champagne, where after World War II 62 percent of growers belonged to cooperatives and furnished 40 percent of the grape crop. An increasing number of members joined a cooperative cellar to have their grapes pressed and the juice fermented. Among them was a growing class called *récoltant-manipulant*, a title as complex as the growers' activities, for they were both grape growers and producers of sparkling champagne. They are, therefore, grower-bottlers. In the spring following the harvest, they withdrew their wine from the cooperative and put it through a second fermentation in bottle in order to turn out a finished product. These vignerons were owners of two or more hectares of vines, not the average grower with under one hectare who had to be content with the still wine that most coops sold to shippers. They formed an elite, enjoying a sizable revenue derived from the high prices they obtained either by direct sales or from merchants. Encouraged by these high prices, more cooperatives began to make sparkling champagne for their members, and even to market it for them. When they did this they competed with the grower-bottlers, whether members or not. They suffered, unless their members were widely dispersed, from one serious drawback: their membership came from only one or a few nearby villages, and therefore they did not have access to the variety of grapes brought in by the major companies to create a *cuvée*. Yet a lot of consumers were attracted by their lower shelf prices and have not at all been put off by a less elegant beverage that is just as bubbly as the best.[15] No wonder there is practically no abandonment of the land. And cooperatives have become a major retaining force. Young people, especially heirs to vineyards, have remained to help work the vines; where else could they enjoy a truly high income from such small holdings. Prosperity, however, has undermined somewhat the associative spirit; in 1985 membership was down to 34 percent and production to 35 percent. This decline of course is relative to the expanded viticultural population, the recent doubling of the vineyard, and constantly expanding production, save for the early 1980s. Table 5.2 shows that in absolute terms all aspects of cooperation flourished from 1980 to 1985.

Vignerons of the Loire Valley were not as fortunate, but they did not look to collective action to improve their economic conditions. Certainly cooperatives expanded there too, but while an increase in their number of 57 percent looks impressive, the actual number rose from a mere fourteen in 1950 to a mere twenty-two in 1964 and twenty-five in 1985. In 1950 they vinified not more than 2.2 percent of the regional total; in 1964 this had risen to only 7 percent, and in 1985 to 18 percent. The number of members had risen by an impressive 18 percent, though their total came to only 3 percent of growers in 1985. More important was their general move to turn out quality wines, whose volume rose as a result. But in 1985 they marketed only 8 percent of the valley's total of fine wine. Although limited in capacity and number, they were moving boldly to enhance the value of their beverages. Of course, cooperative leaders cannot take all the credit for this evolution; nonetheless, their enological achievements encouraged all vignerons.[16]

The viniculture cooperative movement had its beginnings in southern France. Over a span of more than seven decades it has, like a giant vine, crept into every major area of grape production. Although created to make wine, it has markedly influenced viticulture, serving as a means of spreading information about the application and usefulness of new techniques and chemicals. Cooperatives have become major employers of highly

Table 5.2.   Aspects of cooperative wineries in Champagne

Aspects	1980	1985
Number of coops	123	140
Membership	9,862	10,421
Storage capacity	901,000 hl	1,163,000 hl
Hectares of members	8,950	9,459
Production AOC	300,368 hl	412,121 hl
% of zone's production	34	35

SOURCE: *Annuaire des caves coopératives de France.*

trained people, thereby helping agricultural schools to place their graduates in good jobs. These technicians, given the grapes most of them had to work with, undoubtedly improved the ordinary and low-level appellation wines they turned out, profiting from better-equipped cellars and enological skills far beyond those of the hordes of small vignerons who constituted the membership.

And yet, cooperatives have increasingly been less successful in overcoming certain weaknesses that have restrained their contributions to improving the product. To a certain extent, these weaknesses were built into their initial organization. I have only mentioned the raw material—the grapes—that they transformed into wine. One drawback was linked to the architecture of their wineries: from earliest times their loading platforms were rarely spacious enough to permit the rapid unloading of grapes. When animal power prevailed, members loaded their newly picked grapes into wooden wagons, made the rather long trip to the winery, and, once there, waited in line, often for an hour or longer, to be unloaded (see figure 5.1). A great deal of conversation and joking went on during the interval under the brilliant sun of September or early October, but socializing went on at the expense of the health of the grapes. Not only the heat but also flies and bees bore down on the skins, causing fissures and the spread of bacteria. Generally, members were not inclined to spend money to speed unloading operations with additional platforms and crushers because these, like presses, went into frenetically busy operation for one brief time, and only once a year. Since the 1950s tractors have replaced animals, but the bottleneck remains, especially in the semitropical south. Costly improvements have taken place, of course, but chiefly in regions where vines of good value bring in a profit allowing further investment (see figure 5.2).

Another serious obstacle grew out of the original concept of cooperation. Originally set up by small producers with limited capital and limited knowledge—men still highly individualistic who would not transfer their vineyards to cooperative or collective cultivation by specialists—vinicultural cooperatives accepted the grapes of their members with only two concerns, weight and sugar content, and ignored the other conditions of the fruit. Everybody's grapes went into the same vats. Careful growers were therefore penalized by the careless. And it was not uncommon for growers to sell their best grapes to merchant wine makers and send their worst to the coop. The founding of a cooperative winery did not necessarily mean that the founders were cooperative in spirit. Since the 1950s, some wineries in France have adopted rules by which quality grapes are accorded a higher rating and monetary return: the higher the sugar content, the higher the value; likewise, the more valued the grape variety, the higher the vigneron's return in the form of supplemental payments. But this new system exists in a small minority of coops that produce AOC wines. In Languedoc, on the other hand, rules of this sort have been rejected in practice even when the membership accepted them in principle. Boulet and Laporte relate an example of resistance to selectivity.[17] From 1965 to 1970 the leaders of a cellar in Hérault urged members to replant their vineyards in grape varieties recommended for improving wine. The general assembly agreed almost unanimously to try the experiment to see if higher prices could be obtained to cover the higher costs. But, as it turned out, only one member out of seven actually replanted, covering only 4.7 percent of all members' total vine area. Only medium and larger growers were really serious, and they were the younger, full-time vignerons with a higher level of education.

This brings us to another obstruction: the inevitable aging of the membership. In many cooperative wineries, more than half the members are sixty years of age or older. They lack initiative, fear change, and own vineyards that are simply too small; they would lose them if they had to make wine as well as cultivate grapes, or if they had nothing but grapes to sell to merchant wine makers. They simply do not have capital or are not willing to invest in replanting. Unlike the example cited above, they vote against renovation, and since they are numerous and each member has only one vote, they can resist change effectively.

Their numbers are reinforced by another kind of member, the part-time grower. Many of these men—and some women—are young, and they either inherited a small vineyard, which they keep to supplement an income from another source, or they, as urban dwellers, invested in a small one for any number of reasons: prestige, second income, or summer residence. They are absentee owners. By no means do all these part-timers or absentees resist change. Unlike the old men, they have some capital and they use the vineyard's income to improve it because they have another income, usually the principal one. But the fact remains that in coops making ordinary wine, part-time growers tend also to resist renovation, and many of them are retired, living on a pension, and depend on the income they receive from their vines. There is a common belief among them that quality is not an advantage, that negotiants simply will not pay the higher prices required to cover the higher costs entailed in cultivating recommended grape varieties. This belief is not entirely a myth, but it was more accurate in earlier times when members tried to sell their share of wine on their own. Since the 1960s cooperatives, especially those with a central sales office, have obtained better prices and have proved that quality does pay. What no longer pays is the *gros rouge* that too many meridional coops sell to merchants as blending wine.[18]

It has become increasingly evident that producers of low-grade ordinaries face a bleak future, and it is especially the cooperatives that flood the market and find it difficult if not impossible to renovate. The professional full-time growers have become a minority in the membership. They usually own about half the vineyard area of the membership; therefore they contribute a large share of the harvest, yet each has only one vote when decisions are made. They usually dominate the elected administrative council, but the general assembly must approve their recommendations. Many part-timers are so indifferent that they do not even attend the assembly meetings, so no quorum is available to reach a decision.

These weaknesses have become serious, particularly in Languedoc-Roussillon, where cooperatives have not resolved the continuous crisis in the VCC market. Neither has the resort to violence and massive demonstrations that have become almost endemic since the late 1960s.

These same problems exist elsewhere but, except in the Rhône Valley, are less acute. And undoubtedly the future of the wine industry in France, more so than its European competitors, is highly dependent on cooperatives. Their share of total production, 55 percent in 1985, has continued to grow, and the skills and knowledge of their salaried technicians are indispensable as vinicultural processes and equipment become more complex and expensive. Only recently has the influence of vinicultural professionals in the Confédération Nationale des Coopératives Vinicoles been strengthened by the passing of a generation whose heirs sell their vineyards, making more land available for the authentic growers. This has been a slow evolution, but it is underway and already notable in the economics of wine.

CHAPTER SIX

The Economics of Wine

CRISIS AND RECOVERY

The cultivation of wine grapes has always been part of the general agricultural economy in France. Not until the later decades of the nineteenth century did specialization in viticulture become extensive, a tendency that entailed risks and was limited mainly to lower Languedoc and Roussillon. Vignerons who did not make wine, who sold their grapes directly to *négociants-éleveurs*, rarely enjoyed a comfortable income. Like general farmers in an industrial society, their monetary revenues were seriously lower than the level of the national income, rising rarely above 70 percent of the latter.[1] Their situation was better if they transformed their grapes into new wine, which brought a much higher price when sold to the merchants who matured, bottled, and distributed it over various markets. Wine, considered an agricultural rather than industrial product in France, enjoyed fourth place for its value in the early twentieth century, behind meat, milk, and wheat. Although a "manufactured" or, if you like, an "elaborated" commodity, it has always been classed with agricultural produce. To the French, it is an alimentary substance (*aliment*), a natural part of a meal, nearly on a level with bread.

Before 1914 wine's total monetary value was estimated at 1.355 billion francs. This was a large sum for that time, before the onset of serious inflation, and provided some support for roughly one-fifth of France's total farm population.[2] For more than half of these growers, however, grapes could not guarantee full support, so they devoted land to food cultures as well, relying on grapes or wine as their chief cash crop. Cash was not often abundant during the economic crises that fell upon succeeding generations after 1914, with the result that the value of grapes and wine fell, pushing them downward in value from fourth to fifth place. On the eve of the Second World War viti-viniculture was responsible for about 8 percent of total agricultural income, with a value of roughly two billion current francs.[3] But since these francs had been devalued by roughly 75 to 80 percent, they were worth only about 500,000 pre-1914 gold francs. This meant that grape growers, like farmers in general, suffered a relative decline in their living standards. What made this decline relative rather than absolute was the tumble of all prices, including those affecting the vignerons' costs of cultivation. Other mitigating factors were cheap land, easily purchased by those with some cash or credit, and the paying of old debts contracted before the war, when money was expensive. In addition, the landed could grow their own food, and enjoy it with their unsold wine. And yet the elderly men I interviewed recalled the interwar as a time of troubles—of monetary instability as cabinets deflated and inflated the currency; of shrinking markets; and of political turmoil and widespread frustration. The outbreak of war in 1939 seemed to be the apex of their bad luck. When defeat came in 1940, there was no longer an army to purchase stocks; there were only Germans, confiscations, and rationings. Nearly all vineyards experienced a period of crisis in the 1940s and early 1950s. During these hard times, there was a general exodus from rural centers toward urban ones, leaving villages abandoned, land up for sale, and the slow beginning of vineyard concentration.

This was also a period of hard decision making within the post-1945 planned economy. Where viticultural syndicates were run by forward-looking growers who could pressure the mass of landowners to follow them, they moved toward the growing of fine wine and securing an appellation. They emphasized replanting with the most promising grapes, the adaptation of mechanized processes, and, often, the reorganization of the local cooperative so it would turn out superior wines. The costs of replanting, refitting, and mechanizing absorbed most profits. State subsidies helped, but growers ran up heavy debts. In fact, borrowing among vignerons really came into its own now, became almost respectable; at least it was recognized as a necessary fact of modern production. In areas with a tradition of quality, innovative syndical leadership imposed discipline to improve value. Such was the Union Viticole de Beaujolais (UVB). When in the early 1950s Midi growers, whose syndicates continued down the path of ordinary wine, began to experience the troubles of imbalance between production and consumption, the Union marked its distance from southern representatives in the Fédération des Associations Viticoles, and demanded separate statutes for VAOC and VCC. With the representatives of other AOC areas, they wanted neither limits on production nor compulsory blockage, and, in addition, absolutely no price controls.[4]

This does not mean that Beaujolais growers had no local problems. AOC rules were rather loosely drawn, allowing the production of too much juice of low quality. In 1954 syndicate leaders declassed wine that outrageously surpassed the ceiling on yields, and it was sold off at low prices. The UVB also recognized that some unscrupulous merchants, chiefly those of recent origin, according to M. Loyat, were using beaujolais labels on ordinary wine. Union heads demanded they be prosecuted for fraud and that official tasting of wine take place to determine its authenticity. These measures have been only partially successful, and false beaujolais continues to flood foreign markets. Nevertheless, beaujolais growers have enjoyed steadily rising values and a sizable expansion of their world sales since the mid-sixties. The same situation occurred in the rest of Burgundy—Golden Slopes, Chablis, Pouilly-Fuissé—where rising prices have generally more than compensated for rising costs.[5]

More so than in Burgundy, viticulture was the leading product of Bordeaux agriculture, making up 40 percent of the total vegetal production, and covering nearly 12 percent of the surface of the Gironde department. Viticulture suffered considerably during the war. Much of the southwest along the Atlantic coast was occupied by German troops who either confiscated or bought at ridiculously low prices the best growths and more elementary classed wines. This burden was merely the latest in a long list.[6]

In fact, the Bordeaux wine industry had lived through hard times since the 1880s, and only in the 1950s did prices begin to allow a comfortable profit. But these same profits had to be invested in renovations. Vines were old and run down; among them were many hybrids, even in the best properties. Equally run down were many of the country houses, and at Château Latour, bought by two British companies in the early 1960s, workers' cottages still had earth floors. Given the greater quantity of Bordeaux wine as compared with Burgundy, it was difficult to reactivate sales just after the war. The great châteaux were bound by contracts with shipping firms that maintained prices at the levels of wartime regulations, and these same shippers cunningly convinced many growers to accept moderate prices to encourage buyers.[7]

With the rising costs of labor and materials, growers became desperate. They turned to publicity, setting up wine fairs, founding an Académie des Vins to stimulate public interest, and finally creating the Commanderie du Bontemps de Médoc et des Graves, whose convivial meetings were widely written up in the press. And yet, unable to survive, many little vignerons emigrated; their number fell from 8,000 in 1939 to 5,600 in 1955.

Undoubtedly these activities helped the revival that began in the 1950s. This revival was as yet modest, since burgundy prices rose twice as fast as those of bordeaux, but still sufficient to tide growers over the catastrophic freeze of the 1956–57 winter that killed tens of thousands of vines. Replanting began at once and, for good or for bad, yields rose, thanks to the vigor of younger vines as well as to new cultural practices. Thanks also to a revived world economy and the end of the economic drain of French colonial wars, buyers had more money to spend on fine products.[8]

Unfortunately, economic prosperity encouraged inflation, which in turn induced people with money to purchase material objects: gold, above all, and art, jewelry, and fine wines. By 1969 classed growths had become objects of speculation and bordeaux nectars became "red gold." Merchants warned growers not to become greedy and not to demand exorbitant prices, but since the war growers had watched merchants grow rich at their expense and would hear nothing of moderation. Up to 1971 a grower, even if he sold all his crop, had to borrow money to finance his operations for the following year. But after that date he was able to finance them by the sale of only one-half his crop.

In 1961 first growths were fetching over 26,000 francs per *tonneau* (nine hundred liters or one hundred cases). By 1972 they averaged 95,000 francs. Because these were speculator prices they did not accurately represent the true quality of wines, and first growths shot up way above the solid clarets of lesser breed. Seriously widened gaps appeared between the hierarchic layers of growths. In 1971 first wines went for 117,917 francs, seconds for a mere 26,977 francs, and regional AOC Médocs for 4,559 francs. Next year first growths sold for 150,000 francs, and these were new beverages needing years to become drinkable. Of course few people drank them; they were resold later for even higher prices.

What happened to wines happened to vineyards. Several eminent vineyards became far too expensive for local shipping firms; they were taken over rather by negotiants from other parts of France or by investors who had no economic ties to either vines or wines. Local shippers were rather hard put to find the cash and credit they needed to pay the enormous prices exacted by growers. Some whose finances were shaky had to sell one or more of the châteaux their firms had acquired in earlier times in order to raise funds. Small merchants without adequate financing simply went out of business, since they were unable to buy from vengeful growers. They were helpless in a price spiral that was fueled by frantic buying, both among international and domestic merchants.

Speculative, euphemistically called "venture" buying was itself stimulated by a relative shortage of fine bordeaux. In 1963, 1965, and 1968 wines were execrable, and harvests were under average until the huge crop of 1970; but 1971 was smaller. So 1970 notwithstanding, good AOC wines were limited in supply. In contrast, authentic burgundy was always in limited supply, which explains the continuous rise of prices, and even mediocre burgundy was always valued as a luxury item. But for the best growths of bordeaux, prices had stagnated in the 1950s and went up modestly in the next decade, when the cost of everything else had leaped ahead. The so-called greed of growers, an epithet used by shippers in the early 1970s, was really a desperate need to catch up, to recover their losses and pay their debts. Of course the oil crisis exacerbated inflation. Oddly enough the unprecedented leap in prices affected chiefly red wines; the whites climbed modestly at best. This was a great misfortune. There had been a trend toward drinking white wine after the war, and many vignerons, when replanting in Gironde, had expanded their white vines. Now, with the fall of prices, they uprooted these new plants and turned again to reds, except for the better locations in the Entre-Deux-Mers and Graves, where whites had long been traditional.

As it turned out, they could have saved themselves both trouble and expense. Prices for all wine began to fall in 1974, even to tumble, when American and Japanese speculators backed away to await future price increases. Buyers who drank rather than speculated were finally enraged and reacted against prices that had no relation to real value. Most likely the situation was made worse by the discovery that the house of Cruse, an old and once honorable shipping company, had been falsifying labels. Buyers became distrustful, but they did not cause the sudden fall of sales. Growers may have gone too far, but so did merchant shippers. It was the latter of the Chartrons district who suffered most, at least those who had not yet sold all their wine. They were stuck with bottles acquired at bloated prices and whose value then collapsed like the proverbial house of cards. Heavily in debt, they had to reduce personnel, close warehouses, and cut costs. P. Ginestet Co. is an example. The company had contracted to buy fine new wine in 1972, but as was customary, the wine did not emerge from the cellars until 1975, when prices had collapsed. In desperate need of capital, it had to sell its prize holding, Château Margaux, to André Mentzelopoules, head of Félix Potin Co., a grocery chain, really the first large chain set up in France. His widow now reigns over the chateau with a splendor reminiscent of the eighteenth century, but it is her daughter who directs it.

This crisis was perhaps too intense to last long. During 1975 prices began to move up, more modestly to be sure, and soon the crisis was over, at least for the survivors. Even the Cruse scandal of 1973 was soon forgotten. The vignerons who had augmented their incomes to undreamed heights, who had enlarged their holdings and had acquired the machines and technical knowledge needed to grow grapes, were in a strong position and have steadily strengthened it since.

The happiest of growers have undoubtedly been those in the northeast, where emphasis on excellence has been maintained by highly organized syndicates and merchants. In Alsace and Champagne, very active publicity campaigns have implanted in the public mind the association of the region and of quality. Undoubtedly Alsatian wine has been the most sugared of all French wines, yet it has been carefully made by cooperatives, individual producers, and firms and enjoys far-flung markets and good prices that doubled between 1966 and 1970. Yet it is cheap compared to champagne, the ultimate beverage of some enophiles. With demand far exceeding supply, even vignerons who contract to sell grapes, hardly profitable elsewhere, have become well-to-do in Champagne. The higher the price, the higher the demand, for in the public mind, champagne is truly a luxury item, and luxuries are *supposed* to be expensive. There is no poor man's champagne in France and the large firms, in cooperation with vigneron syndicates, direct their publicity and appeal toward the wealthy, their chief market. This left a sizable number of eager buyers for the increasing number of grower-bottlers whose progress in sales has been notable. Merely about a thousand in number before 1939, they and the few cooperatives that champagnized wine made 26 percent of total sales of champagne, chiefly in the domestic market. By the 1980s that figure nearly doubled. Taking into account the rather small size of their holdings, they must surely be the most affluent growers in France, at least as regards the amount of property they own.[9]

At the opposite extreme, both geographically and economically, are the Languedocian vignerons. Like the Bourbons restored to power in 1815, most of them forgot nothing and learned nothing. Unwilling to follow the actions of producers in most other wine regions, they paid little attention to quality and returned to the mass production of simple table wines. The postwar crisis that plagued all vine areas was for Languedocians a catastrophe. In 1950 France's grape crop produced sixty-three million hectoliters, Algeria sent fourteen million, and six million remained unsold in cellars. Elsewhere, prices declined slightly or ceased to rise; in Languedoc they collapsed. Yet rampant inflation raised costs, debts could not be paid, and privation spread. In July 1953 vignerons burst out in frustration and anger, barring highways, staging mass protest demonstrations, and fighting with the police. The pattern was initiated as a revival of 1907, and has not yet ended. [10]

The Laniel government, like governments of the early 1930s, responded with a decree in September that marked a return to the Statut de la Viticulture, but not fully. Subsidies for stocking excess wine to keep it off the market were revived, as was massive distillation, but not so the periodic release of stored wine, nor the exemption of small producers from blockage. As already noted, this decree designated the IVCC as the agency to subsidize the uprooting of vines as a means of reducing production. The decree had some effect: prices were finally stabilized, but at a level too low for growers consistently to cover their rising costs. In fact, the years in which prices rose comfortably above costs were those of viticultural disaster: 1957–58, after the great freeze when wine was in short supply; and 1968, when extreme cold and rain descended on most of the country.

Given this situation, why has wine remained the dominant economic force in the region? To answer this question we must consider social and psychological as well as economic factors. The Mediterranean vigneron places a high value on viticulture. His ancestors cultivated grapes and made wine centuries before the unprecedented spread of vines in the nineteenth century, and much of his cultural life and his festivities were and still are integrated with the annual routine of the vineyard. There is an attachment to the soil that is deeply imbedded in the vigneron's psyche which helps to explain why so many of them, despite their impecunious condition, remain on the land.

As elsewhere, those quitting the land are young and lack this traditional sense of the vineyard. Those still remaining have found ways to survive. About one-third of them are full-time growers whose holdings are large enough to provide them with sufficient revenues; many of them have planted in choice locations, make VAOC or VDQS or belong to coops that do, and have the skills and technical knowledge that designate them as true professionals. Another third are there part-time, usually holding jobs as skilled laborers in a nearby town or on a large estate, and cultivate their small holdings in their spare time. Another third are retired and either rent or sharecrop their vines to full-timers to supplement their pensions.

It is the younger and middle-aged of these growers who resort to demonstrations, who block highways to the annoyance of tourists, and who sometimes violently destroy public and private property in an outburst of rage that scandalizes northerners and politicians. As one character in the regional novel, *Caminarèm*, put it: "Financiers, the money grabbers who lead Europe and France, decided that the Midi was no longer profitable. We have to leave, make place for vacation villages. We won't do it. We're going to show them that this region is still alive."[11]

But on what is it going to live? The above outlook has seriously hindered conversion from grapes to other crops. Part-timers and old men, of course, want nothing to do with conversion. They would have no income after uprooting vines and waiting for fruit trees to mature, and truck gardening is not held in high esteem. Even though economic planners partly subsidized a system of irrigation canals drawing water from the Rhône River, diversification has been largely confined to larger growers with excess land on which they could plant fruit trees or raise tomatoes and vegetables. But they soon discovered that there were often surpluses of these crops and, like farmers elsewhere in France, they dumped the excess fruit and vegetables on national highways as a means of calling attention to their plight.[12]

Hard times alternating with good times have always been the farmers' lot, and vine growers are no exception. The postwar decades have brought both in varying degrees to various viticultural regions. Vignerons, despite their gaiety and stubborn persistence, tend to be natural pessimists. Perhaps that is due to their long-time ignorance of accounting. In fact, in the national accounting figures of French agriculture, grape growers have participated in the general rise of prosperity that began in the 1950s. The value of their produce rose from 3.354 million to 19.304 million current francs between 1959 and 1970 and represented about 8 to 10 percent of total agricultural value. Wine made from their grapes attained a value of 103 million current francs in 1974 and 193 million in 1980. Ordinary wines accounted for 40 to 45 percent of these values, VDQS wines for a mere 5 percent, and appellation wines for 35 to 40 percent and in 1985 nearly 60 percent.[13]

The far smaller number of AOC growers and merchants, now sharing over half these values, enjoyed larger incomes than the mass of producers of VCC, but, of course, their costs were higher, sometimes much higher. They were the most successful in augmenting their prices and thereby in defending their living standards from erosion by inflation. Growers of VCC have been less fortunate, partly because of declining markets, as we shall see, partly because the government's planned economy placed a ceiling on their prices, exactly to hold down the inflation that has been a constantly disturbing factor in postwar France.

DETERMINANTS OF PRICE

The focus of nearly all studies of wine economics is price.[14] And some of these studies have influenced politicians to share that focus. The result is a vast legislation intended to stabilize prices at a level profitable to growers and merchants, and affordable to buyers. As we have noted already, the statutes of viticulture and of wine, dating back to the 1930s, have sought to bring about a balance between offer and demand, an idea that is supposed to provide growers with adequate incomes. Let me emphasize here that all of this legislation concerns ordinary red wine, *gros rouge*, and chiefly that grown in Languedoc and Roussillon. This region produces about two-thirds of France's VCC, most of it as red as the politics of the multitude of petty vignerons living there. One does not find controls or price supports for ordinary whites and rosés, nor for appellation wines of any color.

As far as politicians from the Midi are concerned, the most significant force determining price has been yield, the amount of wine resulting from the grape harvest each year. The economists who have used econometric techniques to study prices have consistently come up with correlation coefficients that mathematically prove that harvest size has been the major determinant for VCC prices. They also tend to believe that imports from Algeria until the late 1960s and from southern Italy since 1970 have not had a marked effect on price, a notion that Languedocian vignerons deny most hotly, and I think that they have a valid argument. The problem here is the fact that governmental intervention—required stockage, price minimums, forced distillation—have had an impact on prices in ways difficult if not impossible to measure precisely. The various statutes have long ended a really free market and have been successful to the extent that prices have not fallen for long below the minimums decreed for each crop. But these measures have not brought prices up to the ideal level, and they remain far below the maximums.

The misfortune of southern vignerons producing VCC lay in the fact that government policy has been multifaced. Therefore, when, because of seriously short supply, as in 1958, prices headed toward the legal ceiling, the government encouraged the import of foreign wine to restore a balance between offer and demand. This step quickly reduced prices. Unfortunately for table wine producers, their beverage has been included in the 259 articles used to calculate the SMIG, the official measure of the urban cost of living or price index. And worse for vignerons, wine is overweighted as a component so that a marked rise of its price pushes up the SMIG significantly. When this happens, industrial and farm workers feel entitled to higher wages to keep up with inflation. No government wants that. Growers therefore have been caught between two arms of government: one that supports prices at a low unprofitable level, and one that pushes them down when they approach what growers consider a just level.[15]

There is, of course, another arm, that of wholesale and retail merchants. *Négociants*, when calculating an opening price, include their costs and the level of retail prices. If the latter have been held down by various forces, the negotiant will make a low bid in order to defend his own profits. Since the end of World War II, VCC prices paid to small growers, unlike those obtained by wholesalers and retailers, have simply not kept up with inflation, particularly the rising costs of the industrial products needed to cultivate grapes and make wine. If vignerons belong to cooperative cellars, the costs of construction, repairs, modern equipment, fuels, wages, and land have all risen at a faster rate, two to three times faster, than prices for their wine.[16]

Not all VCC producers suffered equally. Everywhere large growers fared better, especially owners of about forty-hectare properties in the south who were able to cut costs and enhance productivity by mechanization. It was small consolation, if at all, that producers in the lower Loire Valley were as adversely affected as their fellow growers in the south. They too, suffered an average deficit of 6,826 francs each in the 1950s. Their perilous condition was worsened by their failure to set up cooperatives to protect them from shippers concerned mainly with their own profits. As noted in the previous chapter, Loire growers have not turned readily toward mutual enterprise, and only very large cooperatives can bypass shippers.[17]

Prices of fine wines have been determined by forces far more difficult to measure than those of ordinaries. Harvest quality certainly plays a role in the free market of VAOC. In very poor years, many of the best growths are declassed and sold in bulk as second wines with a simple AO or as ordinaries at ridiculously low prices in relation to their high costs of production. In years of high yields and varying quality, scrupulous growers will bottle and label only the best and sell the remainder under another label at a much lower price. This rigorous practice, requiring a steel discipline and commitment to defending quality associated with a label, plays a greater role among wines already enjoying a prestigious place in the hierarchy of fine beverages.

However, it takes a lot of money to create a favorable image of a particular wine, which is the drawback for some excellent appellations of the southern Côtes-du-Rhône, where growers have found it difficult to raise prices to cover their ever burgeoning costs. Improvements have come about chiefly since 1945, but the local syndicates have not invested heavily enough in publicity. Quite the opposite are the cases of Châteauneuf-du-Pape and the northern section, areas that have created favorable images of their wines, thanks to their well-endowed syndicates. Some sparkling beverages of the Loire Valley, although as good as medium-quality champagne, cannot command a third of the price of a bottle from the Marne. Clearly neither quality nor quantity are more important than public image in opening the wallets of most buyers. In the past, reputations have been created by shippers and large-estate owners who have long spent heavily on advertising. This tradition continues, and in imitation, associations of cooperatives have begun campaigns to make the public aware of their produce.

Economists generally agree that the market for fine wines has been more elastic than that of ordinaries. That is, a marked and quick rise in fine bordeaux prices, as in the early 1970s, has provoked a marked decline in sales, whereas a 20 percent rise for ordinaries will provoke only a 2 percent decline. Unfortunately for VCC growers, the obverse is also true: a 10 percent fall in price raises demand by a mere 1.2 percent. So a marked drop in price has induced only a slight rise in consumption—and lower income for the grower.[18]

CONSUMPTION IN FRANCE

The steady and apparently irreversible decline of wine consumption in France has been an economic fact since the nineteenth century. This phenomenon is not limited to France; it is a trend common to all vinicultural countries, where wine has been heavily consumed for centuries. Fortu-

nately for growers, consumption has increased in nations where production
is scarcely significant.

Reasons for drinking have changed. In the past it was not only safer
than water in that it was less germ infested, but it also provided a complement of the calories needed by a population engaged in heavy labor. In
1875 the average rate of wine consumption in France reached 150 liters
per capita, which would mean about 190–200 liters for persons over fourteen
or fifteen years of age.[19] Even more if we include the nontaxed wine not sold
in the market.

A large portion of this wine was consumed by agricultural workers and
small farmers who made it themselves or who bought it cheaply from
neighbors who were vignerons with a surplus. Urban workers were also
heavy imbibers of cheap wine, most of which came from the south of
France after railroad transport drastically lowered its cost of shipment. The
farmers and workers, chiefly in the north, who were more accustomed to
beer and distilled spirits, learned about wine when, as we noted, the army
began to issue a wine ration during World War I. The result was a recovery
of consumption after it had fallen during the phylloxera crisis. From under
100 liters in the 1880s and 1890s, the rate of intake began to rise after
1900 and reached 155 liters of taxed wine in 1925. This high rate was
exceptional, not a return to pre-phylloxera intake. Untaxed wine, made
for home consumption and included in workers' rations, has never been calculated precisely and varies with the harvest. When there is an excess,
growers keep more for themselves and give some to friends; when there is
a shortage, they must sell more in order to maintain their incomes, given
that the rise of price is rarely significant. Experts in France estimate that
on the average, growers retain one-fourth to one-third of their production
for personal needs.[20]

Although acknowledging this, Professor Milhau has refused to include
this wine in his calculation of the income of Languedocian vignerons, ar-
guing that only their monetary revenues indicate their purchasing
power.[21] On the other hand, reserved wine could contribute to a higher
standard of living by "purchasing" various services in the underground
economy. Small-town and urban artisans often exchanged their skills for
produce such as wine.

And yet, Milhau is correct to emphasize the monetary revenue as decisive because vignerons in the monoculture of the Midi needed the means
of buying nearly all their food, clothing, and absolutely all of their equipment and chemicals. Consumption by the public at large therefore was of

major importance. It averaged about 117 liters per capita between the wars, following a modest sawtooth trend of sales, with peaks in 1925 of 155 liters as noted above, and of 123 liters in 1936, the year of the Popular Front and extensive strikes. Believing in a second coming of social reform, workers in town and country downed their fill.[22]

World War II had a marked effect on old drinking habits; in fact, the years 1941–45 form a turning point. Wine was rationed and hard to obtain, even on the black market. So much fake "wine" circulated, often made from various dried fruits and disguised and preserved by noxious ingredients, and sold at such high prices that many people simply fell out of the habit of drinking it. Per capita consumption never recovered, even though the French have retained the dubious distinction of having one of the highest drinking rates in the world, along with the highest rate of cirrhosis of the liver.

The rather swift and far-ranging transformation of the French economy and social life following the war was a major factor influencing traditional habits. Despite the heavy drain of wealth toward the wars in Indo-China and Algeria in the late 1940s and 1950s, the French economy steadily grew stronger and national income rose. With the retreat from Algeria in 1960–62, the economy became one of the most prosperous in the world, making for a rising standard of living and enhancing a demographic revolution that was a dramatic departure from the interwar, when there was an absolute decline of population.

The effect on wine has been a steady reduction in the absorption of ordinaries, now called "table wines" instead of the clumsy *vin de consommation courante*. In 1950 the rate was 109 liters per capita; it peaked at 140 in 1956, then slowly went down to 117 in 1965, to 93 in 1980, to 80 in 1985 and to 75 the following year.[23] These figures are somewhat misleading because they are based on the entire population, including infants suckling from their mothers' breasts, not from a wine bottle. Table 6.1 reveals the numbers for the population over fourteen years of age in liters per head.

During this same time frame, total consumption per head for the over-fourteens fell from 173 liters in 1960 to 90 in 1985, a drop of 92 percent. It is evident from the information in table 6.1 that most of this precipitous decline was caused by the unrelenting abandonment of VCC. There is another element to consider; these figures are based only on taxed wine. Consumption would be higher if I included data on untaxed wine, that is, the part of the crop set aside to satisfy family needs, and the part given to

Table 6.1.   Annual per capita consumption by classification (population over 14 years of age)

Time Period	AOC Wine (in liters)	Other Wines (in liters)
1960–64	12.6	114.5
1965–69	14.3	112.6
1970–74	14.7	103.4
1975–80	18.2	90.9
1981–85	23.7	72.9

workers in addition to their monetary wage. But it, too, fell drastically in quantity—even while it improved in quality—from over 13 million hectoliters in 1960 to 5.4 million in 1983, the last year for which I have data. Assuming the data are accurate, they indicate, on the one hand, an abandonment of family vineyards by polycultural farmers and, on the other, the marked decline of workers entitled to wine rations. Deterioration has been constant: there was no pause in the decrease of VCC drinking. However, the first half of the 1970s did constitute a limited pause in the AOC category, a result of weak purchasing rates from 1972 to 1974, when prices leaped abruptly and excessively for the consumer, if not for the producer.

The changing structure of France's population also had an influence on patterns of consumption. During and especially after World War II, France underwent a population explosion that greatly increased the number of children under fourteen who normally did not drink any alcoholic beverages. As this young segment grew in age, many of them did not develop a liking for wine; their taste preference went toward fruit juice, carbonated soda drinks, mineral water, or—to be fashionable—strong drinks such as Scotch whiskey. Those who did turn to wine as they became gainfully employed opted for less wine but of a higher quality. The most significant tendency, as just noted, has been twofold: a decline in the consumption of cheap wine and a steady rise in that of various appellations. This younger generation, therefore, has not followed the drinking habits of its parents, and certainly not of its grandparents, unless family tradition and higher income had early emphasized quality over quantity. A general rise in living standards has reenforced this trend toward superior wines.[24] So far, rising prices have not become a major deterrent, and should not, as long as they do not rise too suddenly, as in the mid-1970s. When that happened, nearly everyone cut back on purchasing.

As postwar babies became married adults and their birthrate declined, quantitative data do indeed suggest an absolute reduction of wine drinking. The 1980 total of ninety-three hectoliters per capita was already menacing for jug wine producers. A serious public survey was carried out by the Ministry of Agriculture in November–December 1979 and included 3,729 households containing 11,176 persons. The survey was conducted by ONIVIT (Office National Interprofessionnel des Vins de Table) and INRA (Institut National de la Recherche Agronomique, of Montpellier). Their findings are highly instructive. At least 96 percent of the sample drank a beverage with meals. However, only 46 percent imbibed wine, about the same number (43 percent) preferred tap water, and a smaller number consumed mineral water (23 percent). Fruit juice, beer, and cider drinkers amounted to only 12 percent.[25]

Most revealing was the discovery that about a quarter of wine drinkers water their wine, or perhaps a more accurate statement would be that they wine their water, since most of them put more water than wine into the blend. This suggests that they try to improve the taste of tap water, as well as reduce the alcohol content of wine. Such a baptism, of course, is reserved for table wine taken with weekday meals. The use of fine wine for these drinkers is reserved for special occasions: Sunday lunch and meals with invited guests. Three-quarters of wine drinkers have no desire to dilute the contents of their glass but rather seek to fill that glass with a liquid of higher quality.

A second opinion survey, carried out, like the ONIVIT and INRA surveys, under the direction of Daniel Boulet and J. P. Laporte in November 1984 and February 1985, reveals further deterioration of the national wine market.[26] This tendency becomes clear in a comparison of the two surveys for a sample of persons over the age of fourteen (table 6.2).

In the quinquennial the wine industry lost about two million consumers, and these were the traditional drinkers of the blended wines. Regional wines and all those bearing an appellation improved their positions in a

Table 6.2. Changing French drinking habits, 1979 and 1985 (in percentages)

Category	1979	1985	Variation
Drink wine regularly	46.0	37.7	− 18.0
Drink wine occasionally	29.0	31.4	+ 8.3
Never drink wine	23.2	29.9	+ 28.9

declining market; for one hundred persons over the tender age of ten, the survey simply confirmed a marked trend (table 6.3).

There can be no doubt about the diminution in the number of drinkers who habitually have wine with meals. From nearly three out of four persons, their number has fallen to one out of four. Those responding to pollsters listed most frequently concern for their health as the reason for imbibing less. There were, however, other factors of which the respondents were probably not fully aware, objective factors belonging to a changing lifestyle.

Among these latter are a hierarchy of new values. The younger generation expends more on food, clothes, cars, entertainment and vacations, and less, proportionately, on wine.[27] With more money in their bank accounts they spend it differently than the well-to-do of former times, and are less attracted to expensive old wine. Keeping a cellar of wine was once a part of upper middle class life, and bottles, as well as tasting habits, passed from generation to generation because families held together and identified themselves by location. The wine cellar, therefore, remained with generations of the family, like servants.[28] Since the war, however, geographic mobility has separated age groups, as do differing values revealed by middle-class student rioting in May 1968, when young sons and daughters denounced their middle-class parents' devotion to complacency and the good life.

Their choice has had a marked effect on both production and sales. They make up the category referred to as "occasional" consumers. They seek out superior wines to accompany superior meals in their search for gastronomic adventure. They exist in a sensory world far removed from that of the everyday guzzler of jug wine. The wording here is perhaps unfortunate. Not all buyers of jug wine are guzzlers; they simply cannot afford the higher-priced appellation beverages. They are not entirely resistant to the

Table 6.3. Wine consumption by categories, 1979 and 1985 (in percentages)

Category	1979	1985	Variation
Table wine consumption	80.7	76.9	− 4.7
Blended wine	(71.7)	(61.8)	− 13.8
Regional wine	(9.0)	(15.1)	+ 67.8
VDQS	3.4	4.3	+ 26.5
VAOC	7.6	12.9	+ 69.7

charm of classed vintages, however, and more of them are turning away from the large containers with metal or plastic closures and enjoying the slightly higher attractions of regional table wines stoppered with a real cork. There is, psychologically, far keener pleasure in the exertion of extracting a cork than in breaking fingernails trying to pull off metal caps. The rise in the purchase of regional table wines has softened the near free-fall of *gros rouge*, but has not halted it.

To satisfy the demands of middle and upper working-class drinkers, merchants and cooperatives have increased their production of better wines, but, as already noted, they make these wines to be consumed earlier. Modern apartments are rarely in a building with a cellar suitable for laying down bottles for aging and are inhabited by a class of wage earners who are not specifically white or blue collar, but open collar. They are the relaxed generation, and think of wine as a relaxative.

Population changes have affected wine sales in other ways too. In the past farmers were big drinkers, but the rapid fall in their number as their children moved to cities reduced the once extensive rural market. The urban population has grown significantly, a result of an increase of office jobs taken over by a sedentary and salaried class. These people are horrified by the large caloric intake of active workers in field and factory, three to four thousand calories per day, with wine providing about one-fourth of that. More informed about diet and health care, office workers, including men, have reduced their alcohol intake. Women, of course, have always been far more abstemious than men, a reticence probably going back to ancient Greece, whose culture permitted a husband to punish his wife severely if he smelled wine on her breath. Office workers in large cities increasingly take lunch in their company's canteen where wine, if available, is sold in one-fourth liter bottles, further cutting back consumption.

Even the artisan class and the blue-collar proletariat, once large consumers of jug wine, have been dwindling as a result of new technologies that replace men with robots, and robots do not consume wine. Mechanization in the field as well as in the vineyard has greatly reduced the number of rural workers; and even among those who remain, driving a tractor demands fewer calories and arouses less thirst than hoeing or struggling to guide a horse-drawn plow.

And finally, the wine industry has often been its own worst enemy. Headlines about mislabeling, the use of harmful chemicals, and other fraudulent practices arouse widespread distrust. Temperance movements and a large section of the medical profession have made use of these scandals to condition public opinion against all alcoholic beverages and to praise mineral water, much to the profit of water bottlers. Interprofessional committees of merchants and growers have spent lavishly to counteract these forces. Anti-alcohol champions are the *bêtes-noires* of those in the alcohol business, who would willingly drown them all in a huge vat of wine. Yet, worry about the authenticity and quality of wine has undoubtedly had an effect. A poll taken in the 1970s in Montpellier and Toulouse, two wine-drinking cities, indicated that from 1968 to 1978 the number of wine drinkers had fallen by 10 percent, and that 15 percent of them had reduced the quantity they consumed. Two to six times fewer people began to drink or to increase their daily intake. Among those questioned, only 20 percent expressed concern about quality, yet 45 percent believed that wine had declined in popularity because of low quality. Evidently their minds had been conditioned by this view. Polls taken at various times since the 1960s, and especially the major one of 1979, reveal that the French are perplexed and inconsistent about their thoughts on wine.[29]

Among merchants, there is a widespread belief that most drinkers do not want to buy young wine and lay it down for aging; they want it ready for consumption when purchased. Therefore, they urge producers to make early-maturing wines. This explains the rash of *vins primeurs* from all vineyards of France, meaning a wine that is best when only a few months old. They are all imitations of "beaujolais nouveau," a grapy beverage that hits the market regularly on 15 November, amid a lot of fanfare. But a poll taken in Bordeaux and concerned with the local production indicated that for the people questioned, bordeaux means red wine that is best when old. Whites, when mentioned, are preferred sweet, and are not well known. For the Bordelais, the local wine is "good for your health," "doesn't make you drunk," "won't give you a headache," "easily digestible." The terms used for burgundies are "velvety," "full-bodied," and "alcoholic"; those for beaujolais are "light" and "fresh." Most of the respondents rejected the idea that a true bordeaux should be made to be drunk young: a quickly maturing wine, they affirmed, would be *soupe*, a product of a *cuisine chimique*, a concoction full of chemicals.[30]

Bordelais do not necessarily represent the rest of France, and yet national polls undertaken by SOPEXA in 1969 and 1979 came up with similar results. Most informative was the French preference for red wine.[31] Of the families questioned about the type of wine they drink, the responses shown in table 6.4 are enlightening.

For the French, wine is red, dry, and consumed chiefly with meals. But

Table 6.4. Wine consumption by type, 1969 and 1979 (in percentages)

Type	1969	1979
Dark red wine	42	86
Light red wine	37	n/a
Rosé	4	5
Dry white	2	3
Sweet white	1	0.4
Nondrinkers	14	n/a

at the time of the surveys, red wine no longer signified mainly *gros rouge*. Consumers of low-class ordinary, even though they were accustomed to spending up to a peak of about 11 percent of their food budget on wine, like the miners in the Saint-Etienne coal pits, could not compensate for a diminishing market. Blue-collar workers have always spent a larger proportion of their wages on alcoholic drink than white-collar workers.[32] In the Lyonnais they consumed the "little wines" from the lower Beaujolais; in Paris and other western industrial centers and port cities, they savored the muscadets from the lower Loire Valley, as well as others equally unpretentious. These were the over-the-bar beverages that workers enjoyed with their buddies after work, albeit independent artisans often began their friendly libations about midmorning, a habit that is dying out with the disappearance of artisanship and small workshops that used to be so numerous in working-class neighborhoods. Still legion are the delivery men who stop their small trucks at their favorite bistro to lift a glass with a convivial group. When workers and petty bourgeois used to return home for the noon meal, a practice still customary in small- and medium-sized provincial towns, they opened a liter bottle of simple red wine that the wife or one of the children had just filled from a spigot in a barrel at the corner grocery. This buying practice has all but disappeared over the past thirty years. Supermarkets, and even the corner grocery, now sell ordinaries in glass or plastic liter containers closed by a metal and plastic cap. Working-class families continue to absorb more wine than middle-class families, and they form the largest market for *gros rouge*.

Lower-echelon employees also consume *gros rouge* with their meals, but will offer themselves an appellation wine on Sunday. This might be merely a VDQS with a fancy label, a type of wine that has a fairly constant clientele. Its consumption has been stable since 1951, albeit with marked ups and downs. These wines, 80 percent of which come from Languedoc-Roussillon and lower Provence, can be a much better bargain than many lesser AOC wines that command higher prices, at least according to some of the persons I interviewed. This social group also regales itself on anniversaries with sparkling wines from Saumur, Vouvray, and Die.

It is not necessary to belabor the point that the more expensive AOC wines are consumed by those in the upper middle class, who will open a bottle two or three times a week and who serve even more expensive appellations to their dinner guests. They make up the bulk of the thirty-five to sixty-four year age group who imbibe 60 percent of appellation wines. Working-class and lower middle-class families usually do not have dinner guests; they have family feasts, and these do not raise the qualitative level of their beverage. But such gatherings have often raised the quantitative level, especially in provincial towns where family ties remained strong until the seventies. At the upper echelons of society, the most sophisticated consumers have traditionally been high-placed bureaucrats, office managers, and well-to-do people in the liberal professions: lawyers, doctors, stockbrokers, engineers, university professors in the sciences, people in public relations and communications, white-smock technicians in computers and electronics. Their expense for wine comes to a modest level of their total budget, about 5.7 percent as compared to the workers' average of 7.8 percent. Since their incomes are ample, they spend, in absolute numbers, more money on wine than do other classes, both in the Parisian basin and in the provinces. If their cellar in their principal residence is unsuitable because of the vibrations caused by the Paris Metro or the furnace in a central heating system, they store their fine vintages in their secondary homes in the country. The fact that the number of families in this category steadily increased after 1950 helps to explain the steady rise in consumption of very fine growths. It was especially in this upper category that the high-priced white wines of Burgundy and of the Graves of Bordeaux found their consumers. According to polls, very few wine drinkers are aware of fine, dry, white wines. The French, I think, know less about their country's wines than most Anglo-Saxon wine buffs who, per capita, drink far less than the French, but who are often more discriminating. It is not surprising to note that while the inhabitants of rural communes and small towns under ten thousand in population consumed more wine than urban denizens, the population of cities over one hundred thousand drink more appellation wine, along with more heady apéritifs and liquors—and more mineral water. Perhaps the water compensates for the higher alcohol content of fine wines. Northerners, who buy more bottled wine than others, tend to prefer robust wines of around 12 degrees alcohol.

Consumers of appellation wines, including the younger partisans, tended to be rather traditionalistic in their choices of wine. Those with money to burn went in for the very expensive burgundies of Côte d'Or, first-growth bordeaux of Médoc, and, for bubblies, turned up their noses at any beverage not from the old firms of Champagne. Châteauneuf-du-pape became acceptable, thanks to promotional campaigns and the reputation of its leading promoter, Le Roy de Boiseaumarie, who, after all, was a baron. Vineyards and wines associated with noble families benefited from out-and-out snob appeal. Recently improved vine areas, such as the Côtes-du-Rhône, with neither a long history of renown growths nor a titled leadership, found it difficult to profit significantly from the general tendency toward better quality. Of course, producers in the Côtes increased sales, but chiefly because their traditional customers augmented their consumption and because some urban devotees of Bacchus in Lyon, Grenoble, and other nearby cities discovered that the price-quality ratio was exceptionally favorable.[33] Their principal competitor, however, was Bordeaux. In the race for clients, Rhône growers sought to moderate prices, but discovered how decisive established prestige could be. When their wines sold for an average price of 3.35 francs and bordeaux for 4 francs, they lamented, not only because their profit margins barely covered their costs, but because middle-class buyers willingly paid a little more for mediocre bordeaux, buying its label, which enjoyed more distinction. Not until the Bordelais pushed their prices up to dizzying heights in the 1970s did more consumers turn to côtes-du-rhône appellations. Bordeaux prices rose 38 percent, other VAO 22 percent, but côtes-du-rhône rose only 9 percent. Sales of the latter jumped 15 percent in 1972–73, an unprecedented leap, and growers surpassed their Atlantic competitor in the number of bottles sold. Unfortunately for them, drinkers returned to bordeaux when prices moderated, yet growers and merchants of the côtes had put both feet in the market's door and have begun to enjoy a greater success in sales. Indeed, the 1980s have witnessed a decided turnaround in the market for all Rhône Valley wines. Price increases for every appellation rose 4 percent, but 10 percent for better côtes-du-rhône. In 1988 they shot up 20–25 percent and now slightly surpass generic bordeaux. Their foreign markets have also expanded, thanks to more aggressive promotions.[34] And yet there are misgivings among shippers and some growers who fear that prices have risen too rapidly and buyers will return to generic bordeaux.

Stocks of generic côtes-du-rhône are seriously diminished, and this in itself will push prices higher, while the Bordelais have ample stocks and can hold prices firm. This gives them an advantage in the national market. In the Rhône Valley voices are rising to demand the right to higher yields, from fifty hectoliters to seventy, which is the average in the Bordeaux region. Producers of fine beverages, however, warn that quality will decline and clients will turn away from their deep ruby reds.

Growers of whites and rosés have problems of a different order, for who has been drinking their beverages? Apart from Parisians, it was people who lived in or near their area of production. Consumers of the Parisian basin drew their whites, chiefly dry or slightly mellow, from the Loire Valley, from Alsace and the south, as well as from the west. Other drinkers were inhabitants precisely of the regions supplying the capital. Rosés were widely favored in Languedoc, Provence, and the Côte d'Azur, where they were most easily grown. Since these were famed summer vacation areas on the Mediterranean coast, consumption was abundant in July and August. The whites of the Atlantic coast between Bordeaux and the Loire estuary also enjoyed their most profitable sales when the sun and hot sandy beaches urged vacationers to cool off with a chilled drink, and to find a suitable beverage for the seafood dishes that made up the menus of coastal restaurants. Reds, of course, were not neglected. Even for native southerners and westerners, red was the wine for all seasons.

CHAPTER SEVEN

The Commerce of Wine

DOMESTIC TRADE AND ADVERTISING

The nineteenth century was not only a period of major viti-vinicultural change, it was also a period of almost feverish commercial activity. In the second half of the century, the major and the main secondary railway lines had been laid out and were in use. At first large casks or tuns containing several thousand liters were loaded onto flatcars (see figure 7.1) and sent out to markets formerly unattainable except by slow barge and wagon transport at high costs—too high for any but the finer, expensive wines. With the putting into service of tank cars in the late nineteenth century and tank trucks in the early twentieth century, the domestic market, already transformed, underwent a nearly complete revolution. The very cheap, mainly red wines of Languedoc and the Midi in general invaded even the most remote corners of France and put out of business the local wine makers who had, for centuries, struggled against the adversities of more northerly climates and supplied their local markets with fairly cheap drink, but not cheap enough to compete successfully. When their revenues were reduced and their vines destroyed by the phylloxera, they turned their vineyards into pasture or plowland. Wine grapes survived mainly where their owners could produce outstanding wines for a larger than local market, and they too benefited from cheap transport. Production of ordinary wines continued, however, in areas suited to vines and close to large cities, especially industrial or commercial cities. There growers could produce a superior ordinary, the *vin à trois sous*, a little wine, fruity and light, sold over the bar in lower-class cafés, suburban *guinguettes*, and neighborhood restaurants. The popularity of these cafés, cabarets, "pleasure palaces," barrooms—eateries, if you like—made for active markets and brought prosperity to vintners in the Loire, Rhône, and Saône valleys, the lower Beaujolais, and the interior vineyards east of Bordeaux. Since World War II, however, their number has been declining. They were in competition first with the cinema, then with television. At first they attracted numerous customers with televisions placed inside their establishments, but then the sets became affordable enough for home viewing. They have also suffered from the unrelenting spread of supermarkets and chain stores with ample shelf space devoted to all kinds of alcoholic beverages to be bought there and consumed elsewhere, usually before the small screen at home, where watching sports matches was a more attractive pastime than barroom chatter.

This enormous development of chain stores beginning after World War I and of supermarkets after World War II had a marked effect on the organization and structure of the wine trade. Traditionally, the selling of wine employed a host of middlemen between the vigneron and the drinker. Closest to the vigneron was the *courtier* or broker, a local agent who had to know all the local growers and, above all, be intimately familiar with their wines. Most were independent businessmen, with minimal expenses, working out of a home office, who prospected, recommended, and arranged for the sale of wines to a wholesale merchant in return for a commission of 2 or 3 percent. Some specialized in ordinaries, others, the elite, in fine wines. There was little exchange between these two categories, even though they had belonged to the same guild in the past, and to the same professional organization more recently. Each had to have, apart from a license, a keen sense of taste, smell, and color, not only for evaluating quality, but also for determining authenticity. Upon finding a type of wine that conformed to a wholesaler's description, the broker offered a price and arranged to ship the produce.

A new element in the trade since 1945, sometimes but not always a broker, is the *commissionaire* who, unlike the broker, stocks wine for those who need it but have no or insufficient storage space. Holding these wines, he has become a powerful figure in some wine areas and a speculator on wine prices. These men are not numerous and serve a limited clientele, such as supermarkets and chain stores.

A far older type, and more important both economically and professionally, has been the regional wholesaler, the merchant-vintner. He was usually located in a regional capital city or major wine center and used the services of the *courtier*. He too stocked wine in his sizable cellars. Traditionally he bought new wine after its first alcoholic fermentation, stored it

FIGURE 7.1. Exterior view of one of the earliest cooperatives, Vignerons Libres. The large casks are attached to flatcars for transport to Paris. Later, tank cars made of acid-resistant metal would replace them.

in his own containers, and matured it, whence his title, *négociant-éleveur*. The final product was as much his creation as the vigneron's. This used to be as true of the finest growths of Bordeaux and Burgundy as of the jug wine that flooded the domestic market. As always, his main function was that of blender of various types of wine to obtain a final product that hardly varied year after year and which became his brand with his label. He studied the tastes of his clients and made his mix accordingly. The advent of estate bottling ended his traditional role in château beverages, but he continues as their distributor, and as blender-shipper when he handles ordinary wine and village or regional appellations.

France has long had at least two schools of thought about wine making, and they have been voiced over decades of time, more recently in a symposium held in 1966. One group held that producers should make wine to conform to customers' taste; if drinkers liked "plonk" then growers must provide it. Louis Orizet, once at the podium, asserted "that's the lazy man's solution." Rather, he argued, the grower should make the best wine possible and educate the consumer: "It's an expression of civilization to teach him to drink better [wine]."[1] However "civilizing" Orizet may have sounded, he was going against a tradition centuries old. Wholesalers had long studied tastes and concocted, not to say doctored, wines most likely to satisfy local tastes, both in France and abroad. The force of the market is not a recent phenomenon. For the domestic market, they knew that the rural and working classes preferred alcoholic beverages at low prices. So they blended the weak reds of Languedoc with alcoholic wines, first from Algeria until the mid-1960s, then with equally heavy reds from southern Italy. Bordeaux negotiants sometimes had added darker, heavier Spanish wines to local pale ordinaries, even to some expensive wines, and merchants in Burgundy poured côtes-du-rhône into fine and not-so-fine beverages from their region. It was precisely to end this practice, which in the case of château labels constituted falsification, that owners of fine vineyards began château bottling on a large scale during the interwar, and made it obligatory for classed growths in 1972.

It has long been a practice for regional wholesalers to sell some of their wine to retailers nearby, and the major share to other wholesalers in large cities, especially Paris, for distribution to small retailers. French specialists refer to the first as *négociants-expéditeurs* (shippers) and the second as *négociants-destinataires* (distributers). It was not unusual for the distributer to carry out the blending and to create his own brand and label. Such a firm was Postillon, founded in 1906 by a vigneron of the Béziers region who went to Paris to sell his and other growers' wines. Before its recent move outside of the city, distributors in the Parisian basin stored their wine in the Halle aux Vins, covering thirteen hectares, or in Bercy, covering forty-two. There were depots also at Charenton, Ivry, Neuilly, and at other sites along the Seine River, a geography of storage that indicates how important river traffic used to be in the Parisian basin and elsewhere. By 1925, however, railroads carried over 77 percent of wine destined for Paris, trucks only 8 percent, and river barges 14 percent.[2] Since World War II, water transport has faded into nothing more than a memory, and tank trucks steadily overtook tank cars on rails in number and load. In the depots, wine storage followed the same evolution as wine making: huge wooden vats that allowed some evaporation, and therefore loss of wine, gave way to glass-lined cement vats, or more recently stainless steel, far easier to clean and airtight. Mechanization, of course, especially electric pumps, has taken over jobs once carried out by human labor. A blender has only to flip a switch to empty a vat, or blend various wines from several containers and pump the mixture to a bottling line. Wine is not retained for long periods, nor aged in the depots where costs of storage have always been quite high. It is sent out as rapidly as possible to merchants selling directly to the public.

Retailers were a highly mixed lot. Several large merchant firms set up their own retail outlets, selling only wine. Such was Nicolas, using its brand name as well as the place names of appellation wines printed on its labels. Nicolas began doing business in the nineteenth century, and by 1938 sold about 600,000 hectoliters from its stores—and far more since World War II. It even delivered to the home, so there was no need for its clients to stock a personal cellar. In the 1950s it had 322 stores in Paris and 440 in the provinces. Most of its sales were good ordinaries. Other early retail chains usually did not specialize in wine but sold fine foods and tended to offer finer wines to complement them. The pioneer in this activity was Félix Potin, and then Damoy. Most retail outlets were corner grocery stores that specialized in *gros rouge* sold from a large barrel to customers who brought their own empty liter bottles and corks. In these stores about half the wine buyers have been women who shopped for groceries at the same time.

Other, more specialized retail outlets were managed and owned by individuals whose knowledge of wine was highly developed and whose counsel was sought by their upper-class clientele. Men like Jean-Baptiste Chaudy were both learned and enterprising. They did not wait for wholesalers to propose vintages; they went out from their urban stores to the rural producers, talked to them, tasted their offerings, and bought a barrel or two directly, thereby avoiding the huge expenses of middlemen. They were adventurous buyers for a clientele that was equally adventurous in seeking out novel and different beverages. They even provided for tasting because their customers bought in larger lots than the single-bottle buyers of grocer retailers. It was in their stores that fastidious and monied drinkers found the best and sometimes the lesser known wines of France. They sold exclusively in bottle and handled the wine carefully, laying down the bottles, keeping them out of bright light, and holding reserves in a cellar.[3]

The tremendous increase in the number of supermarkets and the expansion of chain stores had two results: this double phenomenon put many independent small grocers and also many small wine wholesalers out of business. They underpriced the grocer who was not supported by a chain organization offering credit, commercial advice, and large-scale buying. They also were able to bypass one or even both of the negotiants. Profit was their aim, fast turnover their watchword, and large-scale selling their reason for being. They reserved a fairly sizable shelf space for alcoholic beverages of every description; and wine, chiefly table wine, was a profitable operation. For rapid sales and low prices, they reduced the costs of transferring wine from the grower to the drinker by going either directly to one wholesaler or to the *commissionnaire* who could provide them with sizable quantities, several hundred thousand hectoliters at least. They never bought in small lots. They bargained among growers only with those able to furnish over five thousand hectos. For wine-department managers, cooperatives were made to order since they could provide large quantities of good, consistent, sturdy wine at low prices, in liter containers of glass or, more recently, of plastic, with metal and plastic closures. They also bought wine in corked bottles that store personnel would never dream of laying on side because of rapid sales. Unfortunately, turnover of more expensive wines was not always fast enough, corks dried out in standing bottles, and the wine became oxidized.

Undoubtedly the emergence of chains, supermarkets, and department stores with wine space—Prisunic, Monoprix, Casino, Coop, Genty, Docks, Galéries Lafayette—contributed to the emergence of vinicultural cooperatives. They naturally complemented one another. Until recently, each cooperative sold wine as an individual unit. The great majority of them sold most of their production to regional negotiants, as they still do. This was the easiest way to proceed because their presidents, general secretaries, and councils knew little about commercialization of wine and even less of market conditions. Some of the larger firms set up sales committees, but it was not infrequent that when orders came through for an immediate delivery at a specified price, the committee as well as the administrative council had to be summoned. When this procedure required several days, the hurried buyer went elsewhere, usually to a *commissionnaire* or wholesaler. Only since World War II, and really only since the 1950s, have groups of coops begun to form large regional organs specifically to commercialize their wine, leaving their managers and councils free to concentrate on production. Vigneron cooperators in southwestern France were early to move in this direction. Forty Girondin and Perigourdin coops created the Société Vinicole d'Organisation Technique et Commerical des Caves Coopératives de Bordeaux et du Sud-Ouest, quite a mouthful and wisely reduced to SOVICO; some twenty odd years later in 1979 it assumed the simple title of Union Centrale. Like all of these organizations, it not only marketed the wine of member coops, it also provided managerial and enological services. On a smaller scale were the Union de l'Entre-Deux-Mers, UNIDOR for Dordogne, and UNI-Médoc. In the Bergerac appeared PRODUCTA, which handled sales for ten cellars and sold strictly in glass. A bottling center was completed in 1965 to handle 2.5 million units, a figure that has since grown to 7 million. Before long, UNIDOR absorbed PRODUCTA and sent out fifty salesmen *multicartes*, that is, representatives offering several brands to buyers. Continuing the trend, it joined the Union Centrale to further centralize sales. In Bergerac it has nearly replaced declining wholesalers and has become a strong force encouraging vignerons to pay greater attention to quality.[4]

This kind of centralization has not characterized other viticultural regions producing both AOC and table wine. Cooperatives have federated to defend their common interests; several in the Côtes-du-Rhône have even set up a central bottling plant near Tulette, but most of them continue to deal with wholesalers or have built tasting rooms where tourists can evaluate their wines and buy a carton of three or more bottles. In Suze-la-Rousse, the Drôme department has helped set up a Université de Vin with a respectable enological laboratory for analyzing wine and a permanent staff that organizes courses in every aspect of wine making and sales. It is not an authentic university, but an educational center where professionals can expand their knowledge in several fields. This is not specifically a cooperator's venture either; much of its support, excluding departmental subsidies, comes from the local vignerons' syndicate.[5]

Not even in the viticultural sectors of the Midi have coops been able to centralize sales effectively. An exception is COVIVAR. It was set up in 1973 in the Var department, chiefly by the cellars that turn out a rather nondescript if not downright mediocre wine, quite distinct from the wines classed as côtes-de-provence. Most of its sales are to negotiants. Another is URCAM (Union Régionale des Coopératives Agricoles du Midi), which sold one out of every twenty-five bottles produced in the Midi. Individual members of cellars finally began to allow their coops to sell their wine because these organizations could store wine and hold it until prices rose, so that negotiants usually accorded a higher price to cellars than to individuals, at least for VCC. They awarded the better quality and consistency, and shared the economies they realized from mass purchases.[6]

Concentration went ahead at a faster pace among wholesale private firms than among cooperatives. Small companies missed out on large sales because they could neither finance them nor store the wine. Their costs were too high as a result of their limited purchases and the egregious expense of transferring wine from a large number of petty producers. After World War II the wine trade became extremely competitive. Companies with small turnover found it difficult to raise capital to modernize, and as their owners retired or died, heirs did not step in to replace them. Many simply went out of business in the early 1970s when they could not raise enough money to buy wine at the enormous prices demanded by growers everywhere in France. The coup de grace for the financially weak came in 1975, when prices plummeted and they were forced to sell at a loss the wine they had previously bought at inflated prices. As noted already, even old, established firms were shaken—but not shaken out—by this crisis.[7]

Concentration went at a rapid pace especially in Champagne. This process really began on a notable scale in the 1960s, when the house of Moët et Chandon began absorbing smaller competitors: Ruinart in 1963 and Mercier in 1969. The directors then began to diversify—a strategy that has gone hand-in-hand with concentration—and bought heavily into the perfumer Christian Dior of Paris and New York. Finally, in 1970 the biggest maker of Champagne blended with the biggest distiller of cognac, J.A.S. Hennessy, creating a most remarkable financial *cuvée*. In the next year appeared the holding company (*groupe*) Moët-Hennessy, a giant of proportions hardly deemed possible in a luxury trade. Moët et Chandon alone garnished about 34 percent of net profits of all champagne sales in 1968 and 37 percent four years later. In 1978 its gross profits were 600.306 million francs, its net 34.256 million. It is five times bigger than

G. H. Mumm, the second largest company in this special field. Mumm, following the same trail, bought a controlling interest in Perrier-Jouet and Heidsieck Monopole in 1972, but then in turn fell under the control of the Seagram Company of Canada, a major distributor of whiskey. While insiders were buying into or fully taking over other insiders, outside groups, well financed, began penetrating the champagne trading organization. Thus when Piper Heidsieck acquired 96 percent of Fournier in 1970 and 34 percent of Canard-Duchène in 1973, the Groupe Pernod-Ricard, in liqueurs and apéritifs, absorbed Charles Lanson. Rémy Martin, of cognac, took over nearly 22 percent of Pommery-Greno. Foreign firms also entered the attractively lucrative field: Martini and Rossi of Italy bought into Champagne Cazanove as well as into makers of sparkling wine in the Loire. Möet et Chandon also own 70 percent of Cazanove.[8]

Another tendency was diversification within the same category of beverage, and consisted of champagne firms buying companies making sparkling wine (*mousseux*), chiefly in the Loire Valley, above all in Saumur and Vouvray. Veuve Clicquot, for example, won control of Vieux Moustier, and Taittinger acquired Monmousseau in Saumur and Bouvet in Vouvray, properties that together possessed two hundred hectares of vines. Bollinger and Piper Heidsieck made similar acquisitions.

The move toward concentration had the effect of making the giants even bigger but was checked by several counter forces. Most important was the Comité Interprofessionel des Vins de Champagne (CIVC), which strictly controlled both market and supply of grapes in the interest of all the firms, and the leading houses have thus not been successful in creating a grape purchasing monopoly. It is even doubtful that they saw in concentration the means of achieving a monopoly. Another force was the ability of both medium and small producers, such as Bollinger and Krug, to show high profits. Both of these firms were family managed and renowned for their excellent vintages, and were able for a time to resist true takeovers; however, Rémy Martin has recently acquired an interest in Krug, whereby it deepened its penetration into the region.[9]

Despite their large share of cash flow and net profits, the two giants—oligopoly is the proper word for the position they held—controlled, until the immediate postwar decade, only 23 percent of sales, leaving ample opportunities for the smaller enterprises, which numbered about 140. But recently the ten biggest firms have enlarged their share of total sales: from 46 percent in 1955 to 70 percent in 1982. One hundred thirty firms, then, had to survive on 24 percent of sales. Their salvation lies in their share of a gross income of 2.649 billion francs in 1973, a total that has since grown by at least 10 percent annually. The house of Krug, with a small rate of sales, provided the family with a handsome return. This was thanks to the high quality of their wine, the most expensive on the market and supported by a faithful clientele of bon vivants who would find life dull without it.

Traditionally, the reputation of a regional, communal, or estate wine was made, or destroyed, by wholesalers. Although several regions of France had already enjoyed a certain fame since the Roman conquest of Gaul (that is what local specialists claimed in their applications for AO status), large-scale commercialization of fine wines really began in the nineteenth century. The publicity campaigns that established the reputations of Bordeaux, Burgundy, and Champagne were financed by the larger negotiants and wine-producing firms able to make use of an emergent mass newspaper and magazine trade enhanced by the perfection of the steam press. By the twentieth century, the means of informing the public took on much larger dimensions, moving beyond the daily press and into the slick pages of the myriad weekly and monthly magazines that appealed to a broad variety of middle-class publics, from readers interested in home improvement, women's fashions, and culinary arts to interested consumers of alcohol willing to learn more about vineyards and wine. The wine revolution, it is evident, did not occur in a vacuum. Rather, it was part of a broad process of modernization in industry, agriculture, and public communication. Success or failure depended on how effectively these novel forces were exploited. Growers and merchants emphasizing quality were bent upon using publicity to allure educated, discriminating readers, and they used all the latest findings in regard to public appeal, including snob appeal. The government, considerably enriched by its taxes on wine, also entered the promotional field in December 1931 when it set up the Comité National de Propagande en Faveur du Vin.[10] It was reorganized in 1948 and 1957, and long presided over by Emile Claparède, senator from Hérault and mayor of Béziers, a major wine center for the VCC of Languedoc. It was a consultative body in the Ministry of Agriculture. Its objective was to support publicity abroad in favor of wine and, at home, to favor a reasonable consumption of good wine while emphasizing that "reasonable" meant moderation in the use of alcohol.[11] It reflected conflicting opinions within the cabinet and the bureaucracy, with the Ministries of Agriculture and of Finance urging consumption, and the Ministry of Public Health laying stress on sobriety and the benefits of mineral water. The committee promoted and published research on the dietetic, biological, and hygienic effects of wine. After all, once the social security system was finally set up in the 1930s, the public cost of medically treating cirrhosis of the liver absorbed a large share of the government's revenue from wine taxes. The committee also served as a center of information for the restaurant and hotel trade in France and abroad. The costs of liver ailments notwithstanding, it worked with other forces to propagate the image of wine as the national drink of France. Its early activities also included annual wine festivals (*fêtes de vin*), attended and hosted by socialites such as Mme Fould and Princess Murat, who served only wine at their soirées. In the *fête* of July 1935 the Louvre put together a show with the theme "la vigne et le vin dans l'art." A collection of the displays was published under the same title. All of this was very expensive, and the wine press complained about cost restraints imposed by the finance ministry. Abroad, such restraints were less hampering, and commercial attachés were liberally financed and expected to expand foreign sales.[12]

That publicity sells wine as well as an image of wine cannot be doubted. The wine of lower Beaujolais, taken up by merchants of Lyon as an inexpensive, light, and fresh beverage, was launched in the 1920s as the lawn bowler's wine. Probably a quarter or a third of the lower middle- and working-class male population have for decades spent their Sunday mornings bowling out-of-doors. Numerous taverns and cafés set up packed earth or lawn-covered lanes in shady yards to attract this clientele and, of course, sold beaujolais by the glass or the pitcher. Because bowling was not practical in cold or wet weather, beaujolais was promoted as the "bistro wine." As such it could be drunk year round by convivial men seated around a table, playing either cards or dominoes. Since World War II, it is "new beaujolais" that has been pushed before the public on a massive scale by large distributor firms, and money is not spared for advertising since about 40 percent of beaujolais, up from one-third of sales, are composed of this new or early wine that is put on the market precisely on November 15 each year. "Papa" Bréchard can insist that "it's not by publicity, it's by cordiality that we've made ourselves known collectively." But attracting public attention has become a major challenge among producers since the second great war.[13] Before 1939, the announcement that new beaujolais had arrived did not attract any notice, save in Lyon where lower-class cafés offered it from barrels that no one dared seal lest they explode as a result of carbonic gas emanating from the still-fermenting wine. Rather, the promotion of new beaujolais was taken up by shippers of Beaune and Mâcon in the 1950s, and they gave it its reputation. Their burgundies had become too expensive for rapid turnover, so they sought out a medium-priced beverage capable of fast sales and of bringing in the cash they required to pay for their purchases of new fine wine that needed years to reveal its noble qualities. Restaurant owners and supermarket managers stocked it because it was uncomplicated and easy to sell. Doutrelant quoted a seller who joked, "Name me a more intelligent wine. Hardly harvested, it's bought, drunk, and pissed."[14]

The public learned of it through massive publicity campaigns. Several weeks before mid-November shippers offered cases of the new wine to journalists, radio and television programmers—anyone in communications—to write articles and programs in praise of the vintage. When the precious liquid was flooded into bottles, barrels, and cubitainers, they really went into action at a frenetic pace. Each merchant, impelled to get his wine to market exactly on November 15, hired railway cars and trucks to carry it. In 1976, as Hubert Piat testified, over a hundred trucks left one bottler to diffuse their precious cargo. The more crazed among them even had cases and barrels parachuted or sent by wind-blown balloons in order to attract attention in Paris. Famous racing-car drivers made symbolic and highly publicized runs to Paris with a few cases. Cargo planes were charted to rush the vintage to foreign capitals overseas.[15]

Since the 1960s a kind of fever has spread each year throughout the vineyards and commercial houses as mid-November approaches, a fever that soon communicates itself to cafés and retail stores whose owners stock up and hang large signs in their display windows: "The new beaujolais has arrived." Since the 1970s the new wine gradually began to determine the price structure of other beaujolais that would not enter the market until spring. It therefore assumed the same role played by wine of the Hospice de Beaune when auctioned in November, when quotations shouted by buyers assembled from all over the world set the trend of prices of most other burgundies. Both types of wine have led the steady rise of prices, enriching the burgundian growers and shippers far beyond the real value of their produce. Small wonder that winemen in other vineyards have attempted to imitate the practice, but with far less success. If Piat is correct—and he is a well-known merchant—the costs of advertising and all the hoopla have risen to absurd levels and now just about wipe out the profits of these early sales for shippers. The growers benefited considerably from the elevated prices, and since about 60 percent of the appellation "beaujolais" was disposed of rapidly, there was little chance that prices would fall later.

The promotion of beaujolais became a continuous process undertaken by both growers and shippers. When Monsieur Bréchard referred to cordiality rather than advertising as the means by which the beverage acquired its reputation, he had in mind both individual syndical leaders such as Jean Laborde, a deputy and vigneron, and growers like Claude Geoffroy of Odenas, Jean Petit, and Bréchard himself. Their efforts led to the creation of the Compagnons du Beaujolais, an organization of honorary members, celebrities in many fields, who have sworn, during an elaborate gala, to spread the fame of the wine. Growers have set up tasting fairs, especially for the new vintage, accompanied their produce to foreign cities, and introduced it themselves while offering free glasses of it. The Maison du Beaujolais, located on national highway 6 near Belleville, cost them twenty-three million old francs in 1952. Tourists who came could buy a light lunch and taste all the wines on display. More recently, at the annual Paris agricultural fair, growers offered samples in small glasses to visitors who have consumed on average twenty-five hectoliters gratuitously. In the tasting centers founded in thirty-five cellars in Beaujolais itself, growers have offered free samples. Some half-million glasses annually, representing about forty thousand bottles, have been served at Villié Morgon, and nearly thirty thousand have been passed out, for a modest fee, at Juliénas. All of these practices date from the 1950s and are evidence of how active vignerons have become in promoting their own wines. For the Beaujolais, they have put the area and the wine on the viticultural map of France.

In 1950 most beaujolais enjoyed local markets only; none but the best *crus* attracted a clientel in more distant places. Regional merchants at this time took 60 percent of it. But as the appellation grew in renown, this high rate dropped to 10 percent in 1968 and the national market grew from 15 to 30 percent. And then came the foreign buyers, chiefly the Swiss, who absorbed 60 percent of every variety they could find. Within a generation the entire image and sales picture had changed beyond the most utopian imaginings of the natives. The wine improved, certainly, but the science of communications more so.

The natives of Beaujolais began this kind of promotional fervor belatedly, and growers in the Côtes-du-Rhône, like those in Anjou, Provence, the Jura, Savoy, and Garonne Valley still had much to learn. In the vernacular of the young, they simply were not with it. Far more seasoned and sophisticated were the Champenois, whose incredible promotional antics for their sparklers began in the nineteenth century.[16] Bordeaux also enjoyed a world market. To expand it, producers and negotiants began in 1908 the first of a long line of annual wine fairs that attracted international attention; this was perhaps Bordeaux's response to the publicity engendered by the wine auctions at the Hospice de Beaune.[17]

This kind of intense publicity sometimes creates fads or fashions that thrive and eventually fade. And when they fade many vignerons can be left with a lot of wine that no longer sells, and worse, thousands of vines trained to produce a particular style of wine. Such was the case in the Bordelais in the 1960s when white wine became the rage. It was softer, touted as being less fattening, and an excellent apéritif. Then, in the 1970s, the novelty paled and hundreds of growers had to root up their vineyards and replant with red varieties. And vines, unlike new garments or car fashions, cannot be renewed in a year. The land has to rest for several years before replanting, and the vines require at least five years growth before their grapes produce a suitable juice. The fault was partly that of the growers who responded to demand by raising yields and churning out *gros blanc* that did not at all live up to the image created by publicity. Merchants then stopped buying it and turned to the whites of Charentes or of Italy.[18]

In this case growers and merchants were in conflict, which is in the old tradition of their relations. Since World War II this conflictual relation has continued, but is largely if not exclusively limited to areas of *gros rouge* and *gros blanc*. In the Midi especially, growers' organizations are forces of combat. They view merchants as the enemy, indeed as subversive elements, as the equivalents of a Trojan horse, allowing the enemy, Italian wine, to enter the city. Elsewhere, on the contrary, relations between growers and merchants have become more complex, certainly more cooperative as a result of mutual efforts to create flavorful wines and to publicize them.

This conciliatory tendency was, in part, the outcome of the Vichy regime's efforts to create a corporative organization among all groups of society, including wine growers. Professional contacts in Champagne were especially tense, due to the lack of sales by the firms during the 1930s depression. Both sides were highly organized, and had been since the late nineteenth century: growers in the Syndicat Général des Vignerons de la Champagne Viticole, and merchants in their own syndicate, the Association Viticole Champénoise. Between 1941 and 1942 the two sides were brought together to form a Comité Interprofessionnel des Vins de Champagne (CIVC), a sizable body consisting of delegates of vignerons and the firms, plus technicians and a representative of the government. Since its founding it has grown stronger and controls, in the full meaning of the term, the cultivation of vines, grape prices, and the production of champagne. It is responsible for drawing up the two annual contracts that bind grower and merchant, the first obligating the vigneron to sell a given weight of grapes, the second obligating the merchant to pay a price per kilogram based on the previous year's price per bottle. It classes vineyards according to site, exposure, soil, and grape variety and fixes prices for grapes according to this classification. Since champagne prices have been rising each year, growers have enjoyed a steady, almost soaring income. In no other vineyard can cultivators with merely two or three hectares of vines live so well. The CIVC is also engaged in advertising the merits of champagne and hosts numerous visitors. But the big firms like Moët et Chandon, Veuve Clicquot, Besserat de Bellefon, Krug, Lanson, and so on, have sizable budgets of their own for publicity and entertainment, as well as crews of salesmen circulating in France and abroad.

Advertising consistently emphasizes champagne as a product of the highest quality—a good value, therefore, for the high price. Some firms, like Krug, project their particular brand as a luxury item and as naturally expensive, made indeed for persons who do not pinch pennies. The message is simple: if you quibble over the price, you can't afford it. This sounds like snob appeal, and it is to a certain point. On the other hand, fine champagne is not merely a luxury item, it is a great wine. Underneath the bubbles, which are not so lively as to deaden the taste buds, is a beverage of the highest quality, extremely costly to produce—a serious wine, which is one of the images projected on the public. And yet champagne as a drink has a long advertising history as a source of gaiety and frivolity— of the high life of the leisure classes—and has been associated with their sporting life: racing cars, thoroughbred horses, tennis, pool-side gatherings, casino night life, and elegant dinners. At a lower social level, it has become identified as the beverage indispensable at births or baptisms, communions, graduations, weddings, and anniversaries. I have not yet seen it recommended for funerals.

Behind this image were the actual wines. Some lived up to it: Krug, Pommery, Bollinger, Roederer, and others sought to preserve quality even during the mid-seventies crisis years, when a general economic setback stiffened buyers' resistance to continuously rising prices. But this was only a temporary setback, and as demand rose, the AOC vineyard nearly doubled in size. Growers augmented yields by using more fertilizer, and less scrupulous firms began admitting immature and sometimes even slightly rotten grapes into their vats, relying on large, very active bubbles to disguise an inferior taste and conducting an intensive sales campaign, especially in France. For unlike the firms with solid reputations that exported half or more of production, a large number of firms sold mainly to French markets. In fact, since World War I a reversal of sales orientation has occurred, away from foreign markets and inward to the national one. This shift has probably influenced quality adversely, for several fine wine makers have insisted that selling in foreign markets is a stimulant to achieving and maintaining quality. Domestic consumers have rarely been as demanding as foreigners. And what has been true in Champagne has been equally true in Burgundy and Bordeaux.

The CIVC, located in Epernay, has been perhaps the most successful organization in overcoming the mutual distrust between grower and merchant. It has become, as a consequence, a model for other regions, but none of them has achieved the same level of control over the conditions of production with respect to quality. Viticultural Champagne produces no VCC, and prices both for vignerons and firms have risen almost annually. In Bordeaux the CIVB enjoys the use of spacious quarters in the Maison de Vin in the central quarter, across the street from the main tourist office. It therefore can welcome a large number of visitors and distribute folders glorifying the value of local wines. Like other interprofessional committees, it has designated certain roadways as *routes de vin*, guiding tourists to and through the main vineyards. But neither in the Bordelais or anyplace else does the visitor penetrate wine-making establishments as one can do in Champagne, where the major firms offer free guided tours of their cellars and vinicultural facilities and a complimentary taste of champagne at the end.

Big shipping companies in Beaune (Burgundy) approach this system, but Bordeaux is a place of walled, closed châteaux, and neither growers nor shippers have shown serious interest in direct sales of a few bottles to tourists. The CIVB from its beginning in 1948 to the mid-1970s was mainly an agency to register sales contracts of AOC Bordeaux and to publish global data on monthly commerce. Reorganized in February 1976, however, it won a greater measure of control over prices so that contracts between growers and merchants can now prevent the kinds of sudden price rises that had occurred early in the decade, and sudden collapses, like those of 1974–75. Equally important was the right it obtained from the Ministry of Agriculture to block the sale of AOC wine that seriously exceeds the maximum yield allowed by official decrees. It could also urge—but not compel—both growers and negotiants to sign three-year contracts at prices established by its specialists, a goal accepted for the 1978 harvest, but not successful. It also carried out continuous studies of market conditions, as well as public attitudes and buying habits.

These activities of interprofessional committees were costly. Bordeaux's CIVB budget in 1978 came to 7.492 million francs. Its chief source of income came from "parafiscal" levies on wine sales (85.4 percent), plus income from securities (7.9 percent) and a subsidy from the General Council of the Department of Gironde (6.7 percent). Its expenses came to 8.543 million francs, of which over 54 percent went for publicity and 36 percent for administrative costs. It also had to pay 10 percent to the National Committee for the Wines of France, the master organization that enjoyed considerable influence over law makers. By 1986 the total budget had leaped to 51,445,940 francs, an advance of 587 percent, well surpassing the roughly 10 percent annual inflation rate. Now parafiscal taxes brought in only 37 percent of income, and producer fees added 54 percent. The remainder came from subsidies and diverse sources. Total expenditures had risen to 55,814,000 francs, with nearly 73 percent spent on marketing and advertising. Administration costs had fallen to 19 percent. In a general way, the interprofessional committees were charged with safeguarding quality, but the real controls of quality, that is, tasting, were in the hands of viticultural syndicates. This kind of control gave member growers the right to print "Appellation d'Origine Controlée" on their labels, a phrase that many buyers assumed to be an added guarantee of authenticity and quality.[19]

The existence of interprofessional committees brought about more collaboration between big and medium producers, on the one hand, and merchants, chiefly big and medium, on the other. The relation has been amicable, perhaps because wines have been selling well at profitable prices for both sides, at least for appellation types. Yet large numbers of growers have sought, with some success, to sell their wines directly to consumers. This is possible where growers are close to or in the center of popular vacation spots, and where the *routes de vin* have indeed guided tourists toward vignerons. There tasting rooms await them, and family members are willing to devote time welcoming visitors, pouring a little wine for tasting, and writing out an order for a mere three to six bottles. Many small producers sell about 10 percent of their supply directly in this way.

What results is that growers build up a mailing list and send out their literature—a list of types of wine and prices—as Christmastime approaches. And mail orders are much larger because of economies of shipment in bulk. This type of selling is often combined with a more aggressive approach, when the father or his sons go out to contact restaurant and café owners as well as independent retailers, in order to sell directly on a greater scale. This has been a fairly successful endeavor. Among Médoc producers, direct sales of this sort came to over 16 percent of total volume in 1969, and rose to over 31 percent in 1976. This increase owed much to the large cooperatives who sold simple bordeaux directly to supermarket and chain stores, especially in the Paris region and the industrial north where demand is for both reds and whites.

On the whole, ties between growers and shippers have become more conciliatory and cooperative since the formation of interprofessional committees, even in the Côtes-du-Rhône where merchants did little or nothing to promote the local wines until well after World War II.

In Languedoc-Roussillon, as mentioned briefly above, there is much evidence of continued bitterness between them. Merchants seem to pay more attention to buying *gros rouge* low in alcohol and therefore very cheap. These they blend with equally cheap Algerian or south Italian wines, and obtain a higher profit by shipping out this nondescript mixture in bulk, to be bottled at the place of consumption in liter or three-liter containers. Although consumption of this type of drink has been declining, it continues to outsell all other wines. Vignerons who have sought to improve their produce, as in Minervois, Corbières, and the Aspres of Roussillon, complain bitterly that local shippers refuse to pay prices high enough to cover their costs, forcing them to sell superior wine at inferior prices. Merchants blend it with foreign wine and sell the blends as superior ordinaries. Negotiants, however, have shown no interest in promoting these beverages. The blends were hardly promotable, being a concoction with no identity either through the grapes or the region. Cooperatives for decades did nothing to change this situation, since most of them churned out simple reds.[20]

Vignerons complained but felt helpless. Their frustration finally burst out in violent demonstrations and attacks on public property or on merchants cellars when they felt they were victims of fraud. Only since the 1970s have growers making better wines begun to promote and sell their own wine for which they obtained either an AOC or VDQS appellation or a *vin de pays* label. Their tactic was to set up a GIE (Groupement d'Intérêt Economique), that is, a legalized grouping of entities with the same interests who can promote and sell their separate products in common. One of the first to be set up, in 1975, was called Vignerons de l'Aude. The departmental chamber of agriculture aided in the creation of another two years later, with the more imaginative title of Grand Vins en Terre d'Aude. Funds emanating from vignerons themselves, with some departmental subsidies, not only created these entities but encouraged a new sense of unity needed for large-scale commercial operations. On a much larger scale was a GIE set up in 1979 as part of the VI.LA.RO., short for Vignerons Languedoc-Roussillon. It included the Society of Producers of Blanquette, numerous cooperatives, the Vignerons Catalans, an association of Roussillon growers, and others.[21]

These several organizations sent sample bottles to regional and national wine tastings, set up stalls in vinicultural fairs, and encouraged members to bring their beverages to offer free samples to the public. Both leaders and followers actively participated in large-scale promotional activities, not only at fairs, but in supermarkets as well, such as the *hypermarchés* at Marseille and at Montpellier. Vignerons, in a sense, became their own promoters and salesmen.

Several large wholesalers soon became aware of this thrust toward quality among some producers and began to seek their better wine, and to sign contracts with cooperatives. The large firm Chantovent in 1976 signed with ten cellars in the Minervois. Five other cellars there refused to join because the contract gave too much power to the firm over conditions of sale and price, and left the growers in a weak position if conflicts of interest arose. Other coops signed contracts with another firm, Trilles, which handled about eight million bottles a year, far less than Chantovent, but sufficient for the medium-sized cooperatives. For other areas of the Midi several other GIE's appeared. All these efforts represent a new approach to commercialization that still affects only a small percentage of vignerons. Given the saturation of the French market, they have begun to prospect foreign markets for their AOC wines.

FOREIGN TRADE: INTERWAR

The golden age of French wine exports came to an end with the invasion of the phylloxera. Although the aphid had begun its ravages in Languedoc in the late 1860s and 1870s, it did not yet affect the fine vineyards elsewhere that produced most of the wine shipped by merchants to foreign countries. Its advance, however, was relentless, and by the beginning of the twentieth century most vineyards had to be replanted on American rootstock. But the restoration of the vineyards did not bring about the rebirth of foreign trade. In the 1870s France exported over three million hectoliters. This volume fell to under two million in the 1890s, and recovered to over two million in the decade before World War I. But the war and its revolutionary aftermath so upset the world market that not even the prosperous 1920s could bring revival. On the contrary, unprecedented political upheavals seriously displaced channels of trade. First, Russia of the tsars collapsed and the victorious Bolsheviks were more given to vodka than wine. A catastrophe of equal magnitude occurred when the United States, in a moment of sublime aberration, voted for the Nineteenth Amendment, which prohibited the sale or fabrication of alcoholic beverages. Anti-alcoholic movements appeared in other states—even in France—but won some success in changing drinking laws only in Scandinavia. Apart from this limited success there were moral victories in that temperance advocates won more followers, with the result that many moderate drinkers became complete abstainers.[22]

Yet there was an alcoholic impulse in the 1920s generation; the mass of men who had fought in the mud of the trenches, and who survived, had acquired a taste for wine, and not only in France. The Belgians too had tasted that invigorating red liquid and felt the need to buy it after the delirium of war had ended. British Tommies had also substituted wine for beer, at least for the four years of hostilities, and learned that port and sherry were not the beginning and end of the vinicultural universe. However, they also learned, on returning to Britain, that wine was far more expensive at home than in their army canteens.

French exports went up with the recovery but never reached prewar levels, the average for the 1920s coming only to 1.6 million hectoliters and then plunging to a mere 800,000 hectoliters in the 1930s. The blackest year was 1932 when exports dropped to just 700,500 hectos. From this low level they steadily rose to just over one million hectoliters in 1938. Then came Hitler's invasion of Poland and war, and exports then plunged to 482,000 hectos in 1940, before climbing again to just over a million, with nearly all of the increase going to pro-German and neutral countries. Some reached Britain via Spain, but that channel soon diminished to a trickle.[23]

Wine exports played an important part in the French economy; in the late 1920s they were valued at about two billion francs, and ranked second, just after silk. The major market was Switzerland, a tiny country with a thirsty people whose per capita consumption ranged between sixty and sixty-five hectoliters. Belgium stood next and then Germany. Unfortunately for the French, both countries bought more wine from Spain and Portugal. Germany, burdened by war debts, laid heavy taxes on imported still wine to limit consumption, a policy followed with a vengeance by the Nazi rulers after 1933. The Nazi rank and file were beer drinkers. Fascist political alliances also favored Italian and Spanish wine over that of France, a potential enemy.[24]

The British Tommy returned to beer after the war. It was the middle and upper classes, although inveterate consumers of port and sherry, who remained the most faithful and most knowledgeable consumers of fine French wine, chiefly bordeaux and champagne. After Portugal, France was their main supplier, high import duties and internal taxes notwithstanding. Of course, the beverages that French shippers or British importers sent across the Channel were often blended with heavier alcoholic wines coming from Portugal, Greece, or Spain in order to give them "body," and to satisfy the British traditional penchant for alcoholic beverages. This was a very old practice, as noted already. As also noted, official wine policies were changing. Since French, especially Bordeaux negotiants, imported blending wine from Spain, the parliament in Paris voted to prohibit the use of foreign wine for mixing with French, a law that went into effect on January 1, 1930.[25] The act provoked bitter trade relations across the Pyrenees, but since it also safeguarded Algerian blending wine from Spanish imports, it was considered a defense measure. Competition from the Hispanic peninsula declined anyway when civil war broke out there in 1936. These blending practices, therefore, have nearly disappeared, a result of more restrictive legislation and, just as important, improved viniculture.

In the 1930s French shippers confronted a far more competitive world market. In that black year, 1932, exports dropped by 75 percent relative to those of 1901–10. Spain, even during the civil war, remained the leading wine exporter as regards quantity; then came Portugal and France, both of whom benefited from Spanish turmoil. But not by much. The fine wines that had enriched France in the past were now too expensive in the markets that had favored them; worse, trade tariffs went up everywhere, including France, further raising imported wine prices.[26] And it was precisely in the early 1930s that French grape harvests rose drastically, and other non-European countries, in South America, Australia, and South Africa, increased their production. The world market became glutted.

French fine wine growers created various commissions to carry out large-scale publicity campaigns. There was a steady expansion of commerce as economies slowly recovered and nations signed trade treaties to encourage mutual exchange. And yet exports, standing at 3 percent of national production in the 1920s, fell to 1 or 2 percent in the thirties.

Champagne producers, as we briefly noted already, were heavily dependent on exports, and suffered the worst setback. Tariff rates on sparkling wine, since it was always considered a luxury, were three or four times higher than on still wines. Exports fell from 14,238,159 bottles in 1929–30 to 4,370,667 bottles in 1932–33, a total below that of 1850. Since this latter date, however, the geography of the trade had shifted: a majority of companies turned inward to the domestic market, where sales of AOC wine rose above exports by two to three times. The oldest major houses, however, continued to rely heavily on foreign markets, if only because native drinkers would not pay the high prices they demanded.[27]

Bordeaux shippers suffered an equal adversity since they sold abroad roughly 20 percent of the area's production, which came to 38 percent of France's total wine exports before 1930. In this year exports fell to only 7 percent of production, the lowest in history. So Bordeaux negotiants, like those elsewhere, tried to sell more in the domestic market. But foreign markets remained a major source of income, and hoping to profit from the quality of their produce, negotiants encouraged growers to expand the supply of appellation wine and reduce ordinaries. This tactic did not support higher prices, and total value of exports fell from 234.7 million francs in 1929 to 64.4 million in 1935, the lowest of the decade. The huge grape crop of 1934, added to the excesses stored in growers' cellars, upset the market. In the domestic market VCC sold more easily than classed growths. As a result, more growers and merchants had to sell their châteaux wines at bottom prices; some even had to sell their châteaux properties—also at bottom prices.[28]

FOREIGN TRADE: POSTWAR

World War II had less effect on wine exports than its more deadly predecessor. Manpower losses were not as catastrophic, and not all markets were closed. The German invasion of 1940 was of course a disaster of huge magnitude, worse than that of 1870, and exports fell to a mere 482,000 hectoliters, shipped out chiefly before the fatal summer of the German invasion. Throughout the war the victors confiscated large amounts of fine wine for the officer corps; the common soldier drank his beer ration. Thereafter exports rose to the level of the 1920s, nearly double those of the 1930s. A good deal went to neutral countries like Switzerland and Spain, far too much for native consumption, an indication that it was shipped out again, even to belligerent countries, so that Britain and the United States, and, incidentally, Latin America, received French wine in 1941, 1942, and 1943. Thereafter trade seriously deteriorated, falling to the 1930s level, a condition lasting until 1950–51, when normal trade channels were once more established, especially after France abandoned the colonial war in Indo-China and pulled out to concentrate on Algeria.

During the 1950s grape production, as already noted, increased and became mechanized. Wine making followed the same trend, and there was an increasingly plentiful supply to satisfy a growing world population. Exports followed a steady upward trend, as revealed in table 7.1 The greatest profits derived from exports were obtained from the markets rich enough to demand the truly great beverages, the most expensive, all grown in the three major appellation districts: Bordeaux, Burgundy, and Champagne.

The time when bordeaux represented a major part of these shipments ended with World War II. During and after the war, Bordeaux merchants and an increasing number of regional growers turned to their fellow nationals, sending their largest shipment to the industrial north, the Parisian basin, and the southwest.[29] By 1951 their foreign sales came to only one-fifth of all French wine exports, down from 38 percent in 1930 and declining to 14 percent in 1979 for volume, and 20 percent for value. The

Table 7.1. French wine exports by volume, 1950–85 (annual average, in thousands of hectoliters)

1950–54	1,980
1955–59	2,040
1960–64	3,870
1965–70	3,757
1971–75	5,936
1976–80	10,164
1984	11,159
1985	11,617

SOURCES: France, Ministère de Commerce, *Tableau général, commerce spécial*; Food and Agricultural Organization of the United Nations, *Trade Yearbook*, annual.

great growths composed 44 to 48 percent of Bordeaux total exports in the fifties, then, in the richest markets, rose to 59 and 63 percent over the next two decades. By the mid-seventies sales came to 700 million francs for a volume of about one million hectoliters. After the brief crisis of 1974, as noted already, came very prosperous times for the vignerons and shippers who survived. Merchants sold roughly 80 percent of this wine, half of which had formerly been sent to the United States, Canada, and Belgium-Luxembourg. By the 1980s a turnaround occurred, and the European Community absorbed about three-fifths of it.

Bordeaux's main competitor has for centuries been Burgundy. Bordeaux, oriented westward to the Atlantic, naturally did well in markets easily accessible by water, including Great Britain. Burgundy, in comparison, appears landlocked. Indeed, until the digging of canals linking France's major rivers and the creation of an extensive railway network over a century ago, Burgundian shippers were rather isolated and only their finest beverages enjoyed prices high enough to cover egregious transport costs. Postwar wealth and improvements in transport and highly aggressive salesmanship enabled Burgundians to surpass their Bordeaux counterparts. In 1961 they exported 390,000 hectoliters valued at 109 million new francs (the new francs of President De Gaulle), well above Gironde's 331,000 hectoliters, valued at 98 million francs. These were the two giants in the domain of still, appellation beverages.[30] All other AOC wines sold out of France came to 173,000 hectoliters for a value of 41 million francs.

Between 1970 and 1980 fine exports rose from 564,800 to 934,592 hectoliters, a jump of over 60 percent. Burgundy gradually fell behind Bordeaux in volume of exports, but did not suffer a corresponding loss of place as regards value. Prices rose sufficiently, perhaps even more than sufficiently, to provoke buyer resistance to increases between 1978 and 1979. This explains why volume suffered a relative diminution, and even an absolute fall of over 15 percent if we exclude the produce of Beaujolais, where moderate price rises led to a leap in volume of 23.4 percent, and in value of 25 percent. Like the Bordelais, the Burgundians relied upon export markets to maintain high prices. Their foreign sales equaled only 10 percent of volume, but like Bordeaux, 20 percent of value. In 1969 they sent out just over 51 percent of their beverages, in 1972 they raised that figure by nine points, where it has more or less remained stable. Not all Burgundian areas were so actively engaged in foreign commerce. The appellations Burgundy, Pouilly-Fuissé, and Châlon attained the highest success and the highest prices, while Beaujolais depended somewhat less on non-French buyers (45 percent), and Mâcon dragged at a mere 30 percent.[31]

The region of Champagne did not suffer as much in the second as in the first great war. An even greater difference between the two eras was the paradox that Germans not only whetted their taste for the wine, but they enjoyed rapid economic recovery after hostilities, creating the wealth that enabled them to purchase a considerable quantity of the stock available from the 1950s on and rise to fifth rank among importing states in 1970.[32]

To meet the postwar demand, vignerons and some shippers began a massive campaign of planting in 1954, which ended by nearly doubling the area of appellation vineyards, from 11,800 hectares to 21,000 in 1975, and to 25,000 at present. Production rose from 380,000 hectoliters to 1.27 million. No other vineyard of quality expanded at such rates: 47 percent for the land and 30 percent for the wine. Champagne producers in general had ceased to export more than half of their bottles after 1914. Like Bordeaux, their fellow Frenchmen became their chief market, and this tendency encouraged an increase of *récoltants-manipulants*, who found the national market readily receptive to their more moderately priced wine. Since the 1920s exports have rarely exceeded 30 percent of total production. In 1970 they were down to 25 percent.[33]

Distinct from the grower-bottlers are the major shippers who buy grapes and still wine in order to create their special *cuvées*, their blends, that are kept secret. These houses, creators of the *grandes marques*, ship out about half of their bottles. A few of them rely more heavily on non-French enophiles and export 65 to 70 percent of their supply, for it is only this worldwide distribution into the richest urban populations that enables them to maintain the extremely high prices they command.

Not only do the finer champagne makers practice a policy of high prices, they also limit shipments to their national as well as international markets. It would be erroneous to assume that they limit supply in order to raise prices. They do not have to resort to this kind of trick because they, like all appellation growers, have a legalized monopoly both of supply and the market. There is only one threat to their dominance: imitation champagne. They limit market supply because they must maintain reserves of old wine that are essential as ingredients of their *cuvées*.

Data furnished by the Food and Agricultural Organization of the United Nations indicate that France, during most of the twenty years after the war, imported more wine than it exported and paid out more francs than it earned. These data, however, are deceptive because most of the "imported" wine came from North Africa, chiefly Algeria, which was politically an integral part of France. When Algeria won independence in the early 1960s, natives began uprooting vines as French Algerians left to settle in Corsica and southern France. By 1966 the supposed trade imbalance had ended and exports steadily rose over imports both in quantity and value. Of course, southern Italian wine took the place of Algerian to blend with weak native wine, but this exchange has never assumed the volume or the value of the Algerian exchange. The favorable shift becomes clear by studying table 7.2.

France's best customers are not difficult to pick out if we use the data of the annual issues of the *Tableau Général de Commerce Extérieur*. In 1950 the United States became a major buyer, a reorientation important enough to shift the geography of exports somewhat more toward the West, since Britain also remained the leading consumer of still wines. It is curious that neither country had a high per capita rate of wine consumption; the mass of their populations preferred beer and hard liquor. And yet their middle and upper classes considered it more fashionable to drink wine as aperitifs and with meals. This marked an unprecedented shift for Americans, who had felt more venturesome drinking whiskey and gin during Prohibition, and had hardly changed their habits after the end of Prohibition in 1933. I think that the millions of soldiers who fought first in Italy and then in France picked up a taste for wine, and this time did not abandon it after the war. If I may interject a personal recollection, the first word I learned

Table 7.2.   Value of imports/exports in U.S. dollars

Year	Value of Wine Exports (in U.S. Millions of Dollars)	Value of Wine Imports (in U.S. Millions of Dollars)
1960	112.2	271.8
1965	169.5	271.2
1966	191.6	171.9
1970	285.1	176.8
1971	351.0	99.2
1972	519.5	166.8
1973	811.4	232.1
1975	709.8	256.7
1979	1,657.5	401.9

SOURCE: Food and Agricultural Organization of the United Nations, *Trade Yearbook*, annual.

as a G.I. upon arriving in Italy was *vino*, and given the difficulty of finding pure water, I more readily filled my canteen with the peasant wine I obtained in exchange for C-rations. Perhaps this also explains why Americans have persistently imported the less expensive beverages.

On the other hand, the British, in line with a long tradition, purchased the best and most expensive bottles, at least until import taxes raised the retail prices of appellation beverages enough to put them out of reach of all buyers save the wealthy. A liter of wine costing four francs when leaving the shipper's cellar paid over eight francs of import duties. A switch came in the 1970s, when modestly priced wines made their appearance in British supermarkets. Between 1976 and 1980, sales in these large retail outlets rose from 22 to 50 percent of all sales. Chain stores, most of which now belong to large breweries, the major importers, have lost about 10 percent of their trade, as have independent retailers who concentrate on brand labels.[34] France has remained the prime supplier, with Italy and Germany (given the preference for white wine) competing for second place. By 1978 Britain was the leading client of French producers.

Less burdened with taxes, which varied from state to state, Americans have steadily increased their consumption both of French still and effervescent beverages since 1950. For roughly twenty years these imports dominated the markets of New York and California. Far less wine penetrated interior regions, save in major urban centers such as Chicago and New Orleans. But the 1970s marked an adverse change when French prices rose to the heavens and Italian shippers sent massive amounts of inexpensive wine, most of it from the Po Valley provinces of Emilia and Romagna. Slightly sparkling, slightly sweet reds, called Lambrusco from the principal grape, made up over 70 percent of exports and put Italy in first place for volume of shipments but in second or third for their value. Yet Italian shippers have steadily improved their prices in all their markets: in 1967 their export revenues came to only 38 percent of France's; in 1970 they rose to just over 48 percent; in 1972 to over 63 percent, and then they more or less stabilized.

French shippers, after the crisis of 1973–74, aggressively expanded their commercial penetration of the United States. In 1982 Americans absorbed 8.7 percent of the volume of their total global shipments and paid out 16.5 percent of the value. As regards profits, America has become the prime market. And yet Americans, when they returned to French wine in 1975–76, began imbibing more ordinary or table wine of a superior sort, VDQS and regional wines under four dollars per bottle, and it was these that grew to constitute about 78 percent of the total. In 1979 the United States was France's third largest customer, Sweden or Canada alternating as the second. The strong dollar of the early 1980s has helped to prevent serious price increases. However, the weakening dollar in 1985 led to halving imports the next year. And as the dollar continues to fall, exporters will have to cut profit margins or suffer declining sales.[35]

The French have sought to meet the American fad for light, fruity white wines. Here, as in Britain, women have come to equal men in purchases and in consumption, and they are partial to whites. Hence the enormous jump in sales of white beverages from Alsace, Burgundy (chiefly Mâcon), the Côtes-du-Rhône, and muscadet from the Loire.

Also less burdened with taxes and profiting from highly dynamic postwar economies, the Belgians and the Luxembourgers were active importers. The growth of the drinking rate did not result from a significant increase in per capita consumption but from the spreading acceptance of wine among broader segments of the population, chiefly among persons between the ages of thirty-five and forty-nine, and those enjoying comfortable incomes. As in France, their preferred type of wine was red (75 to 80 percent of imports) and imbibed during festivities. In Belgium, French wine was king. The hardly significant wine growing in Luxembourg, dry whites, accounted for only 3 to 4 percent. Belgians, although only ten million in number, have absorbed over 15 percent of French exports. Combined with Luxembourg it is France's largest market for appellation wines, both AOC and VDQS. This does not mean that Belgians have taken to drinking only classed growths. On the contrary, the bulk of French exports there are shipped in bulk, then bottled locally after some blending because these northeners, like the British, prefer a rather full-bodied, alcoholic beverage. Hence the predominance of bordeaux in both countries, for it lends itself to "improvement." Full-bodied côtes-du-rhône have also begun to claim an important place; they are good and less expensive. Burgundies, given the steep rise in prices, have steadily fallen out of favor. France's chief competitor has been Italy, whose exports have steadily risen since the giant jump in prices of French wines in the early seventies. However, the Italians have not been highly successful. In 1980 France enjoyed nearly 72 percent of the volume of imports into Belgium-Luxembourg, Italy 18 percent. In value, the French advantage was nearly 83 percent, Italy a mere 8 percent. In 1979 the Belgium-Luxembourg economic union was France's fourth largest buyer.[36]

The picture changes entirely for the German Federal Republic. West

Germans import on average slightly over half their foreign wine from Italy, roughly 10 percent of their red wine from Yugoslavia, and 10 percent of their white from Austria. French shipments have ranged from 29 percent in 1973 to 37 percent in 1977 to 25 percent in 1982. Reds progressed rather slowly from 22 to 29 percent, but whites have declined from 26 to 20 percent. The German preference for white is an old tradition, as is their taste for moderately sweet beverages, whatever the color. They of course produce most of their own white wine, and much of the white they bring in is bulk wine, Italian or Austrian in origin and used to make *sekt*, a bubbling beverage, sugary, low in alcohol and acidity. French champagne, highly favored in the 1960s, has steadily lost out because of the extreme increase in price over the years. Gallic *mousseux* sent to the Republic is the cheap, low-quality liquid, usually the product of the closed-vat method. A commodity of this sort has to survive in a highly competitive market. Fine wines from France constitute only 3 to 4 percent of total imports.

By 1957 the "westernization" of exports was more marked, with the United States, Britain, and Canada buying roughly half of shipments and providing over half the revenue. These figures declined to around 40 percent by the late 1970s as Belgian, Central European, and Far Eastern markets expanded when economic conditions improved. These data refer to wine shipped out in bottle.

The geography was significantly different for wine exported in barrels or in any containers over five liters capacity. The compass directions were east into Switzerland, northeast into West Germany, and north into Belgium-Luxembourg. Six times more wine went out in large containers than in bottle, but since it was one-half to three-fourths cheaper per hectoliter, it brought in only twice the revenue of bottled wine. Belgium was, in a sense, a kind of pivot, buying heavily both in bottle and in bulk, the latter in particular to be blended with Spanish, Greek, or Italian wine and shipped out under authentic brand labels or French imitation labels. They, as well as the Germans, bought large quantities of still wine from Champagne, refermented it in bulk, and sold it as *sekt*, sent out usually under a brand label. But there were merchants who passed it off as "champagne," hoping to escape the vigilance of the Comité Interprofessionel de Vin de Champagne. In this latter endeavor they were rarely successful; the CIVC had to devote an inordinate amount of its budget and energy suing the violators in courts throughout the world.

The patterns of trade that began in the 1950s continued, and the 1960s were prosperous for exporters. There was a more or less steady increase in volume and prices. Positive forces that were more numerous and helpful in expanding sales were the following:[37]

1. Retail outlets increased. In the 1960s and 1970s supermarkets appeared everywhere, especially in suburbs where high-salaried classes, including skilled workers, resided. Traditionally wine connoisseurs of the upper class probably did not exceed 15 percent of the population but consumed about 70 percent of fine wines. A new market appeared among the lower middle and skilled working class. France's ordinary wines and regional wines attracted their attention. The decline of Italian imports can be partly explained by the rise in consumption of these lesser breeds of French wines at cheap prices, which are light of body, fruity, deeply colored if red, crystal clear if white, and more sweet than dry. Wine chain stores, especially those owned by large corporations like the breweries in Britain, had dominated retail sales until supermarkets appeared and took over at least 50 percent of the sales of these lesser wines shipped in bulk, blended to suit local tastes, and sold in bottle under a trade name. By the late 1970s the volume of VDQS was expanding at 12 percent annually and the value at 11 percent. More spectacular were the advances of superior table wines, leaping ahead at 31 percent in volume and 29 percent in value. Côtes-du-Rhône's lesser AOC's rose by 15 and 13 percent, respectively.[38] France's viniculturists had learned quickly how to defend their place in foreign markets—even in supermarkets.

2. Wine sold in supermarkets was bought mainly by women who did the family grocery shopping. Their tastes therefore became an important element in viniculture. As noted above, they preferred white wine, low in alcohol, fruity with some sweetness, and very low acidity. Lesser wines filled their needs, exported at first by Italians, then by Frenchmen who had to make up for their greater production of reds, heavy and alcoholic. Only Belgian and German women accepted these. The 1970s witnessed a western revolution in wine fashion, and the Anglo-Saxons of both sexes abandoned their demand for alcoholic, deep red, heavy wine—even sherry imports declined—and went for the "light," that is, those low in alcohol.

3. The substitution of light sweet wine, chiefly white, for the cocktail as an apéritif added to volume of sales. The big rise of simple sparkling wine, far cheaper than champagne, also reflected this change of taste. Wine sales have grown, in part because seasoned drinkers consume more, but in greater part because there are more unseasoned people bringing home a bottle to take either before the meal or along with it. The consum-

ers of these lesser wines have been young, chiefly between twenty-five and forty-five years of age. The future of the wine industry lies with them. Shippers hope that these newcomers will improve their earnings and mature their knowledge, so that they will eventually become more sophisticated buyers of finer beverages. Britain is fairly indicative of the spread of wine drinking. In 1970 the average drinker imbibed only two liters, while in 1980 it rose to eight liters, and presently ten liters, chiefly on festive occasions or with Sunday lunch. This represents a fivefold increase, but it is a drop in a big glass compared to the French, who used to drink ninety-two liters on any and all occasions, even though they now drink only seventy-five liters. In 1985 the Portugese surpassed them, but the French recovered their prime place the next year and held it despite the drop of consumption.

4. The undertaking of massive advertising campaigns by syndicates of growers and by shippers pushing their own brands has opened the public's interest. The same is true of the appearance or expansion of various organizations whose purpose is to educate the public, such as the International Wine and Food Society, the Friends of Wine, each with numerous local chapters, as well as the increase in wine columns in the popular press and of slick magazines specializing in spreading both information and misinformation about wine.

PROBLEMS OF WORLDWIDE CONSUMPTION

Wine commerce beyond the hexagonal frontiers of France was intimately related to patterns of wine consumption in foreign states. Since the end of World War I, syndicates of growers, cooperatives, and shippers undertook sizable publicity campaigns to encourage sales of corked bottled wine, not "corked" wine, that is, wine that usually enjoyed some kind of appellation. Both in and out of France their efforts eventually proved fruitful: consumption of appellation wine rose steadily, and more than steadily after World War II.[39] The interwar, as we noted already, was a troubled time. Among European states, consumption per capita of all kinds of wine remained stationary over two decades, or tended to decline, except in France, Germany, Portugal, and on the Balkan peninsula, where growers expanded vine planting and improved their techniques. Latin American countries also expanded their vineyards, and Chileans and Argentineans began drinking more homegrown wine, creating a serious predicament for major European producers and exporters. Soviet citizens, like Americans, almost abandoned wine. Asians never seriously took to it.[40]

Small wonder that merchants in Bordeaux, Burgundy, and Champagne turned toward their domestic market after 1918. But even there, several factors discouraged sales: the limited incomes of the French, heavily taxed by ministers who woefully discovered that the Germans would not or could not pay the full costs of their wartime destruction along the Western front; the large number of French farmers who had planted Franco-American hybrid vines and made their own wine, a quantity that added to the large commercial output by one fourth, or at times a third; the galloping inflation of the 1920s; the depression of the 1930s; and the uncertainties about the future, exacerbated by the Popular Front, the Civil War in Spain, and the menace of Nazi Germany. Despite all of these perturbing factors, French per capita consumption remained remarkably stable during the interwar, ranging from 140 to 162 liters, if homemade wine is included.[41] Most of this drinking was focused on ordinary table wine, the *gros rouge* bought right from the barrel at the corner grocer's. This was what the soldier drank in wartime and after demobilization. The problem for growers of better wines and their shippers was the continued minuscule rate of wine drinking in foreign countries and the incalculable difficulties of exporting alcoholic beverages. Laws governing vine and wine growing have become increasingly complex, but not more so than the legal jungle of foreign rules and restrictions on alcoholic imports. In addition, since the horrendous inflation of the 1920s, there have been fluctuating rates of monetary exchange, unstable markets, delays of transport resulting from social instability that ranged from dockers' strikes to political revolutions, and the ever rising tax rates levied on imports.

Of all France's foreign markets the United States has remained the most difficult. Not only was there federal law to contend with, there were forty-eight—and more recently fifty—state laws, differing drastically as regards the sale of all alcoholic liquids; some were "dry," others "wet," and there were even county laws within each state that either favored or disfavored alcohol. In many central and southern states the era of prohibition did not end in the early 1930s. "Old time" religion retained its hold over two public activities: education and drinking. Hypocrisy thrived in these areas; everyone knows that Mississippians voted dry as long as they could stagger to the ballot box. So the laws prohibiting or restricting consumption remained on the books. Traditions of wine consumption were important, indeed influenced the law: Americans, like the English and Canadians, were habitually beer and whiskey drinkers. There was also a native American wine industry, concentrated chiefly in California. It retained about 70 percent of the wine drinkers, most of whom absorbed the jug wines of Gallo, United Vintners, and even Almadén. At this lower echelon of quality, the Italians with their lambruscos and simple chiantis far outsold the French. The latter, of course, had made certain regional names household words by massive advertising dating back to the nineteenth century. This is why American producers referred to their wines, even their jug wines, as rhine, burgundy, chablis, and champagne. This was a favorite practice before Prohibition, and it was immediately resumed after Prohibition. The French were furious, and their numerous syndicates complained to the United States government. The latter was not unresponsive and a bill soon emerged from Congress, the Federal Alcohol Administration Act, on August 29, 1935. Of more concern to us is the amendment that passed both houses on June 26, 1936, which did not deny American vintners the use of French or any other European regional names on their labels if the local wine was of the same type. This was an innocuous restriction, but at least it required that the name of the American state or other area be added in lettering as conspicuous as that used for the French locale.[42] For this reason there appeared a host of wines bearing the sobriquets of "California burgundy" and "New York chablis."

Given the size and variability of such an immense American population, French firms after 1945 began grouping their efforts and resources and concentrating on successive promotional campaigns by region. Since 1974 a group of large exporters has spent four to five years penetrating certain key territories, chiefly large metropolitan centers. Recognizing the ferocity of competition among wines under about two or three dollars, they have promoted those selling retail between three and six dollars. Their aim is to sell good table wine and VDQS rather than appellations. In this way they hope to familiarize the public with brands as well as with grape regions, and to associate French wine with a price slightly higher than that of California jugs and Italian lambruscos, to suggest that bottles from France offer much higher quality at a minimally higher price. The great classed wines sell themselves to an elite clientele; it is the little wines with a brand label that must be promoted actively, in large wine stores, supermarkets, and restaurants.

Since most Americans buy simple table wines, champagne firms have found the market a particularly difficult one. Despite pouring huge sums into promotional campaigns, the French have come to recognize that

Americans and Canadians as wine drinkers rank last among the industrialized populations of the West, consuming a mere 0.04 bottles per head. Yet the Americans rank second in the number of bottles imported (9,718,538 in 1983), and the Canadians eighth (993,048). The population of the United States has been so large that even the few drinkers faithful to champagne formed a sizable clientele. The British consumed 0.16 bottles of champagne and ranked fourth in per capita consumption but first in the number of bottles imported. Yet the market was largely limited to England. The Scotch and Welsh are far less attracted by wine, making up a sizable part of the 40 percent of the British population who have never put a glass of still wine, not to mention champagne, to their lips.[43] The average annual rate of consumption for still wine in the early 1980s did rise, thanks to Britain's entry into the common market and the EEC's prohibition against discriminatory taxation on imports by its members.[44]

The formation of a common market for wine in 1970 certainly abetted international trade. Yet it did not magically put aside all the barriers, and the volume of sales continued to depend on policy and action. Since the 1940s or 1950s every major AOC viticultural region has had an interprofessional committee for wine (CIV) that sought to discipline growers to maintain standards and to assist shippers with advice and market surveys. It also sought, sometimes without much success, to limit price increases in order successfully to compete against American, Italian, and Spanish sellers. The CIV of Bordeaux failed dismally to control prices in 1972–74, and the CIV's of Champagne, Burgundy, and Alsace have hardly tried to control them. Growers, above all, demanded increases to cover their ever rising costs in prestigious vineyards whose yields remained moderate, and their voice resonated in CIV meetings.

In general, French wine has always been the most expensive in foreign markets, a situation making the sellers' job all the more difficult. Large-scale promotional activity has become a necessary adjunct to the in-store campaigns that use posters, tastings served by representatives, and elaborate galas for wine writers, journalists, large retailers, and socialites. I have mentioned some of the tactics already and shall not repeat them here. What must be underlined are the ever rising costs of selling by publicity and tastings. In 1983 the CIV of Champagne spent forty-five million francs for promotional campaigns both in and out of France, one-third of its budget. A fraction of these funds come from state and departmental budgets, because wine exports have almost always helped balance France's foreign commerce. In 1981 champagne alone equaled 2.3 percent of agricultural exports, 25 percent of all wine exports, and 31 percent of appellation wine exports. It also constituted 33 percent of the exports of the Marne department.[45] These figures are roughly also valid for bordeaux and burgundy wines.

The major share of the costs of selling, however, have come from the treasuries of shippers and vignerons who pay a fee to their syndicates, based on the size of sales for the former and of harvests for the latter. On the whole, France has become the best-known producer of wine, the homeland of Bacchus. Drinkers with discriminating palates tend to pay more for their wines because the expectation of good value motivates them. Not even scandals like "winegate" turned them away for long. After all, nobody died from the wine of the Cruse company, an aftermath almost benign when compared to the scandalous adulterations recently perpetrated in Austria and Italy. Small wonder that the average vigneron has profited from his labors.

Conditions of Life: Propertied Growers

WAYS OF LIFE DURING THE INTERWAR

The vignerons who were able to leap with unblemished joy at 11 A.M. on November 11, 1918, and could emerge from the stench and filth of their trenches, still sound in body and mind, were indeed a happy and lucky array of homesick rustics. Like the hordes of demobilized farmers, they returned to home and land. There they found their families: wives fatigued from overwork, children older and active on the land, and vines in diverse states of neglect. Because they did not reach home before winter had set in, the harvest having been completed two or three months earlier, they put aside their uniforms—or used them as work clothes—and began pruning. If their weapons were not transformed into plowshares, they were, perhaps, forged into pruning shears. In the spring they would undertake the delicate task of replanting to fill in the all-too-visible gaps left in their vine rows. The great majority of them were family heads, owning land, crop sharing, renting, or combining two and perhaps three of these categories to be able to support their dependents. Many of them were petty vignerons with two or three hectares of vines; they put up for sale from 150 to 200 hectoliters, a quantity that in good times made possible a level of life referred to as *décent*, a term vague enough to indicate that a family was housed, fed, and clothed in accordance with the lowest level of human needs.

As noted in Chapter One, the interwar was not the best of times for winegrowers. Save for a brief period in the mid-1920s, their revenues were meager. There was rarely enough in the proverbial woolen sock—most likely a small savings account by the 1920s—both to live well and to buy more land. So the wise among them lived badly, purchased a few ares, and

planted them in vines in anticipation of better markets to come. The vigneron labored hard himself and expected his family aides to imitate the
work ethic he followed before the war. During his absence his wife, children, grandparents, nephews, nieces, cousins, uncles, aunts—all had tried
to maintain the family vineyard. The veteran's return did not ease the
family's tasks. Depending on the region and the family size, work was the
measure of life. Whether the vineyard was one or two hectares in a fine-
growth district, or five to six in an area less esteemed, family members
carried out most of the tasks, from the most painful to the most exacting
in skill. They carried uphill, often on their backs, the soil washed down
by rain; they pruned; they tied canes to wire trellises, chiefly women's
work; finally, they picked grapes, also a woman's job, with men brought
in to carry heavy loads. Many hefty women accomplished these jobs more
easily than decrepit old men who had nothing to keep them going save
their pride. Whether petty, medium, or large owners, all of them underwent changes, but it is difficult to identify the social category that underwent the earliest modifications, and to discover the pace and nature of
change.[1]

Perhaps family diet was slowest to change, for rural people have always
been extremely reluctant to alter their eating habits. Certainly peasant
vignerons consumed the same kinds of food as their distant ancestors.
Bread remained the staple, the *matière sacrée*, as Bréchard put it.[2] In areas
of vine monoculture, wives bought bread at the baker's, sometimes for
money, sometimes for wine, a practice very common in the Midi and
Champagne, where growers had abandoned in the late nineteenth century
the cultivation of crops other than grapes. In the Rhône and Loire valleys,
in Burgundy, and in Bordeaux, vignerons still cultivated some cereals
from which they could obtain flour at the miller's and either made bread
at home or had the baker make it for a price. They also attempted to grow
fodder for their animals.[3]

Bread appeared at all meals. At breakfast, it accompanied *la soupe*, a
thick liquid heavy with vegetables and fatback. Bread that had become too
hard to be bitten into was chopped into pieces and dropped into the bowl,
where it softened as it absorbed the liquid, helping to thicken it. Only
vignerons who were truly polyculturists could produce vegetables in sufficient quantity to feed their families. Their occasional resort to white
bread was a sign of progress in either income or pretensions. They abandoned cereals other than wheat, but it is likely that most families continued to consume brown bread, chiefly whole wheat, save on Sundays or

during festivals when white bread was displayed with pride. On ordinary workdays the noon meal, if taken at home, was the main one. As usual, it consisted of broth, potatoes cooked in every way known, and a small chunk of pork; many vignerons, like other peasant farmers, still raised a pig or two in a small sty, and salted its meat to preserve it. The finest pieces, as well as sausages, were reserved for Sundays and *fêtes*. Vegetables and legumes like beans and peas also appeared at the daily meal, and cheese was as common as bread. The amount of wine that growers consumed depended on the market. When prices were low and sales lagged, they drank more of their own production. In this way they could be assured that their barrels would be emptied for next year's crop. In extremely dry seasons, when they lacked water, some of my interviewees recalled washing themselves in their wine, especially in areas that produced light, low alcoholic wine that could easily turn sour in extremely warm weather. Most growers simply did not have cellars that were cool enough for preserving mediocre beverages. Perhaps the wine was mediocre; still, it was real wine, pure and uncontaminated, not the *piquette* that was the beverage of petty owners and workers when busy in the vineyards.

Perhaps the picture I am painting is too somber. In truth, vignerons who sold wine in a nearby urban market acquired city tastes, and this contact, reenforced by ample army rations during the First World War, led to some improvement in diet after 1918. Not only vignerons but the rural population in general began to consume more meat. Even monoculturists continued to raise rabbits and chickens, meat items formerly sold for cash but now more abundantly partaken of on Sundays. At times, roasts other than pork were put in the oven before the wife left for church, and then enjoyed for Sunday lunch; what remained graced the dining table on the following days. Gradually, bread ceased to be the principal item of the meal, and the tastiness of food increased as wives or grown daughters took more time away from field work and improved their culinary skills. Cookbooks had appeared in greater numbers since the early nineteenth century, and although they were destined for literate ladies of the middle class, by the turn of the century more vigneronnes were literate. They began to procure at least one of these tomes or, more likely, found novel and flavorful recipes in the magazines and newspapers that used to be read in cafés, and now in the home.

During the late 1920s the traditional monotony of meals, the same kinds of insipid food day after day, was giving way as more rapid transportation brought wider choices to housewives. Fish entered the diet on occasions other than Friday, but did not find wide acceptance in the countryside. The exception was sardines, at least on the southern coast, where they were eaten during the harvest with grapes and old Cantal cheese.[4] More frequently enjoyed were various vegetables: spinach, celery, artichokes (the complicated eating of which put off many a peasant), tomatoes (which rural lore had formerly damned as poisonous), green beans, cauliflower, and mushrooms. Thanks to the popular press and mass literacy, wives discovered not only recipes for a particular dish but full-scale menus for an entire meal, and gave more attention to ways of adding savor to food by using spices, cream, or milk to create sauces. When not working in the vines or tending to the *basse cour*, that is, the chickens and rabbits and pig that brought in some cash and provided meat, and, of course, when not raising children, the vigneronne could give more attention to preparing appetizing meals. But she was a terribly busy woman and everyday fare, with rare exceptions, remained dull and monotonous.[5]

In any case, her cooking facilities remained quite limited. Happily for her, she no longer prepared her meals over an open fire; the *marmite*, a large thick iron pot that hung on a hook in the hearth, was almost a relic of the past, save for the most backward regions, chiefly nonviticultural ones. She had wheedled from her husband a heavy iron stove, with an oven and a flat surface perforated by three or four holes on which she placed pots, and which could be closed by thick iron disks when not in use. Fuel consisted of faggots of vine canes that she had gathered when pruning during winter. Canes, alas, burned rapidly, so for more substantial fires she used heavy vine trunks that had been uprooted when replaced by new stock. In addition, there were charcoal, rather expensive, and rough anthracite, which gave less heat but glowed for hours.

This kitchen with its array of pots hanging from wall hooks, with its stacks of dishes in an open cupboard that was either homemade or the product of a local carpenter-vigneron and turned out from local wood, and with its long table covered with oil cloth, flanked by two benches in a modest household and by wooden chairs in the more affluent, was not merely a room for cooking and eating. It was the focal point of family life, combining with its main purpose the functions of a living room and recreation space. For petty growers as well as for skilled vine workers, this was the only room that was ever heated, making it the natural gathering place of the family during winter.

Some old vignerons recalled with keen nostalgia the fireplace before which the family had gathered after the last meal. They missed the intimacy of the bright, lively flames, as warming of the heart as of the body, and a comforting addition to their father's tall tales. Sometimes the forebears of the more prosperous growers had built hearths in the living room and made them wide and deep enough for the old folk to sit inside to warm their bones. This practice still exists in some houses erected in previous centuries.

In warmer weather, many vignerons recalled, families sat outdoors wherever shade was available, and it was not uncommon for neighbors to sit together in order to exchange their views on matters that were familiar to them all. This socializing took place on long summer evenings. During the work day, differing functions separated the sexes: the men plowing between vine rows, silent behind their horses; the women meeting at the wash fountain, chatting and gossiping to forget their drudgery. Washing clothes still took place at a public fountain or at a low wooden pier along a stream's edge. For the 20 percent or so of viticultural families that owned above ten to fifteen hectares of vines, there might be indoor plumbing. But even so, the wives of well-to-do growers often accompanied a servant to the wash place and gossiped along with all the other women. The community of gossip was more powerful than the sense of class, save for the women of families owning large estates. They lived in a world apart.

For small and medium owners, conditions of life tended to diminish any militant sense of class. This of course was more true in villages with a population of a few hundred than in market towns with a few thousand denizens of varying professions. In both, however, housing was not greatly different. The kitchen-living room was almost always the largest room, bedrooms being used mainly for sleeping. Overcrowding was common, parents usually sharing a bedroom with infants and piling all the older children in another chamber. Houses were old, except in Champagne, where rebuilding on a massive scale followed the war's destruction of thousands of dwellings. Elsewhere in rural France, few houses were raised during the interwar. In 1938 eight out of ten families lived in housing that predated 1870, the year of the Franco-Prussian War.[6] These were solid structures, made of stone and intended to last several generations, but primitive as regards sanitary equipment. Peasants, as we noted, spent money to round out their holdings, plot by plot, not to make themselves comfortable. Like their everyday clothing, they patched their houses, stopped a leak in a decrepit roof, shored up a stooping wall, covered their dirt floors with wood, stone or tile, installed new windows in thick walls. Serious renovation was rare with two exceptions: the installation of electricity and indoor running water, the source of which was a cistern or a well with an electric pump. As in the Golden Slopes, new or improved housing with showers or baths appeared in villages nearest a sizable city but remained rare curiosities elsewhere. Outdoor toilets far outnumbered indoor.[7]

Many vignerons' houses had some kind of attached space for pressing grapes and carrying out the first fermentation in wooden vats. Only the most professional and full-time had underground cellars, usually with the door located to the north to avoid warm air currents arriving from the opposite direction. These were the vignerons who matured their wine in barrels before selling it to local shippers. Traditionally, most vine trainers sold their grapes or newly fermented wine immediately to winemaking merchants or, more recently, brought their grapes to cooperatives. Therefore their need for a cellar had vanished. Since most vignerons had carried out their vinicultural operations in a kind of lean-to structure attached to a wall of their house, they could now use this space for other purposes.

Quite different were vignerons in fine wine areas whose mental outlook was formed by family as well as by communal traditions dating back to premodern times. They were more averse to cooperatives than to innovation, because in their view, grape and wine growing were complementary, were indeed so interlocked that doing one without the other seemed a violation of natural law. Inheritors of an almost mystical concept of vine and vat, they were convinced that only the individual grower of grapes was capable of transforming his juice into wine, that cultivating the vine was a connubial insemination, and the changing of juice into wine was a birth, as natural and yet as miraculous as the creation of life itself. These were the self-motivated, independent growers present in all wine regions, but especially in Burgundy, Bordeaux, and Champagne. They owned on average six to ten hectares, spread in rather small parcels over two or three highly rated wine communes, combining a landed inheritance, a wife's dowry, and a series of purchases of several *ares* at different periods in the life cycle of a grower's family, as a contribution of their generation to the future well-being of the next. Simon Loftus, a British wine merchant, and Eunice Fried knew some of them in Burgundy and described them with the broad stroke of the writer's brush. There is Jean Thévenet, resident of the Mâcon appellation village of Quintaine-Clessé. Possessing seven hectares he is a medium producer in his area. Although he found mechanical harvesters useless, even harmful, he was one of the few vignerons to purchase a pneumatic press. He also ferments his wine in stainless steel vats before maturing it in wooden casks.

Pierre Cogny is also a typical Burgundian producer in that he wants to become personally acquainted with his clients. Like many growers devoted to quality, he sells his best wines to his clients, his lesser to negotiants. Although the latter complain bitterly about this prejudice, the vignerons do not trust them. Cogny nurses his wine—even if it is not sick. Fearing oxidation, he tops his barrels every day, refuses to bottle if there is fog, rain, or a full moon; and hates both filtration and cold stabilization, that is, chilling white wine to bring about the precipitation of tartaric acid before putting the wine in bottle.

Among these individualists there are some truly odd characters. Fried met André Mussy, whose fifteen hectares spread over Pommard, Volnay, and Beaune. A scion of eight generations of vignerons, he began working on the family property in 1928 and still turned the earth with a two-pronged hoe, the type commonly used by vignerons before the phylloxera. There were few horses in his village. He later bought one. In his words, the horse is an "intelligent animal and we worked together. A horse does not compare with a tractor. A horse's work is more refined, more careful and meticulous. The horse is man's friend. The tractor is only a machine, and man is a slave to that machine. When I worked with the horse all day I was tired at night, but only physically tired. When I worked on a tractor, I was physically exhausted, but I also suffered from nervous exhaustion."[8] Monsieur Mussy hired two workers to train his vines, allowing him to devote his energies and his knowledge to his cellar. I have spoken with many growers who fondly recalled the days of the horse, for these were the days of their youth as well; but none of them really wanted to return to the past, to trade their tractor for an animal of any sort.

Even now, without having to care for an animal, their days remain long. As independents they have both land and cellar to manage, and after eight or more hours of physical labor they spend their evenings poring over their accounts and corresponding with their clients. Almost every house has a room equipped as an office. Here the wife also spends much of her time, and lucky is the man whose helpmate knows how to use a typewriter. In the Champagne town of Bouzy, Camille Savès is lucky; his wife both types his letters and keeps the books, far more efficiently than he can. Like all récoltants-manipulants he sells his sparkling wine directly to individual clients and to restaurants. He and his wife spend their winter evenings calculating costs and prices, writing promotional literature, arranging purchases of chemicals and equipment for vineyard and cellar, answering queries of clients, and reading the latest professional publications: articles in journals, pamphlets from experimental stations, and books. Just keeping up with all the revised and new viti-vinicultural rules and regulations has become a major task, almost requiring some legal training. And the EEC has added to the complexity.

The vigneron's year is as full as his day. After harvest comes the time for uprooting dead, dying, or excessively old plants and replacing them with new stock to maintain production levels and a medley of vines of different ages. Rotted posts and rusted trellis wires must be replaced. Over the coldest months there is pruning, the most delicate and demanding of operations. There is also the cellar where the new wine demands constant supervision, where leaking barrels must be repaired; fermentation vats, stemmer-crushers, and presses cleaned and sterilized; barrels topped, and their contents racked off the lees. Under great pressure the vigneron at times hardly knows where to begin, or to turn: to the vineyard and its needs, or to the cellar where neglect may lead to a defective wine. Such are the anxieties that beset the independent.

Lucky is he whose son decides to succeed to the property, who grows in strength and learns on the job, attends a viticultural school, and inherits the powerful arms and back demanded by the profession and the mental fortitude to remain even after seeing a hailstorm devastate a whole year's efforts, perhaps even imperil the vineyard's future. Such a son is, like a wife who can type, a gift of a benevolent fate.

Only in late summer, after the last spraying and tying of canes, can the vigneron relax. Then he and his family leave for vacation, an occasion that had rarely arisen for his father or his grandfather. The family needs rest, for they will return to the harvest of September and October, the most physically and mentally demanding months of the vigneron's calender. With grape pickers to supervise, house, and feed, and with continuous cellar work, the entire family puts in twenty-hour days, sometimes twenty-four, sleeping only in snatches. As they say, the full grapes are "jealous," demanding all their energy, all their time during three weeks or more. Mechanical harvesters would spare them much of this heavy labor, but men and women fully committed to the making of fine wine refuse to use them. At least for the present. And yet more and more wives encourage their husbands to invest in a mechanical harvester; not only can she then escape the day-long bending required by picking grapes, she also does not have to prepare the enormous meals that hired help expect at harvest time.

In contrast to the slow, meandering mutations of the past, World War II was a floodgate through which the waters of innovation rushed at a torrential rate. By the late 1950s and 1960s the vigneron was not merely a generation away from the interwar, he was a world away.

Before the formation of free, public education rural inhabitants generally communicated in the language of their region, with a bit of French mixed in. But all of their agricultural vocabulary was purely regional. Those who knew academic French, the language of officialdom, never used it in their villages, homes, or fields and vineyards; it was reserved for contacts with the "outer" world. But the post-1945 generation no longer spoke the old language, the dialect, the *patois* of their elders. The use of proper French had, of course, spread before 1914 and even more rapidly afterward, thanks to elementary schools and more active attendance in them; to the radio, to the popular press which increasingly replaced purely local journals written in dialect; and, finally, to cheaper rapid transport by bicycle, motorbike, bus, and train. Post-World War II developments, such as cheaper automobiles—rare in rural France before 1939 but almost universal by 1970—and television, speeded up these agents of change and added new dimensions. Under pressure from their children to mechanize and modernize, middle-aged producers went more frequently to the city to borrow money to equip their vineyards. They also borrowed to improve their houses with indoor plumbing. Toilets and hot running water were enormous innovations not only in personal hygiene but in comfort. Hot water made it possible to install clothes washers, an advancement that led women to abandon the community wash shed and, to some extent, the conviviality that had reigned there, even if petty jealousies had emerged in some sweetly bitter exchanges. The installation of refrigerators, bought on a time-payment plan like all other machines or with money borrowed from a mutual credit society or the Crédit Agricole, made it possible for families to shop in newly erected supermarkets and to introduce foods for everyday dining that were once considered luxuries, indeed, royal fare.

Increased revenues of the growers who had enlarged their properties earlier, when land prices were moderate, enabled them now to concentrate more of their skills on viticulture. Fewer animals were used, and the enormous time and care they required diminished. Horses and mules went first, being replaced by tractors. Then cows and goats, whose milk and cheese were replaced by produce from the shelves of supermarkets or consumers' cooperatives. Less rapidly but ineluctably women gave up the *basse cour* and the pig, both replaced by butcher's meat. During the 1970s more and more rural families were at last liberated from the care and feeding of animals, allowing them to go on weekend or more extended vacations. Until now this was a practice reserved for the rich, who could hire workers to care for their beasts, though only rarely did these large owners live on the land for longer than the summer months. Now the wives and daughters of resident growers, who no longer had to look after animals and fowl and whose housework was lightened by vacuum sweepers and various machines, could devote more of their time to other tasks such as bookkeeping, bottling, and labeling. This change was most useful for families with holdings not too far from large cities. They began to bottle more of their better wine, and as demand for appellations grew they made greater efforts to sell directly to consumers. Families from Paris and neighboring Bourges, once they acquired cars, drove out to Sancerre and the area around Chablis to buy directly from the grower; or the grower, once he acquired a small van, delivered directly to his urban clients who had placed an order by telephone. In this trade women played a capital role: they not only bottled and labeled the wine and took care of all the bookkeeping, they were the ever-smiling receptionists when tourists stopped to taste and buy a few bottles. This practice was widespread in Champagne also. But these additional tasks did not relieve women from laboring in the vines or from the demands of the kitchen.

The kitchen itself did not escape the transformation of life either. Increasingly it became a room limited to cooking, and this task was now carried out on an up-to-date gas or electric stove. The old iron monster that grandmothers had sweated over when they were young housewives, their hands blackened by handling firewood or coal and by ever-present soot, was gone forever. The placing of a new range, refrigerator, clothes washer, perhaps even a freezer, left little room for purposes other than meal preparation. The act of dining moved into another all-purpose room, a combination dining and living room heated by an oil stove. And in a prominent place facing the large table that was often still covered with oil cloth was the television set. Families dropped conversation during mealtime to watch the news or a serial, most likely produced in the United States.

The *télé* had spread slowly in France and even more slowly in rural communes. In the 1950s and early 1960s, sets were located mainly in cafés and family restaurants. This was a good investment, since whole families went out in the evening not to talk or play cards but to watch television, especially soccer matches. Since each evening of the week offered different programs, there was the Monday night crowd, the Tuesday night crowd, and so on. As a student in France in 1951–52, I was struck by the number of people who could, at the same time, watch television, imbibe meals and wine, and talk. By the 1960s, when sets had come down in price and entered the home, I was equally amazed by friends who could do as they had done in the neighborhood restaurant. They did not actually hold conversation at table, they just talked, most often about events shown on the screen. The ultimate was when in the late 1970s I went to interview a vigneron in the early evening, and he made no move to turn off his set when I turned on my tape recorder. I was finally able to persuade him that the background noise would stifle his recollections as he voiced them.

In the more prosperous vineyard regions where AOC wines have traditionally commanded high prices and enjoyed a fairly steady or rising market, housing conditions improved noticeably. When houses were not renovated, it was because they were torn down and new ones were built, often in the traditional style, but with all the modern conveniences, except window screens to keep out insects.

Postwar Demographic Problems

If we measure a generation by a spread of about thirty-five years, the modernization of life of viticultural France occurred in about two generations—timidly with the first, born before 1914, far more rapidly and aggressively with the second, born just before the German occupation. The second generation broke away from the cultural, economic, and social traditions of France of the Third Republic more defiantly. Unlike the generation of 1914, it did not want to restore prewar conditions: it demanded change, reform, betterment, mobility.

Mobility was upward, especially among owners of classified vineyards. Rise in status came mainly through the land that was purchased for its suitability to the training of the noblest vines. Foreseeing growers had begun gathering plots before the rise of prices in the 1950s, a rise that had resulted from intense bidding for the limited amount of land that met AOC qualifications. These men who had managed, at times by truly painful self-sacrifice and borrowing, to extend their vineyards just before and after the war, were the truly enterprising ones, able therefore to benefit most from expanding markets. Their families suffered privation, but their sons became heirs to a means of livelihood with a promising future, and their daughters married the sons of men who had gone through the same sacrifice. These were the young who reached maturity in the 1960s and 1970s, had gone to agricultural *lycées*, and benefited from both practical training and book-learning. Technically they were far in advance of their parents, and if one was the only direct heir to the land, his future was certainly full of great expectations.

For most of them, however, there was a fly in the wine. Wartime families, and especially postwar families, tended to be large as French couples sought to compensate for France's once lagging population growth and produced more babies, future vignerons or vigneronnes. To encourage the stagnant birth rate the government retained a 1939 law providing married couples with money allocations for each child. The result was an increase in the number of heirs per family. Inheritance laws dating back to the Revolution and to Napoleon required the equal division of property among all children. As applied to a vineyard, it meant that a father who had put together a holding of, say, nine hectares—very large in fine vine areas—and who had three children would have to leave each child three hectares—a worthwhile inheritance only in the best sites of Champagne, the Golden Slopes, and upper Médoc. Elsewhere three hectares could not provide a livelihood for a full-time vigneron. A young woman with even a small allotment could still be a tempting nuptial match, especially if she were also attractive. The sons, on the other hand, were forced to investigate other options. Each could buy additional land, but by the 1960s prices had risen so drastically that, unless a son had inherited a sizable sum of money, at least 300,000 francs, he could not borrow enough to buy a sufficient number of hectares to make a living.[9] He might, like his sister, marry for land; the practice of arranged marriages, land espousing land, was not completely outmoded. And if marriage still did not sufficiently round out his holding, he could either rent or sharecrop several hectares from an owner too old to work, or from an absentee owner. Crop sharing, once not a widespread practice outside of upper Beaujolais, had spread since the war precisely because there were so many sons committed to viticulture, but without an adequate inheritance.[10] Furthermore, laws that reformed the crop-sharing system were passed after the second war and presented an advantage to the tenant that I shall discuss later. On the other hand, the young man could sell his heritage and leave in quest of a city job. This alternative seems to have been preferred to that of becoming a landed wage worker, which signified a fall in status for the son of a landed middle-class family. Acceptance of such a diminished status seriously reduced marriage prospects.

Politicians had long recognized the problems created by the articles on inheritance of the Napoleonic Code. In the interwar the Radical party, once part of the political left had become increasingly ambiguous as regards social and economic programs and tempered its views on landed inheritance. Combining with moderate republicans, the cabinet promulgated a decree law on June 17, 1938, affirming the right of the heir who worked and lived on the family holding to inherit it all, on condition that he compensate his siblings. This was an alternative open mainly to the inheritors of large estates with a sizable revenue. To be sure, legislation in 1960 and 1962 provided for a very extended period of compensation payments, and also made available long-term loans through the Crédit Agricole. Nonetheless, a considerable amount of wealth left the land, limiting the kind of intensive investment required in a program of modernization. In some areas of controlled appellation, as in upper Beaujolais, siblings sometimes united to create a *société civil immobilière*: the relative who continued to work the land received a wage and gradually bought the sisters' and brothers' shares.[11] This, nonetheless, was a devastatingly costly way of transmitting property and could be justified only on political and moral grounds, to wit, that all men and women are equally entitled to inherit regardless of economic consequences. For smaller heirs, the cost of compensation was too onerous, an unbearable burden on a newly independent vigneron. Such cases generally ended with the sale of the vineyard and equal division of the price, or with each heir renting or sharecropping his or her allotment to small owners in need of additional vines.

Vineyardists with petty properties, that is, a holding allowing little more than subsistence, lived under conditions that were far less rosy than those I described above. Indeed, their future was bleak if they devoted their main efforts to ordinary grapes for making common table wine. They could never retire so long as they could work; in consequence, their sons had little to look forward to and left the land. Without young sons to stimulate the family enterprise there was lack of modernization both of equipment and of living conditions. As late as the 1960s, the village of Preignac in the Bordeaux area was still characterized by its lack of comfort. Of 652 houses, 527 had been erected before 1871, the remainder before 1914. Only 9 percent boasted inside flush toilets and 13 percent a bath or shower. According to Monsieur Rajchenbach it was difficult to find a grower under twenty-five years of age; about 80 percent were over forty-five. Out of 138 holdings, only thirty-four had an assured successor; the young were moving outward. The old remained until they could no longer work the land, then they rented or sharecropped it to provide a pitifully small retirement income which, when added to an equally pitifully small social security pension, enabled them to survive with a minimum of comfort.[12]

This observation brings us to another characteristic of postwar conditions of life, especially in the lower south and southwest: the continued activity of vignerons after their sixtieth year, and the outward migration of youths. The conditions of life and work have progressed, but not everywhere sufficiently to retire the old and retain the young. In the past, vine cultivation had demanded a fairly dense population. The vine was hailed as an agent of colonization because it thrived on slopes with thin, sandy, stony soil, and peasants could cultivate it where food and green crops were unprofitable. Before mechanization a family vineyard of about two hectares in Champagne or five to six in Languedoc occupied both parents and the children. Viticultural regions were thickly populated because each unit of cultivation was so small compared to those of cereal and cattle growers. Even though outward migration has been a demographic constant for about four generations, the phenomenon quickened and broadened after 1945. It was a natural accompaniment of mechanization that required greater concentration and enlargement of properties to achieve efficiency, a smaller labor force, and the conversion to other crops of land not truly suitable for vines.

Emigration toward urban centers has seriously weakened the human element in rural society. In the highly viticultural department of Gironde, for example, one out of two villages had a population of under five hundred in the 1960s. Since then these people are even fewer in number and older. Villages like these have become too small to provide services needed by the aging. There are no stores; merchants use vans, going from village to village to sell meat, vegetables, and bread to clients too poor to own a car or too old to drive one. Even priests are ambulatory, saying Sunday mass in seven or eight villages before lunch, often in church buildings crumbling into ruins. The few children remaining are now driven in buses to attend elementary schools too far away to reach on foot. This transport marks an advance of grand magnitude when compared to the long treks of small children in former times to learn their ABCs.[13]

These conditions were not limited to viticulture; they were the problems of general farming as well, although probably not as acute. Vignerons tended to be older than general farmers. In 1979–80 vignerons over age sixty-five came to nearly 21 percent of their profession, farmers to just under 17 percent. Young vignerons under thirty were less numerous, 3.3 percent as opposed to 5 percent of farmers. Within their professional population, young vignerons had larger holdings, over five hectares as against four for the fifty-five to sixty-four year olds. Unfortunately, the younger ones did not possess as much appellation land as their elders: 4.6 hectares to 4.9 hectares per grower, a result of the very high price of such land.[14] This difference was not great, but the fact that many younger VCC vignerons were located in Languedoc and grew nothing but grapes was a disturbing factor in that region, as we have already observed.[15]

Monoculture in itself was not disruptive of social peace. In Champagne *viticole* more than half the growers cultivated nothing but vines. But, of course, there was practically no production of common table wine. Nearly all the grapes went into the making of an appellation, chiefly sparkling, wine. Undreamed of wealth flowed into the area. A standing joke had it that a vigneron was poor if he had to wash his own Mercedes. In this environment, heirs were rarely lacking—if not a son, then a daughter and a son-in-law, or a nephew. Here the problem of depopulation hardly existed. The aging of vignerons was a quantitative phenomenon of little professional or social importance; statistics were often deceptive, for while elderly growers declared their *vendange* each year, control of the vineyard was really in the hands of a son or a son-in-law.[16]

FESTIVITIES

The festive aspect of life, the play element, has always assumed a large role in every society. Until the First World War festivals and other forms of amusement that most directly and frequently influenced vignerons were local, a product of their own or of the neighboring villages, and combined traditional practices such as storytelling, cardplaying, and the maypole, with the newest music and dances. The pattern and pace of village life, its limited contacts with the outer world, determined the form and substance of recreation. The isolation that was part of rural life gave to the various styles of play their rootedness in the locale and their naturalness, their authenticity.

Viticultural France of the 1920s was not greatly different from the France of the Gay 90s. In wine villages and small towns the pleasures of life had not changed much and were still enjoyed as part of village life. I am referring to the open or public activity that went on after work. Within the village setting, vignerons relaxed and sought pleasure both on a day-to-day basis and during certain seasonal holidays.

After their daily labor, especially after pruning during cold winter days, growers often attended a *veillée* or *chambrée*. The *veillée* was a gathering of the members of a small village, or only of several families, each bringing some form of artificial light as well as beverages and food for sharing. Here, the village elders told stories from ancestral lore—often about calamitous vintages or ghosts that shook grapes off the vines or a local achievement that was still part of the collective memory. For the vignerons of Champagne there were the disasters of war, 1870 and 1914, and heroic harvesting in the midst of falling bombs. These experiences, lived and remembered, integrated or bound the group together. Entire families took part in the *veillée*, and young people carried on their courting and decided who was to marry whom. Beverages were usually cooked wines or wines fortified with alcohol.[17]

Equally important was the café or barroom. Even a small village had at least one café, and small towns boasted several. The village café was usually a grubby, ill-lighted, smelly place frequented mainly by local peasant males after work. Married men went there to escape their cramped living quarters and their families. Bachelors went to seek companionship. These were not singles bars. Women rarely set foot in them, certainly not until recent times. But few of them are still open, having disappeared along with the grocer and the baker.

The café, regardless of its decor, used to be the central place for locals to meet. The patrons did not drink much during their stay, and the beverage would more likely be coffee than alcohol. They talked and joked and played cards or dominos and, if inclined, read a newspaper provided by the café owner. Municipal counselors frequented it to learn what their electors were thinking. One cup of coffee lasted the hour or two that its drinker remained among his pals. Grape growers were not big spenders; very few of them made much money and they went early to bed. During long summer evenings and on Sundays, their favorite game was *boules*, or outdoor bowling, in the backyard of the café. The drink on these occasions would be more decidedly alcoholic: a vermouth or brandy in the north, pernod in the south, a *petit muscat* or cheap beaujolais in the eastern central regions. Male peasants living on estates at some distance from the village visited the café only on Sundays, and they were more likely to find their way there than to the parish church. During the interwar, when cafés were often politically oriented, they were as likely to be sermonized by an habitué as vigorously as they would have been in church.

Sunday lunch and various celebrations (marriages, birthdays, anniversaries) were family and often village events. Here, wine, homemade to be sure, came into its own. It is here one sees the important role of wine as part of the ceremonial activities of rural life—a role that goes back to ancient Greece and Rome. What the French (and the Italian and Spanish) inherited from these very distant ancestors was the notion of wine as part of the ritualized aspects of society. Marriages, births, anniversaries were rituals—formerly religious rituals or ceremonies. Wine was a necessary ingredient in religion, and both Greeks and Romans worshipped wine gods (Dionysus and Bacchus). Christians, having early adopted the use of wine as part of their ritual, preserved ancient tradition. They did not have a wine god, but Christ was able miraculously to create excellent wine out of water, a feat unscrupulous wine men have been trying to emulate for centuries. They were the vinicultural sorcerers, the alchemists of the trade, seeking to transform the base into the precious, and always ending with plonk.

I do not want to give the impression that grape and wine growers were given to excessive drinking. I discovered no recollections of Dionysian drinking contests or Bacchanalian orgies. To the question, "Were wine-men heavy drinkers in their reveling?" I must answer that I do not think so. To be sure, the French accept wine as a desirable part of life. Wine is far older than France. It was brought to ancient Gaul—from which France grew—by the Greeks and the Romans. Like them, the French have always believed that wine is a gift of God, unlike many Anglo-Saxons who have been convinced that it is a potion of the devil.

As a gift of the Christian God, wine has played a dual role in French life. First, it is a divine food. In former times the father of the family, before cutting a loaf of bread, made the sign of the cross over it as an act of gratitude. Wine was part of this meal and this sense of gratitude. Among a people who for centuries were more poor than rich, whose diet was often limited, wine was a divine gift of calories.

But wine was more than a food, it was also a part of the ceremonial side of life. This aspect of its influence undoubtedly arose from the Catholic tradition of France, for wine was an essential element of the Catholic mass which was for centuries the unifying ceremony of both rich and poor. From the holy altar, wine moved to the dinner table as dining became a ceremony. Since World War I, many French growers have abandoned the sa-

cred altar of the church, but they certainly have not yet abandoned that
other altar, the dinner table—nor the wine bottles standing upon it like
holy candles. They drink wine with a certain reverence, but chiefly when
it forms part of a meal. In consequence, their consumption has been limited by their gastronomy. Winegrowing regions were not and are not now
beset by alcoholism because much of the wine consumed is homegrown
and low in alcohol. This is fortunate because it is as much a part of work
as of play. Vignerons consume as much as two liters when working on
their vines. They rarely drink that much when dining or during an evening's entertainment. Wine is a natural accompaniment to social ban-
quets, and growers generally organize several of these. On such occasions,
each member brings a bottle and passes it around. This is homegrown,
untaxed wine. Most growers do not possess a great deal of superior wine
for their own consumption, and the best of it they jealously reserve for
seasonal festivities.

In January, either on the twenty-second or the weekend nearest it, took
place the feast of Saint Vincent, the patron saint of most God-fearing and
many agnostic vignerons. In Catholic villages, days and nights were spent
preparing for the celebration. It began with a formal mass in the church,
attended by growers' families as well as any dignitaries visiting for the
occasion. In Saumur there was a growers' fraternity, the Commanderie de
Taste-Saumur, founded by Gérard Nau, who headed the procession following the church service. It was given solemnity by the large statue of Saint
Vincent, carried on the shoulders of four stalwart volunteers. Then came
a band followed by the entire village population. At this time elderly
growers were made "master vignerons" and given certificates as testimo-
nials to their skill. Finally came a big banquet, truly *agapes pantagruéliques*,
to quote Nau, accompanied by the best wine of each vigneron. To prevent
drunkenness, large clay pots stood on the table to receive wine left in
glasses after fastidious and abstemious tasting.[18]

The Golden Slopes had a tradition, begun in 1938, of a Saint Vincent
tournante; that is, villages in the Côtes rotated among themselves hosting
the feast. The village chosen spent weeks preparing for the occasion. Dec-
orations went up along the streets: garlands of juniper and broom, flags,
paper flowers, lamps—a triumphal arch of diverse vegetation to greet visitors from other villages. Upon their arrival, a band struck up music and
a procession formed. The church was always too small for the multitude,
so mass and sermonizing took place out-of-doors (and prayers had been
murmured for weeks begging for good weather). Here old vignerons were

dubbed "knights of the *Taste-vin*." The banquet assumed its usual gigantic and lengthy proportions, and in the evening those two enemies of the vine, frost and hail, were burned in effigy.[19]

In February many villages in the south celebrated carnival. This has always been a time of true reveling, and festivities went on for a week before Ash Wednesday and the beginning of Lent. Sometimes the reveling went on for a month, because February was not a time of work. There were parades with decorated floats made on harvest wagons drawn by mules or oxen. There was dancing in the dirt streets and on the cobblestone square. Young people dressed in odd costumes, all wearing masks.[20] In villages with an imaginative population, there were theatrical farces. These were occasions for the village wit to bring laughter by sly allusions to the illicit acts of his neighbors: the watering of wine, overcropping, sugaring of musts, cheating in trade, and lovemaking among the vines. There was often a troupe of young men dressed in voluminous nightgowns who performed traditional and comic dances that were centuries old.

The grape harvest was also a time of frolicking. Before the advent of mechanical harvesters, picking grapes was a hard, back-breaking task. Yet every evening the youth of the village gathered for dancing and merriment. Music was provided either by a mechanical piano or by local musicians and their instruments: accordion, fiddle, trumpet or flute, and drum. Dances were the waltz, mazurka, polka, and a lively quadrille. In the 1920s came the tango; in the 1930s came jazz and jitterbugging.

Up to World War II (1939 for France), amusements were determined by the technological level of society. In many wine villages, transport was extremely limited, therefore people had to amuse themselves. They could not rely on outside entertainment. Even a village or town ten miles away was very far away when the only means of transport in the evening was walking or a bicycle. Very few grape growers owned automobiles until the 1950s. The Saturday night village dance, therefore, was about the only form of weekly communal fun, as distinct from seasonal festivities. Until the 1930s local musicians provided the music, which consisted of peasant songs that everyone could sing, and there were sing-alongs as well as dancing. By the 1930s the jukebox made its entry. The village could rent one and everybody contributed coins to feed its hungry mouth. It was placed on the village square, not because it was cheaper than live musicians, but because its recordings offered "city music." Peasant songs were now in disrepute, old fashioned, fit only for "yokels."

I have not found a fully acceptable reason why this change in taste occurred. Perhaps it was a result of the economic crisis of the 1930s. Young men and women who had fled their villages in the 1920s to work in the city were suddenly without jobs. So they returned home and brought their big-city ways with them. Naturally, the local folk wanted to imitate them. Peasants learned the Charleston, jitterbug, and Blackbottom. This tendency was reinforced by the spread of radios in households as rural electrification made headway. The advancing technology of communication rapidly broke through the isolation of village life.

This change took place more rapidly and easily in wine areas because they were generally located near lines of major transport and communication. Communication was—and still is—all important in the entertainment business. Before World War II, however, that business was centered mainly in larger cities. In the countryside, it was more of a craft than a mass production enterprise. It did not center itself in one place, but had to be peripatetic; it had to travel to its audience—as did the wandering peddler who carried his wares on horseback until the 1930s, when he began to arrive in a huffing and puffing truck. Entertainment arrived in the same way: the traveling circus as well as the traveling cinema and vaudeville show. Save for the movies and kerosene lamps, such troupes of actors and acrobats had been carrying comedy and drama to rural villagers since time immemorial. The notable feature here was the communal or public character of entertainment. Peasants had fun as part of the village community. They had fun together—this was togetherness as a normal part of life. Housing conditions probably encouraged people to go outdoors, and entertainment was largely an event of the warmer months in wine areas. In colder months, there was the *veillée*.

Since World War II all of this has changed. The automobile and television have ruined the traveling theater and destroyed the integrity of village life. The little community has lost its reason for being and, therefore, its economic independence and cultural creativity. The local craftsmen and merchants have been put out of business by mass-produced goods and supermarkets. Automobiles have allowed peasants to drive into cities to buy manufactured articles as well as groceries at prices much lower than in villages. The village has become a place where people work and sleep; it is no longer a place where inhabitants play. When vine dressers come home from work, what do they do? They dine and go to bed. There are, of course, a couple of hours in between dining and sleeping, and these are devoted to television. Villagers no longer visit neighbors for gossip or exchange of jokes—they stay home and watch the *télé*. Communal life hardly exists; the new technology of entertainment has fragmented the community. Television keeps people closed up in the home; automobiles carry them away from the village.

The technology of transport has also separated generations. Once, young people organized village festivities. Today, they get into automobiles to escape the village. At reckless speeds they rush into the city's cafés and discotheques, leaving their parents at home to watch television. More than ever before, technology has separated the young from the old. In the past, the youth of the village were keepers of the flame of fun. Today, in an age of canned entertainment, they have abandoned that role. Disco dancing is a symbol of the new generation. There is little physical contact; there is barely communication with others. Each dancer does his or her own thing. Hindu philosophers were supposed to attain nirvana looking at their motionless navels. Today's youth attain an exalted state of excitement while beholding a navel that is rocking and rolling in rhythm with sounds so ear piercing and frenetic that they could turn good wine into vinegar.

VIOLENCE IN THE VINEYARDS

Vignerons in appellation regions had ample justification to celebrate. After many difficult years, their living standards began to rise during the 1960s. By "difficult years" I do not mean that grape and wine growers were all starving or that their daily life consisted of an unending fear of the hard times wolf at their door. Appellation producers, as we learned above, came to enjoy a rising standard of living after the second war. These rising standards, of course, were accompanied by rising expectations.

It was unfortunate that the mental construct of rising expectations came into conflict with the reality of steadily declining standards of life experienced by Mediterranean vignerons. There were, and had always been, several layers to the social and economic hierarchy of viticulture. At the bottom stood the growers of common wine in lower Languedoc and Roussillon, and it was they who missed out on the postwar economic advance. But they had missed out for generations, since 1900 in fact, and frustration in the midst of plenty drove them to acts of violence that, as such acts grew in frequency, became a tradition, or better, a conditioned reflex. Now, as was stated briefly in Chapter One, frustration, and the violence it breeds, were not human emotions limited to meridionals. Menacing demonstrations have expressed the anger of peasant populations since time immemorial. The fine texture of French history is scarred by food riots, tax riots, price riots, Luddite riots, bloody conflicts between villages, anti- and pro-clerical risings, police riots against the rioters, political riots, student riots, xenophobic riots, race riots, antimodernization riots, destructive actions by cattlemen, fruit growers, truck farmers. The easier question to answer is not, "Who has resorted to violence?" but rather, "Who has not resorted to violence?" Class distinctions are not adequate indicators of participants: the wealthy, the middle, and the poor classes have all been implicated at one time or another. And no geographic sector of France is untainted.

What I am concerned with here, of course, is violence in the vineyards; and when studying this topic, our attention is naturally drawn to the roots of discontent. Like those of vines, they are deep and buried in the layers of the past. The recent phenomena have causes that appeared before 1914. In the spring of 1907 the vignerons of Languedoc and Roussillon began a series of truly massive rallies as a protest against the sale of false wine. Encouraged by an action group called the Committee of Argeliers or the Committee of Beggars, huge crowds assembled in Narbonne. Then in the summer of 1907 occurred even larger gatherings in Béziers of over 100,000 persons, then in Perpignan, Carcassonne, Nîmes, and finally in Montpellier, where half a million crowded the narrow streets and sweated in the summer heat. Leaders of these rallies did not call for violence, but rather frequently a minority of zealots led by agitators turned to rioting: from burning public buildings, as in Carcassonne, to trying, unsuccessfully, to lynch police agents disguised in civilian clothes in Narbonne.

Far more violent and destructive were the vignerons of Champagne who went amok in 1911. They accused several local companies of using wine from other areas of France, even the Midi, to make champagne. In their fury they either put the torch to wine cellars or staved in the barrels and vats that presumably contained the "exotic" beverage. Only the arrival of troops restored calm to the towns whose streets ran with wine. This was the last resort to massive rioting in Champagne. In 1932 several thousand growers, suffering from the economic depression, marched through the streets of Epernay to express their despair, but no turbulence ensued.[21] Indeed, this manifestation was the last of its kind in the northeast.

In the huge viticultural region of Languedoc, however, the events of 1907 gave birth to a tradition of furious action, bubbling over at times like fermenting must in warm weather. During the interwar southerners did not constantly resort to violence: in the 1920s wine sold rather well, and in the 1930s their condition was perhaps not as desperate as that of the Champenois; they made common wines to be sold in France at low prices, so they were not dependent on the depressed export trade as were makers of appellation beverages. In addition, the state, abandoning its laissez-faire policies out of fear of renewed agitation, put into effect a series of laws that attempted, with some success, to limit the distribution of wine so as to maintain higher prices.

World War II, like World War I, brought problems that could not be solved by mass demonstrations and rebellions. The Vichy state tightened its control over all markets, wine being no exception, and despite the shortage of grapes, growers did not suffer unduly. Rather, it was the return to peace after 1945 and to "normalcy" after 1950 that brought back to the Midi the conditions making for economic malaise.

The postwar years therefore witnessed enraged action on a scale comparable to 1907. In July 1953 a homemade bomb was thrown against the prefecture in Carcassonne, and the major highways of the Midi were invaded by crowds of angry vignerons. In 1961 they once more blocked roads, railways, and cut down telephone poles, this time in alliance with angry farmers in Brittany. Leadership was provided by action committees that appeared spontaneously and directed their excited followers first against the locks of the Canal du Midi to block wine barges, then against retail stores selling, or believed to be selling, wine from Algeria, and also, of course, against high-tension pylons, a favorite target. Riotous action of this sort broke out again in 1963, 1967, 1970, 1971, 1974, 1975, and almost every summer since, although not of the magnitude of 1975–76, when two men were killed in a shoot-out between demonstrators and policemen of the CRS (security forces).[22]

Since 1970 attacks are no longer carried out against Algerian wine, but against that of Italy. Truck drivers and their cargoes are hardly safe, but easy targets of hidden riflemen. And in 1976 the cellars of Pierre Ramel, who blended Italian and French wine, were destroyed by a "commando" from Languedoc, sent by the action committees. Two men were caught, put on trial, and released "in the interest of public peace." The property destroyed was valued at 4.5 million francs. The fine levied on the perpetrators of this destruction came to one franc.[23]

Violence of this intensity is rare and confined to the lower south. Growers elsewhere are not subject to such vigorous competition from imports. Champagne growers are the richest in the world and have conveniently forgotten their moments of turbulence in the past. Only some producers in the Bordelais in 1974–75 imitated the Languedocians and resorted to blocking roads and railways. Some tank cars, believed to contain Italian wine, were emptied. A few main highways were also blocked. There was, however, no real violence but rather smiles as tracts explaining the growers' situation were handed to stranded tourists.[24]

More recently in the spring of 1984, growers in Touraine exploded into violence when state engineers decided to build a new high-speed rail line through their vineyards. Not only were many hectares of vines to be bulldozed, but the underground cellars in the cliffs facing the Loire River would be disturbed by the vibrations caused by extremely fast trains.[25] According to Monsieur Thevenet of the CIV Touraine, this matter has been resolved by mutual agreement: the railway will pass underground deep enough to leave the vines undisturbed. Whether it will pass deep enough to leave the wine in the cellars undisturbed, only time will tell.

The prime cause of collective violence has been the scissors grip squeezing grape growers between the sharp blades of falling incomes and rising costs. At certain critical times the pain became intolerable and mass movements arose. Such critical times were 1903–11, 1929–35, and, for the Midi, the decades following 1960, and elsewhere, 1974–75. Clearly the focal point of violence was Languedoc-Roussillon where response to price declines was far more frequent than elsewhere. What was so special about the Midi?

Southern vine growers, after the phylloxera crisis of 1870–90, made several choices that were fateful to their future. First, they decided that there was no profit in polycultural farming and planted vines on such an extensive scale as nearly to eliminate other crops. During the Second Empire, southerners had grown rich on wine; it seemed reasonable, then, to plant more vines in order to become even richer. Vignerons in other regions were more conservative when they replanted, and careful to preserve much of their traditional polyculture. Wine often remained their chief cash crop, but they continued to cultivate legumes, cereals, and fruits to fall back on during hard times. For the southerner, therefore, a serious and sustained fall of prices was not merely a temporary setback, it was a catastrophe.

In addition, Languedocians in particular planted vines with the highest yields in the rich soil of the coastal plains, where they attained yields beyond their ancestors' dreams. Wine made from the juice of such grapes was mediocre, to say the least—watery, low in alcohol, flat, or excessively acid in taste. Wine of this character had been produced in the Midi in earlier centuries, but on a much smaller scale, and it had been distilled into a salable alcohol. However, with the considerable rise of prices from 1850 to 1900, growers decided to sell it as natural wine and to produce it on a massive scale. After 1900 the vignerons of Languedoc-Roussillon turned out nearly half of France's total wine crop. A varying percentage of this wine could not be sold in its pure state; it had to be blended by wholesale merchants with more alcoholic, solid wines from Algeria until 1970, and from southern Italy thereafter.

The problems of finding profitable markets for this nondescript ordinary wine, not always an easy task before the early 1940s, were compounded by the continuous decline of consumption of ordinaries since the interwar. The Languedocians insist that the excess production that weakens prices is not their fault, that they make just enough to satisfy demand. Rather, it is Algerian and Italian beverages that flood the market, hence their ferocious animosity toward *vins exotiques* and toward the EEC, which opened France's borders to Italian exporters just after the reflux of the Algerian flood.

Another cause of the current crisis is the huge number of small and very small growers. Even though there are many large estates and even wine factories in the lower south, a sizable population of growers has had less than one hectare or one to four hectares of land. None of them managed to make a living from their land; they were also vine laborers on larger estates or held jobs in nearby towns. Economic survival also required that their wives find outside employment. They supplemented their revenues by selling all of their grapes, or they became members of cooperative wineries. In general, they were poorly equipped and either unwilling or unable to find the capital required to modernize and plant vines that promised superior wine. They swelled the ranks of discontented, despairing vignerons, most of whom were full-time growers burdened with debts for expensive tractors, plows, and spraying devices, and constantly pressured by their creditors. They were able to survive one or two bad harvests, but the continuous decline of prices and rise of costs made long-term survival problematic. Theirs has become a truly pitiful, tragic fate. They have always felt deeply attached to their land and to their region. Not many of them still speak the Languedocian form of Occitan, a general term referring to various languages and dialects south of the Loire River. Their regionalism has become a state of mind, an emblem of identity, a symbol of collective memory, a resounding call to action. They are passionate and at times outrageous: the way of life that nurtured them is fast fading away, indeed, is crumbling beneath them; and the nation for which they fought in two wars grants them a paltry handout while mocking their pretensions as well as their southern accent when they speak French.

Wherever and whenever vignerons resorted to action, they had an immediate goal in mind, and usually a somewhat limited, practical one. This does not mean that all growers had the same goals. There was a universal difference between the aims of Languedocians in 1907 and recently, on the one hand, and Champenois in 1911 and the 1930s, on the other. The men of Champagne had a perfectly clear aim: the punishment and banishment of dishonest merchants. Save for a few extremists, they did not display any sense of belonging to a mass movement seeking profound social and economic change; they certainly were not revolutionaries bent on overthrowing the power of the capitalist merchants. The big firms of Epernay and Reims were not molested, suffering neither damage nor reputation. And there was no effort to set up cooperatives. There is even less indication of class struggle in Champagne. The participants there were local people, chiefly small and medium vine owners and some of their hired workers. The enemy was not capitalism but fraud, and in this respect the vignerons of Champagne were similar to the larger owners of Languedoc. But the former differed in that they were not politically touched by these events, so neither political tradition nor social structure were upset by rioting.

There was, finally, another difference between the vignerons of Champagne and those of Languedoc, and it was connected with the quality of their respective wines. The mentality of the average Languedocian was essentially proletarian and Jacobin; that is, he mass produced a common uniform wine, and he had no interest in distinctions of quality nor a sense of history, except for the Albigensian crusade of the Middle Ages. Like the Jacobin of 1793, he was a ferocious egalitarian, distrustful of class distinctions, and antihistorical. He was in revolt against the past.

The vigneron of Champagne, on the other hand, found his fortune precisely in the distinctive quality of his wine. His vocabulary included terms such as "noble" for his own grapes and "ordinary" or "common" for that of other areas. His was a vocabulary of class precisely because he was an artisan devoted to excellence. In addition, he had a keen sense of history. Wine, like man, was the product of centuries of time and labor, carried on by generations of vignerons matching vine to soil and climate. The vignerons of a geographic district, in order to qualify for an *appellation controlée*, had to prove that their wines not only had a long history, but had acquired renown in the past, and that the techniques of growing grapes and making wine in the present were faithful and loyal to those of their ancestors. Such a traditionalist frame of mind of course did not rule out a resort to violence, a viticultural Jacquerie. But once the Champenois achieved their goal, they set out to grow the best grapes and, save in the world depression of the 1930s, abandoned mass demonstrations and rioting. This was equally true of growers in areas striving for fine grapes and classified wines; by the 1950s, they made up more than half of their regional production. Their financial, self-policing, and marketing problems were serious, but they believed that any riotous action would mar the image they sought to impress on buyers' attitudes.

In the past the typical vigneron in Champagne sold his grapes to the merchant shippers who actually made the sparkling wine. Over the past twenty-five years, however, a novel kind of producer has risen to prominence, the *récoltant-manipulant*, whom we have already encountered in cooperatives that carry out the first fermentation of musts. These grower-bottlers are fast becoming increasingly associated with Champagne vineyards. From a mere handful after World War II, they grew to 4,926 in number in 1980, representing 70 percent of the full-time vignerons. Although they account for only 20 percent of the total—full and part-time—they make about half the champagne put on the market. All are middle and large owners. They constitute 55 percent of producers turning out under fifty thousand bottles a year. Just over 67 percent are limited to under ten thousand bottles a year. Thirty percent produce ten thousand to fifty thousand bottles, and only 2.6 percent produce more then fifty thousand. The first group relies fully on cooperatives, the second less so, and the third make their *cuvées* in their own cellars and are also active in their commercialization.[26] All are aggressively persuasive when proclaiming the high quality of their nectars.

Midi vignerons rarely thought about quality. Rather, they were devoted to purity, that is, an absence of foreign wine. Languedocians, until very recently, turned out only 5 to 10 percent of classified wine; the rest was *gros rouge* and its white or pink equivalent. The problem, as they conceived it, was fraud: their mentality remained close to that of their forebears of 1907. Their natural wine could never flood the market; the sale of false wine made the cup run over. They earnestly insisted that any French wine that is mixed with those of Algeria or Italy is fake, and its sale is a deceit perpetrated by dishonest, greedy merchants. In their more bitter moments, Languedocians accuse all other producers of selling fraudulent wine because they add sugar to the must to raise the alcohol level as the must changes into wine. The government allows the sugaring of classified must that is not in oversupply, but forbids southerners to do so because the process does increase, significantly, the quantity of finished wine. Sugar is sometimes dissolved in boiling water before it is added, and only a small amount of water evaporates during the process.

Inasmuch as Languedocians have always been concerned chiefly with fraud, a police matter, they demand that the state serve as the policeman. For this reason they have never been rebels in a true sense. Even when they displayed their greatest vehemence, in 1907 and 1976, they were not re-belling against the state, or even against an entire ministry. They were rather taking action as a highly motivated and sophisticated pressure group to force politicians to implement effective measures against fraud and imports. They were practicing "demonstration democracy."

WOMEN'S WORK

So far I have written about vignerons, without paying adequate attention to vigneronnes. Kipling, an unregenerate sexist, once asserted that the female of the specie is more deadly than the male. Putting aside a meta-phor relevant only to spiders, I feel rather that females were often more hard-working than males, and far less rewarded. Men identified them-selves with their profession; they had, as it were, a niche in the hierarchy of society, their names were carved in the family tree. The position of women was far more ambiguous. In a marriage settlement they were often the bearers of the vineyard, and yet it was the husband who enjoyed rec-ognition in the community. He alone was provided with a profession in the census. The wife, regardless of land ownership, was never more than the *conjoint*, the mate of the male.

Conjuncture was not an easy role to play in the theater of everyday life. At the peasant level the wife participated actively in the family economy; she prepared meals, cleaned the house, maintained the *basse cour*, and bore and cared for children. She was housewife, cook, and mother. In these activities, she did not differ from all the peasant women throughout France, whether they raised pigs, chickens, ducks, rabbits, vegetables, or legumes, along with children.[27] Among the family vines, however, she enjoyed a kind of privileged protection, for she was also a participant in the seasonal labors of vine training. During the winter's pruning, it was she who gathered the discarded branches, bunched and bound them into faggots, and tossed them into a wagon. Before the world wars and certainly during their harsh years of deprivation, she either sold these as fire-wood or kept them for cooking meals, but only for light meals because vine canes burn rapidly. Before 1914 the women of small growers some-times had to carry several faggots homeward on their backs, a practice that had just about ended with the 1920s and had already been rare after 1900.

Since the 1950s various machines were invented to gather canes, shred them, and spread the remains among the vines as green fertilizer. Several elderly vignerons have explained to me that these shredders did not work well, the leavings being washed by rain into drainage ditches where they blocked the free flow of water. Fortunately, recent models are more effi-cient. Most vignerons no longer use faggots of canes for heating or cooking in the home; they enjoy the higher and more efficient benefits of gas or fuel oil. Consequently women, when shredders are not used, simply gather the wood, place it in piles between vine rows, and set it ablaze in the winter-bare vineyards, allowing the men to warm their hands at suitable times during the day's pruning.

Before the advent of mechanical sprayers, women also helped fill the backpack devices of their men, and sometimes they carried the pack and sprayed alongside them. Far more enduring tasks were those not adaptable to mechanization until recently: in May, topping (*ébourgeonnage*) or pinch-ing the tip of fruit-bearing branches just above the highest cluster, remov-ing excess leaves, and tying shoots to wire trellises (*palissage*). It has been generally recognized that female fingers were far more nimble and skilled at performing these tasks. It was rare to see the women of the family en-gaged in truly hard physical labor: digging and plowing. During wartime, of course, they willingly undertook these jobs because there was no one else to do them. But under normal conditions there was a tacitly agreed-on division of labor by gender. This was particularly the case during the *vendange*, the harvest. Picking of grape clusters was almost exclusively fe-male work, although young teenage boys of the family were put to the same job. Harvesting for women and girls was a time of physically de-manding labor, but it was also a time for socializing, gossiping, and riot-ous joking. Teenage girls and young women drew the attention of male admirers, and an ancient custom in the Midi allowed young males, when a female missed cutting a grape bunch from a vine, to smear her face with it. Conditions were far less gay when harvesting took place in cold, wet weather. At mealtime women built fires to dry themselves, at the same time placing small stones to heat in the cinders. When called back to work they put the stones in their apron pockets to warm their hands when nearly frozen by metal shears. In hot weather they suffered from mosquito bites whose sting they relieved with squashed grapes. Today they use lemon juice, or insect repellant.[28]

Older teenagers and younger men pitched in as carriers: they attached to their backs large containers, formerly made of wood or wicker and now of plastic, and the girls and women pickers filled these from their small baskets. When ready the carrier brought the clusters to a wagon or open trailer to empty his burden into it. With the more frequent use of mechanical harvesters, women—like men—are beginning to lose one of their most traditional functions.

Women of a propertied family have long performed these tasks without complaint. With the advent of mechanization, however, they have abandoned all save *ébourgeonnage* and picking. They have improved their conditions of life, above all in AOC regions. We have noted earlier that young sons forced their fathers to mechanize as a condition of remaining on the land. Prospective brides enjoyed the same bargaining power. Enlightened by television, the press, and the broader experience of education and travel, young women, after 1945, no longer tolerated the harsh conditions of rural life as inevitable. Those who did not move to nearby urban centers expected considerable improvements before accepting a proposal of marriage. Frustrated growers, in need of wives, had to agree not only to mechanize vineyard tasks, but also those of the home: hence the appearance of washing machines, vacuum cleaners, gas or fuel ranges, even dishwashers and clothes dryers in the better-off families of fine wine areas, and, of course, television sets in every dwelling. The *basse cour* has nearly disappeared, but not the vegetable garden, although it has declined in size and importance. The demands of the kitchen also underwent radical change: frozen food, even quick foods, began to edge out traditional cuisine, at least for weekday meals. Sunday lunch remained special: either an elaborate home-cooked feast, or dining out in a nearby restaurant so that the wife could enjoy a day off, a phenomenon not really of much concern to independent growers before the 1950s.[29]

Wives, like daughters—indeed like working sons—were rarely paid wages before World War II. The latter were vouchsafed an allowance, a pittance, for labor on the family land. Only when they threatened to leave did they win a higher return. If the son's or daughter's father lived to a ripe old age, each had to be content to follow the *pater*'s orders or else depart the land to seek a better livelihood in a nearby city.

There can be no doubt that the conditions of wives have improved.

Where income has risen above inflation, husbands usually hire workers to tend the vines, and wives contribute by keeping the account books and handling the elaborate correspondence that growers must maintain with an extensive clientele. Wives send out promotional literature, fill orders for wine, and see to its shipment. Once field laborers, they have now become office managers.[30]

At an even higher level of social status, that of the absentee estate owner, women have achieved true middle-class standing comparable to that in a city. In fact, they spend much of the year in an urban apartment with their husbands, who are usually in the liberal professions and hire overseers to manage the estate. Such couples, very rare in number except in the finest wine areas of Bordeaux and Burgundy, are borderline participants in grape and wine growing. They are more urban than rural in habits and outlook, and never really work in the vineyards. Somewhat different are families with vineyards near a city, in a sector with easy transport, enabling the wife to take an urban job while the husband works the land alone or with sons and daughters or with hired workers. The income of these wives has become of increasing value, enabling the family to invest in labor-saving equipment both in the vines as well as in the home.

Before the 1960s female labor in the vines was essential. Since then their work routine continues, but almost exclusively on family holdings too small to mechanize. And females at this economic level, like their husbands, have often resorted to part-time work, either on large and medium estates as wage laborers or in nonfarm employment. For women since the interwar, nonfarm jobs have become more and more attractive, hence the women's steady decline in the rural family work force as it, also, has steadily decreased.

However, women still participate actively in agriculture as well as in viticulture, and their roles vary from heads of farms, or wives of heads, to family helpers in their capacity as daughters, daughters-in-law, sisters, aunts, cousins, or nieces. According to the agricultural census of 1979–80, they were, if we include all forms of agriculture, 2.088 million in number, or 46 percent of the active agricultural population. Of this grand total, 6 percent were heads, 46 percent were wives of heads, and 47 percent were family helpers. They performed just under one-third of family labor as measured in hours per year of 240 days. As regards viticulture, about 9.7 percent were heads (many widows), considerably more than the percentage of female heads in all sectors of agriculture. The wives of vignerons, however, were less active in the vineyard than the wives of farmers in most other agricultural activities: only 12 percent of them take a truly operative part in family work. Those married to AOC growers were more active (13.7 percent) than those married to producers of VCC (10.4 percent). These low percentages are indicative of women's abandonment of field work, especially in viticulture. The decline in the number of vigneronnes was nearly twice that of the wives of general farmers, and an important consequence of the waning use of land for grape culture.

Conditions of Life: Laborers

STRUCTURE AND CONDITIONS OF THE LABOR FORCE

Wage workers, like small independent vineyard owners, steadily declined in number during the eight decades of this century. And for the same basic reasons came the abandonment by their children of a life that offered an uncertain future. As their hope of rising in status by acquiring land declined, so did their numbers. It was always difficult for a vine dresser without property to accept the condition of landlessness. This is why so many of them, really a majority in most viticultural regions, bought small parcels of land in order to become worker-owners. This urge to possess even a few minute plots was almost a primeval instinct among vignerons, a form of planting roots in a community, of acquiring an identity. In the countryside a man without land was like a man without a shadow. He was also a man with a family to support, and with household expenses that rose during the frequent inflationary periods that followed World War II. His wages tended to lag behind the cost of living, and he frequently had to resort to strikes to keep up. Owning one or several small plots of vines was, and continues to be, an indispensable source of income. Possession also raised his status in the social hierarchy.

There were several types of landed workers, and their differing incomes, labor services, and conditions of life naturally placed them in a status structure resembling a bottom-heavy diamond shape. Comfortably situated in a narrow peak was the supervisor of medium and large estates—called a *ramonet* in the Midi, *chef vigneron* or some similar name elsewhere—who was in charge of the work crew. On small estates, with two or three permanent laborers, he worked along with them and was almost one of them. On large estates, such as the great châteaux of upper Médoc, he was a salaried agent, experienced, often a highly trained agronomist, whose rank in the hierarchy of viticulture was at the top, coequal with the cellar master who made the wine. These two jobs were often combined on medium properties.

On sizable estates there were, close to the bottom of the hierarchy, the live-in workers, generally referred to as *domestiques*. Since World War I many of them had been foreign immigrants, living almost in isolation on the property and enjoying little contact with natives in surrounding villages, especially since many knew hardly any French. Lacking viticultural skills, they were usually general workers, the men doing heavy labor with pick and shovel, the women spending their time between the vineyard, the master's house, and his *basse cour*. In the previous century they had been lodged in barns or stables, sleeping on straw, covering themselves with hand-me-down clothing, fed dull monotonous food, heavy in starch, with *piquette* to help wash it down. Their wages, paid by the month or year, allowed them to buy only a few articles to make life more amenable. By the early twentieth century, and after 1914 when laborers became scarce, they were more adequately housed either in dormitories or in small rooms, their hours of labor regulated by law and their work day shorter. These improvements, however, were to be found mainly on large estates, as in Upper Médoc where workers were not highly unionized, and in Lower Languedoc, where they were.

Smaller owners, unless they treated their one or two workers like part of the family, treated them like animals. As late as the 1950s there were laborers, according to Françoise Langlois, still living in stables or attics, lacking adequate sanitation and even basic amenities such as washing facilities.[1] The housing law of 1929 was hardly effective since small employers ignored it with impunity, and hired hands were thankful for any jobs in the 1930s. Far more common was the absence of privacy. Owners of all sizes were not at all hesitant about overseeing the personal lives of their workers, encouraging sobriety, church attendance in Catholic strongholds, and a strict moral code everywhere. Men living under these conditions joined unions at their peril. What, of course, remained unchanged was their isolation and domination by their employers.[2]

Far more independent and enjoying higher status were the worker-owners, occupying the center of the hierarchical diamond. They were usually day laborers, highly skilled, and hired at an agreed-upon wage to carry out specific jobs: planting, pruning, spraying, and harvesting. When the price of wine was high, as during and just after World War I and in the late 1920s, they enjoyed comfortable incomes derived both from wages and the sale of their own grapes or wine. Had prosperous times continued, many of them could have saved or borrowed enough money to expand their vineyards, even to the point of becoming full-time proprietors. In some of the quality vine areas of Burgundy, Alsace, Bordeaux, and Champagne, there were fairly numerous examples of such advancement, at least during the 1920s and soon after World War II, when land prices were moderate and the market somewhat more stable. The great loss of men in the first war, depleting many villages of eligible young males, induced some landowners to put aside class prejudice and to marry their daughters off to their most promising wage workers. But the acquisition of land by dint of hard work and saving was far more rare in vineyards generally, and most uncommon in the mass vine region of Languedoc. Workers lacked capital to make a purchase; they even lacked sufficient working capital, according to Rémy Pech, who views this lack as a "decisive obstacle to social rise" in the 1920s.[3] Langlois noted it in the 1950s. Whatever advancement was made in the 1920s was wiped out by the economic crisis of the 1930s. By 1934 prices of wine had fallen by 50 percent. So in order to reduce costs owners cut down on vine work simply by not replacing dead vines, or spreading manure, and limiting other tasks. They cut wages whenever possible, and if workers went on strike, they cut back the number of work days from 250 to 150, hiring simply for pruning, sulfuring, and applying copper sprays, for they had to preserve their vines as capital. In these lean times, family income declined 43 percent whereas the cost of living fell only 8 percent. Land, of course, became very cheap, but too few cultivators had the means to buy it.

A majority of the completely landless workers seem to have been of foreign origins—Spanish, Portuguese, and Italian in particular, men who were familiar with vine culture. Poles, who were not, had a tendency to break their labor contracts and slip away toward industrial towns. The concentration of foreign workers took place mainly in the south and in the Bordelais region, where they were most likely to live on the estate. Although their lives were closely regulated, they were at least fed and bedded. Thanks to this combination of control and a modicum of solicitude, they rarely left the estate and, of course, they were not eager to become labor militants. It was exclusively those who brought with them a tradition of radical politics who were prepared for class conflict, both at the political and economic levels. They were to be found largely in Languedoc, Roussillon, and lower Provence.[4]

Quite different were the workers in the fine wine region of upper Médoc. Very few of these were foreigners; on the contrary, not only were they French, most of them were indigenous, belonging to old viticultural families with deeper roots than many châteaux owners. On the whole, they were a somewhat privileged working class. They were housed and most of their wants were provided by the hired administrators who really managed these prestigious properties. They were often lodged on the estate, but they were not part of the unskilled *domestiques*. Housing conditions varied from adequate to rather poor. Health care was a regular benefit, along with firewood and a garden for growing vegetables; ever present were the chicken and rabbit cages, and the pigpen. Until recent times each worker was a *prix-faiteur*, that is, he trimmed about three hectares of vines for a fixed sum of money. He was a highly skilled vigneron, and like most of them he tended to be an individualist, distantly supervised by an overseer, yet left with considerable power of decision within his alloted space. He bargained on his own over his wage; he also fixed his own hours and conditions of work. He was in effect an artisan laboring in an artisanal workplace.[5]

This system was also widespread in the finest vineyards of the Golden Slopes, but here, given the small dimensions of most properties, vigneron workers often owned or rented their own houses and lived in the villages that, like beads of a necklace, were strung along the national highway running north and south. If we remove this pattern of village location created by the geography of the Slopes, we find almost identical conditions in other quality wine areas.

Quite different were the laborers of the large properties of the southern coastal plains. They were organized in gangs each work day to carry out one or more specific jobs. Each gang labored under a supervisor who was responsible for setting the pace of work. Men and women in the gang, therefore, had no control over their work space or freedom of decision such as enjoyed by *prix-faiteurs*. This arrangement was different from the assembly line set up in factories; there was no minute division of labor. Each task—planting, pruning, spraying, tying—was carried out at a specific time and often by the same hirees. These people were, like *prix-faiteurs*, skilled artisans. And when not at work they enjoyed considerable freedom, neither living nor dining on their employer's property. Most of them were natives of a nearby village or small town.[6]

Apart from upper Médoc, where the celebrated properties were large and concentrated, the finest vineyards elsewhere were small to medium in dimension and often broken into scattered parcels. The result was that workers, living in villages, had considerable distances to walk or bicycle to the vines they cultivated, and then return home. For this time they were not compensated. If the distance was considerable they naturally did not return home for lunch. Either the owner provided food and wine, brought to them in the vines, a practice common in Mediterranean vineyards where laborers were organized into gangs; or, as elsewhere, *prix-faiteurs* brought their own food. The wine they drank was usually a part of their wage, and since the early twentieth century it was real wine, perhaps not good, but no longer *piquette*. Only small owners drank their *piquette*, not self-respecting workers.

DECLINE OF NATIVE LABORERS

The Second World War was as great a watershed for vine workers as it was for viticulture as a science. This unavoidable and close relation existed because the condition of workers was determined both by wartime experiences and by changes in the methods of grape growing. Wartime circumstances enhanced their militancy; after hostilities ended they were no longer willing to accept pre-1939 living conditions. Technological innovations also dissuaded growers from returning to the past. The innovation that affected wage workers most intimately was the introduction of labor-saving machinery. As the area of vines declined and machines enabled one worker to cultivate roughly four times or more the number of hectares he had worked before 1939, the demand for workers steadily went down. Vine training, of course, continued to be more labor intensive than general farming, but the downward trend in the number of workers that had begun earlier was considerably hastened. This was especially evident in the mass-production vineyards of the Languedocian plain, where nearly every device invented to speed up work could be and was applied. From planting to harvesting, the machine became not quite omnipresent, but increasingly necessary, especially when that most delicate of operations, pruning, was semimechanized, a step decidedly facilitating and speeding up the handwork required for this time-consuming task. From the 1960s on a kind of double and contrapuntal evolution took place. On the one hand, the permanent as well as the temporary work force fell by over half in many communes. On the other hand, many native French wage earners left the land and were replaced by immigrant laborers.[7] First, young men from Portugal, Spain, and Italy came to seek their fortunes; then, as these countries' economies grew wealthier and more able to reabsorb their lost populations, relatively young men came from North Africa—the Maghrébins, as the French call them indiscriminately. Most of them are now natives of Morocco, and come as seasonal workers in sizable numbers. Inevitably they were less trained than native workers and had to be supervised very closely. Very cleverly devised machines, however, made some of the old skills superfluous anyway. For more delicate operations there were always worker-owners, and although they demanded higher wages, they had the requisite skills and were less likely to emigrate, precisely because they could not carry their land with them.

Unlike the immigrants, the native workers were becoming older and not adequately renewing their ranks. Their children found the life offered by viticulture too uncertain and less rewarding than their expectations demanded. Following the example of the offspring of small growers, they either departed, or, given the facilities of travel offered by the automobile, they found jobs in nearby cities and continued to live on the land, commuting up to sixty kilometers a day. And since they had acquired sufficient expertise, they accepted part-time work in nearby vineyards. They therefore had three sources of income: a small inherited vineyard plus membership in a cooperative; part-time labor in another owner's vines; and their regular job. They were very busy men indeed, but they preserved their roots in the soil, and, unlike the foreign workers, felt at home in their native villages. The immigrants, as already noted, usually lived on the estate that employed them and were housed in dormitories or small rooms that were somewhat more modernized than those during the interwar.[8] Isolated on the estates, the first generation of foreigners has barely learned to master the French language, but the next generation is learning it, unless, of course, the worker has left his family in the old country and returns there periodically. The North Africans in particular have come over alone, economized with ferocious determination, and eventually bought enough land at home to return there as independent farmers.

In areas of appellation wines, viticulture was slower to become mechanized and in consequence demanded a more skilled labor force. A holding of over three hectares required one worker as a minimum, unless the owner had sons willing to remain on the land. The near doubling in size of the Champagne vineyard area in the 1960s and 1970s raised the need for a sizable labor force. Both muscles and skills were needed even by small independent growers for this enormous and unprecedented operation, since the newly denominated soil had to be planted in vines. Also as champagne firms, seeking to assure their grape supply, began to buy more and more land, they too had to engage a sizable number of skilled workers. On the whole they resorted to local vignerons, but when faced with a shortage they brought some in from other vine areas as well. There were usually enough locals to fill their needs.[9]

Employing the natives inevitably raised problems of industrial relations. Champagne companies were more accustomed to dealing with landed growers, and sought to treat their hired workers in the same way. Since native labor has become so expensive and unionized, the firms have sought to transform their wage workers into crop sharers. Where this has worked out, the firm gets one-third of the grape harvest, and contracts to buy the remaining two-thirds from the vigneron. This system has effectively reduced labor costs and has been expanding, even against the resistance of some workers who view it as a trick, not only to reduce their income, but to place the burdens of vineyard management on their shoulders.

It is odd that while crop sharing has become more widely accepted in Champagne, where it had no roots, it is declining in upper Beaujolais, where it has long been the most common form of land tenure, going back several centuries. Owners of the finest *crus* have become convinced that the postwar agricultural code that allowed the owner only one-third of the crop was a diabolical socialist scheme. To outwit the central power they turned to wage laborers, hoping to earn higher revenues. They have not fully abandoned crop sharing. They have, if croppers' assertions are valid, ignored the law and continue to collect half the crop. The fact that they make the wine has facilitated their subterfuge. In retaliation, croppers and tenants have formed a union to defend their claims. Revised legislation has strengthened their position, which has sought to change crop sharing into a tenant system that includes renting the land at a fair rent. This the owners absolutely oppose.[10]

In the Golden Slopes owners also sought to transform the very old practice of *prix-faitage* into a regular wage system. Their motive was simple: the enormous rise in prices induced them to retain all the best wine, a limited portion to which *prix-faiteurs* were entitled, and to pay their vignerons a fixed cash wage.[11] Vigneron day laborers in Champagne and the Golden Slopes usually had their own housing in a nearby village, owned some vines, and were often scions of old families. Their parents owned small vineyards, which they were waiting to inherit. Meanwhile they were wage workers on another man's land and family helpers on their parents' small property. They were paid by the day or the job. If they were married, their wives also labored part time in the vines to add to the family income.

The same type of day laborer, a true *journalier*, existed in the Bordeaux area; but in upper Médoc, Graves, and Saint-Emilion, where the finest properties were located, the laborers' condition varied widely.[12] The classed château was more than a property; it was an institution, which explains the persistence of prewar conditions. Although a large number of these châteaux were owned by absentees, and increasingly by large companies, each was a kind of integrated, tradition-bound community. The real manager was still a salaried specialist thoroughly familiar with estate management. He was salaried but also generally entitled to a percentage of profits, which elevated him far above those who worked for him. He was assisted by a cellar master and a chief vineyardist, as well as an office staff. The vine workers, like the cellar workers, continued to be recruited from among natives, almost inheriting their jobs from their fathers. They were deeply attached both to the estate and the people living and working on it, for the classed estates provided not only a wage—always slow to rise—but also lodging, ordinary wine, firewood, free medical services, and land to plant food crops and raise small animals. Nothing changed over time, and intermarriage among vigneron families remained common, further binding the château community together with its focus on the vineyard. As Professor Roudié put it, "The vine here is more than a resource, it is a way of life. It is also an art of living."[13] This community of owners as well as workers has managed to survive hard times and even changes of ownership over the years. Wholesale merchants and shippers, like owners of classed vineyards, have also married into landed families, further tightening professional bonds and holding the chateau communities together. Needless to say, the workers who benefit from such paternalism do not impulsively resort to violent demonstrations or strikes. Independent day workers, however, are sometimes far less timid than live-in workers about work stoppages, but still far more hesitant than their counterparts in the Midi. They inhabit numerous small villages and are a class quite different. They generally own a small plot of vines, own or rent their housing, join cooperatives, and a few also join trade unions. In the upper Médoc, their numbers have risen because they are needed for the intense cultivation now required by châteaux. There are still numerous manual tasks that skilled hands perform with infinitely more care than machines. In classed *crus* one does not find pneumatic pruning shears or the automatic branch cutters that facilitate manual pruning. In areas producing ordinary wines, however, the work force has fallen, but so has population in general, and as everywhere, the young leave first. The girls with some education go in search of secretarial jobs. They are followed by the young men who not only go in search of the girls, but also seek jobs in the secondary and tertiary sectors. It would seem that the more ambitious, and perhaps the more strike-prone, abandon the land. When they are replaced, it is with immigrants who have become seasonal laborers.

During the early 1970s French viticulture employed about 60,000 permanent and about 75,000 seasonal workers, both native and immigrant. These figures represented a decline of roughly 44 percent from the previous two decades, an awesome plunge in a span of about half a generation. As we noted already, mechanization was partly responsible for the reduced need of workers, especially in the Midi. But in a certain sense workers of both sexes voted with their feet against an economic branch that promised them very few positive expectations. With the exception of the privileged, highly skilled men and women working in the best vineyards, most workers suffered either a declining standard of living as wages failed to keep up with inflation, or earned only meager advances in wages that just managed to keep them above the poverty line. Before 1968 their wages were adjusted according to the SMAC (Salaire Minimum Agricole Garanti), a measure of inflation for rural enterprises, and calculated at a lower level then the SMIC (Salaire Minimum Interprofessionnel Garanti), a measure of inflation in urban centers based on volatile retail prices. In 1971 the average hourly wage was 3.85 to 4.54 francs, the bottom of the SMIC. Even the official *Journal officiel* recognized that conditions among vineyard workers left much to be desired.[14] Too many of them, especially in the Mediterranean vineyards, lacked professional training. This situation has not changed greatly, and has hindered their advancement in the hierarchy; and even collective bargaining has been unable to improve their hourly rates because there has been a low demand in viticulture for qualified workers. Only impoverished immigrants have consented to be hired under these conditions.

STRIKES

Since 1945 viticultural wages have been linked to several factors: the skill of workers and the skills required by employers, the prosperity of the wine industry, and the degree of trade union organization and bargaining power. Of course owners' attitudes cannot be ignored, but in general they have been reluctant to raise wages without a marked rise in productivity. For an increase in wages they want their personnel to cultivate a larger area in less time than in the past. That they have agreed to collective bargaining is, in their minds, already a major concession, one made in the interest of better relations and the avoidance of strikes. These are the hard-nosed employers. On the other hand, there are owners whose family traditions are layered in noblesse oblige, a form of paternalism that prefers giving workers material advantages other than high wages and fairly common in many châteaux in the Bordelais. Such dependency appeals less and less to full-time workers, and the postwar development of social security and family allowances has obviated the former need of it. Workers now contribute 13.44 percent of their wages to acquire a state pension, protection against illness and unemployment, and death benefits. This has been one road to freedom. Another has been trade unionism.

Unionism, in France called *syndicalisme*, began in the countryside as early as the 1890s. It assumed a particularly militant form in the Midi, precisely in the mass production vineyards of Languedoc, where a major and highly successful strike movement in 1903–1904 prevented owners from lowering wages. Trade unions, rallying to the then militant Confédération Générale du Travail (CGT), appeared in most of the communes where workers and worker-owners were numerous. Union organization spread to communes in other wine areas before 1914 but without the *élan* of the Languedocians. During the interwar the latter rallied largely to the communist-dominated Confédération Générale du Travail Unitaire (CGTU), a break-away movement from the moderately socialist CGT. Languedoc-Roussillon had an old tradition of left-wing politics, and rural workers, concentrated in villages of the coastal plain where the largest vine properties thrived, were much easier to organize than the more scattered workers in other areas.[15] Adversely affected by galloping inflation in the 1920s, the CGTU called for militant strike action to defend wages, a call that had the irresistible lure of the siren's song in the more left-wing communes. With the highest rate of strikes in agriculture, the southerners were really engaged in class war of an intensity rarely witnessed in the countryside. Employers were also organized into a syndicate since 1921 so that when a work stoppage occurred in one locality, both sides received backing from a much larger number of sympathizers. The longest strike occurred in Valros (January 2 to April 20, 1922) and ended by negotiation only when the time for spraying vines arrived and strikers emerged victorious, having staved off a reduction of wages.[16] Another wave of strikes hit between 1926 and 1928, when wine prices were rising, along with living costs. Again the workers were successful, winning an average wage increase of 15 percent.

Some forms of violence were not absent. In general, however, work stoppages among vineyard workers have been far less dramatic than those in industry, and less destructive than the collective action of rioting small growers. Deliberate resort to violence did not appear often. Most work stoppages were short and enjoyed a high rate of success, probably because workers put forward clear practical demands and enjoyed effective organization, at least in the lower south where they were numerous. In fact, the vast majority of viticultural strikes took place in Languedoc-Roussillon.

When violence occurred, it was generally in the form of intimidation toward nonstrikers, whom the local police sought to protect. Fairly typical of this situation was the work stoppage that broke out in 1928 in Rivesaltes, a small wine center near Perpignan. Most of the vine laborers were members of the communist CGTU and demanded not only a five-franc per day raise but, more important, a guarantee of work on inclement days. Collective violence broke out when some workers, refusing to join the communists, sought to begin the pruning operations. Strikers armed themselves with stones and let fly a few before the local police intervened. These latter, too few in number, called for aid and soon nearly ninety gendarmes, some mounted, arrived on the scene. Their first task was to clear the bridge over the Agly River, the gateway to the vineyards. Several men, many women—some pregnant—and children blocked it by locking their arms together, forming a human barrier. A few women even stretched out in the pathway to halt the advance of mounted officers. This tactic was reminiscent of 1907 when it was used against the army. Once more, however, it was ineffective, and horsemen broke up the women's barrier by simply carrying them off singly.

Strikers met each evening, listened to pep talks, and then paraded down the main street, usually named after a left-wing hero, accompanied by drums and bugles. This activity was not violent, even though it was meant to threaten employers and "scabs." The forces of order were simply too numerous for this to happen and violence was kept under control until the strike ended in defeat in June, six long painful months after it began.[17]

The largest strike movement of the next decade began at harvest time in 1935 when owners, badly hit by the economic depression, decided to economize on costs by lowering wages for grape pickers. Centered mainly in the departments of Aude and Hérault, there were from 8,300 to 30,000 strikers, the first the Paris government's official count, intended for the press, the second the prefect's, intended for the ministry. Within three days the owners gave in partially to union demands, and harvesting resumed on September 12. Workers had learned the critical times for work stoppages: during pruning, during spraying, and during harvesting. They had the owners, not by the neck but by the grape. Additional strikes broke out in the summer of 1936, part of a huge wave of stoppages throughout France that accompanied and embarrassed the Popular Front cabinet of Leon Blum.

All permanent workers won two advantages in 1936: the forty-hour week, and a week of paid vacation. Employers throughout France were hostile to both. To get around the latter, they offered a week off in midwinter at reduced wages. Yet the ever-present menace of strikes restrained them from reducing the wage levels attained in 1936, putting southern vine workers among the highest paid in France, a result of a lengthy and often bitter struggle.

Indicative of trade union activity, the strike rate in other vineyard areas since 1900, as measured by Tilly and Shorter, did not even come close to that of Languedoc (3.7). The southwest, including Bordeaux, was fairly active (0.2) but still behind Champagne (0.3).[18]

In Bordeaux unions did not appear until just before 1914, among independent workers in the Médocan towns, not among live-in workers housed on estates. Until recently the average *prix-faiteur* who lived in had many advantages, if not in cash income, then in fringe benefits, as noted above. Probably the most interesting was partial payment in wine.[19] This was less acceptable in the south, where wine prices were volatile. Wine could enjoy a high price when offered as part of the wage, then drop 50 percent in price when the vigneron wanted to sell it. Wines in classed vineyards at least held their high leading price, with the result that vignerons such as *prix-faiteurs* and crop sharers finally acquired considerable capital to buy land, even if it was expensive. In the Bordelais, five hectares in a minor classed area (*cru paysan*) sufficed to live fairly well; in Champagne (with no *cru paysan*), one hectare was enough.

Since 1945 labor militancy has diminished everywhere. Conditions have changed. In the Midi, native workers have fallen in number and the North Africans who replaced them do not strike, lest they face expulsion. In addition, militancy was transferred from labor issues to violent opposition against imports of foreign wine, as noted earlier. This marked a serious reversal of traditional union strategy. Since 1900 union leaders who viewed strikes as part of the class struggle had sought to keep workers' movements clear of landowners' riotous action, seeing it as a diversion away from the true goal, a socialist society. But this was never successful before 1939 and not at all since. Union membership has dropped even below the 20 percent of workers that it enjoyed during the interwar. The postwar introduced new forms of conflict management, chiefly collective bargaining carried out by high-level union chiefs and owners' representatives, and mediated by government specialists. Hourly wages became fixed by agreement, using a coefficient that places each worker in an enumerated class, ranging from 100 to 180, with each class having an hourly rate attached to it. In 1978 these wages ranged from 10.06 francs for class 100 to 16.20 francs for class 180. It is enlightening to compare class 100 and the next one up, class 125. The first consists of permanent female workers, earning 10.06 francs, the next of permanent male workers, earning 11.25 francs. Collective bargaining has nearly eliminated the huge sexual differences in wages that had existed since time immemorial. Until the 1950s a woman had always earned about half an adult man's wage, even when she performed the same job. Trade unions had rarely acted to change that difference; it is only the modern systems of labor relations that have finally brought greater sexual equality.

But then, the native workers who have remained in the vines are becoming far more efficient and educated. Endowed with traditional notions of viticulture and viniculture, they are often graduates of viticultural high schools and many enjoy a far superior technical and scientific knowledge than their forerunners. They are still a minority, but they also form a new class with considerable bargaining power and great expectations.

FEMALE WORKERS

Since time immemorial, women have occupied a central place in agricultural societies and in the family economy of the rural world. As explained in Chapter Eight, vineyards have been no exception. In France, where before the late nineteenth century the family was the primary unit of production on the land, the contribution of women was crucial to a family's survival, whether it owned a small plot or labored for a wage.[20] Among the rural wage-earning households, from 1856 to the early 1950s, between 39 and 49 percent of all women in the labor force worked in agriculture, and undoubtedly a large proportion of them were in viticulture because of its voracious need for labor.[21] These high percentages can be deceptive, however, unless we note that about 80 percent of females were employed on a seasonal basis. Their work in the vines rarely exceeded one hundred days and was often closer to half that figure, with grape harvesting accounting for most of it.

In the past, women's place in the vineyards varied according to whether they lived in areas of grape monoculture, such as the southern mass-production vineyards, or on smaller, family-run polycultural operations. In the latter they were maids-of-all-work, as active indoors as out. From the 1870s to the early 1950s the Mediterranean vineyards with their heavy demand for wage labor saw relatively large numbers of women active on large estates. Many of them were employed as day laborers (*journalières*). Some of them lived in the villages that dot the south and went out to the vineyards each day, taking their lunch and sometimes their children with them. During harvest, women's labor was particularly in demand, as was child labor. In fact, the contribution of children of both sexes during this time of year was important enough for schools not to open until mid-October, when the harvest was over. Most *journalières* came from families who owned no land of their own, and the wage was their main source of income. Landownership, however, did not automatically distinguish the activities of women. The wife of the small landowner performed the same tasks as the working-class woman who labored on large estates, but she received no wage. These wives, too, were maids-of-all-work.

As Langlois pointed out, women who were permanently employed were subject to harsh conditions. They usually lived on the estate, where their tasks were manifold. They looked after the smaller animals. Then, after laboring in the vines, they helped prepare the noon meal, and while male workers rested, they cleaned the tables and washed the dishes before returning to outdoor work. Their chief daytime rest came during the meal while they sat at the table, being no longer forced to stand to serve the men, as had been the case in the past. Since their job descriptions were vague, best characterized as open-ended, they also had extended indoor tasks, such as serving the master's family on Sunday when guests arrived. And since animals had to be fed every day, they were lucky to enjoy a Sunday afternoon of freedom. No wonder women fled rural labor, and by today their number has decreased almost to the vanishing point.

Women's participation in viticulture, as in general agriculture, varied according to the female life cycle. Women who performed wage work on a permanent basis did so most frequently when they were single or during the early months of marriage before children were conceived. With marriage and the birth of the first child, the tendency for women to work outside the home dropped off markedly. When child care was available from an older child, a neighbor, or a parent, women could more easily continue to work in the vines when children were small. Further, many a young mother took her infant into the vines in a basket when no child care was available and nursed it there. Once youngsters were old enough to work and once they finished primary school, they might actually follow their mothers into the vines, learning the elementary skills of viticulture. Indeed, until recently, most training for vineyard work took place within the family, skills being passed from father to son and from mother to daughter.

Work for women in the vineyards of France, as important as it was to the local and family economies, was usually not seen by women as a liberating phenomenon, but as an economic necessity. It was understood and expected that after marriage, a wife would make an economic contribution (whether or not that contribution involved earning a wage). The same expectation was made of children. Still, even though women's wage work was necessary for the family, both husbands and wives insisted on the importance of a domestic role for women, a feature of family life that seems not to have changed at all.

Perhaps because of its importance as an economic unit, the vineyard family did not encourage young marriages. Nonetheless, ages at first marriage in vineyard regions may have been somewhat lower than the national average. In the village of Coursan, Aude, where laborers were numerous, women married at about twenty-one years of age and men at about twenty-five or twenty-six just before World War I, whereas the national averages for that time were twenty-four and twenty-eight for women and men, respectively. Within the working class, as within the bourgeoisie of landowners, it was necessary for the young couple to be capable of supporting itself. In fact, whatever the class, economic considerations were not always entirely absent from the choice of a mate. The requirement that newlyweds establish their own households did not mean that family connections dissolved. Families continued to provide psychological and sometimes material support in the early stages of marriage. Furthermore, parents and offspring frequently continued to reside in proximity to one another. Close living arrangements were facilitated by the fact that before World War II, most marriages took place between people from the same locality, especially because youths without transportation could not easily meet people from other areas. This form of endogeny was becoming rare by the 1930s, and exceptional situations must have been numerous. Some old vignerons in Chateâuneuf-du-Pape recalled that in the decade before 1940 they had to find brides elsewhere, there being no local girls of a suitable age.

Behind the walls of village houses, which seem timeless in their outward appearance, there have in fact been many changes for women and the family. Since the early 1920s, the number of women in the agricultural labor force has weakened. From 44 percent in 1921, the presence of women working in agriculture dropped to 40 percent in 1936, rose slightly to 41 percent in 1946 because of the war, and then declined again to 27 percent in 1954, to 19 percent in 1962, and to 9 percent in 1979. Women in the vineyard areas of France no longer turn to vines for work. The gains made by agricultural labor unions after World War I in raising the wages of vineyard workers have meant that among working-class families, married women's wages have been less of an economic necessity than they may have been earlier (although this, too, fluctuates, along with the vineyard economy and the national economy in general). Mechanization has also helped to take women out of the vines, and harvesting machines have brought about the monosexing of the labor force by completely removing females. One has to look far and wide to find *journalières* still active full-time among the vines. I have seen women driving tractors on a few occasions, but never in the driver's seat atop harvesters. Finally, the increasing use of male immigrant wage labor and growing opportunities of employment for women in the services have contributed to their withdrawal from the vineyard. Today female wage laborers account for a mere one percent of women generally engaged in agriculture. They have not come a long way; they have simply gone away.

The persons whose lives and endeavors make up this volume belong to three generations: that of the 1910s, that of the 1930s and '40s, and finally that of the 1970s and '80s. The first prepared the way for the unprecedented transformation of grape and wine growing that followed World War I. Their successors, recognizing that a new age had been inaugurated by so devastating a war, were far more foreseeing than their political leaders whose goal was to restore the past. They were the first wave of viticultural revolutionaries, youthful and ready for action. The revolution in which many of them participated so actively, however, was not exclusively of their making as grape and wine growers. In this respect the wine revolution they began differed fundamentally from those that in the past had been of an economic and technological nature.

First, the great commercial, industrial, and agricultural revolutions occurring from the seventeenth through the nineteenth centuries were carried out largely by independent entrepreneurs, highly individualistic and nearly free of government aid and control. The great scientific discoveries of these centuries provided them with information, but in a discontinuous, haphazard fashion. They were above all pragmatists and succeeded or perished as such. Their individual imagination was their stimulant. Great social and economic changes in the twentieth century are quite different; they are often planned and imposed upon entrepreneurs, sometimes partially or wholly financed by state decree. The absolutist states of earlier times, moved by the doctrine of mercantilism, pretended to great power, but rarely possessed it. The contemporary state, whether democratic or totalitarian, possesses enormous control, is indeed a vast bureaucratic sea in which ministers and politicians strive to keep afloat and desperately try to direct its currents. The wine revolution took place in France, where politicians come and go but bureaucrats, like diamonds, are forever. And it was above all the latter, guided by the wine lobby, who channeled the wine industry toward the goals of modernization. The true planning was most often the intelligent work of salaried viticultural experts, agronomists, drainage and mechanical engineers, enologists, administrators, financial planners, and many paper-pushers who, like students capable of sleeping in class with their eyes open, always look busy. Before 1939 such a vast involvement in wine making, or in any other private enterprise, was not readily visible or desired by a majority of politicians. The state was rather dragooned into an active role dragging its heels, and as regards wine, it was the growers themselves, highly organized politically and professionally, seeking help desperately in an age of crisis, who insisted upon a regulatory role for the state.

From the late 1920s winemen repudiated the individualistic entrepreneurs of earlier times as models. They chose state regulation over traditional production and marketing, and added another layer of officialdom, a kind of semibureaucracy, when they grouped themselves into state-directed regulatory bodies designed to control individual growers in the interest of the profession. From ardent individualists they became determined corporatists.

Second, the self-imposed discipline, safeguarded by several bureaucratic agencies, has indeed channeled the wine industry along planned directions, as an element of France's planned economy. One of these directions has been the limitation of volume. Here the wine industry is almost unique. Before significant modernization, the total product, even with the phylloxera crisis, rose by 10 percent from the 1860s to the 1890s, greater than population growth. From the 1930s to the 1960s it grew by a mere 5 percent, far less than the immediate postwar demographic explosion. This situation remains more or less constant even though the annual rate of population growth has begun to decline. The quantity of wine has stabilized in relation to the national market. This means that official policy has forced the reduction of total wine volume vis-à-vis other sectors of the economy. Inasmuch as the area of land planted in vines has seriously declined, only higher yields explain the slight expansion of production.

Third, the kind of wine demanded by an enlarged market has undergone a qualitative change rather than a quantitative one. Save for *gros rouge*, which never seems to change, better wines now crowd store shelves in a world where style has become a decisive factor. Wine is not quite in the same category as clothing, coiffeurs, and automobiles, all of which assume different silhouettes each year. Yet style as a matter of taste has imposed modifications. Without adequate cellarage, consumers in greater numbers are abandoning the big full tannic wines for the more supple, thinner, fruity beverages of post-World War II.

Fourth, this shift in style and taste was encouraged by merchants who, as blenders, exercised considerable control over the kinds of wines put on the market. With lighter, early-maturing beverages, their turnover became more rapid and their storage costs declined. Therefore they used their advertising budgets to encourage buyers to select the "new" wine. The enormous increase in the sales of *nouveau beaujolais* greatly aided their efforts. An astonishing rise in the art and expense of advertising wine accompanied this change; the sums once used for storage could now go into popularizing brands and matching styles to various income and age groups. With the advent of radio, television, and a vast variety of magazines devoted to gourmet tastes—all of which sought to influence styles of beverages—both producers' syndicates and wholesale merchants set out to make the consumption of finer wines an everyday enjoyment.

Fifth, the class structure of modern society not only favored the merchants' new policy, it largely determined both production and marketing. Their publicity was aimed at the ever-expanding middle class that enjoyed, at least after the terrible 1940s, a disposable income that increased and was in search of objects to make life more enjoyable after years of economic depression, war, and occupation. In short, both producers and sellers adjusted their product to find its place in a new society that was basking in more wealth and leisure than their forebears had known. Driven primarily by the market, their goal has become the creation of an image of bottled wine as both a necessity for the good life and a luxury for an even better life. To fulfill this objective each producer seeks to provide his wine with a personality and a fetching label designed to distinguish it from other bottles. Urged by government agencies that offer financial aid to agricultural pursuits, and by the threat of bankruptcy, more vignerons have equipped themselves to grow government-recommended grapes capable of becoming an appellation beverage, even if only at the lowest rung of the appellation hierarchy, *vins de pays*. The combination of state policy, professional discipline, and a large market of appreciative drinkers has led growers, cooperatives, and merchant-blenders to turn out a far greater volume of quality wine than at any time in the past. The search for excellence has motivated the policies and processes of the wine revolution, which has meant a notable increase in quality rather than in quantity, though the quality may sometimes be questionable. Wine has become not merely a drink; it is a political force, a source of considerable revenue, and a social indicator. *Gros rouge* has followed the downward social trend of the rural and urban working classes, its principle consumers. Like the red flag, the Internationale, and the Communist party, its future is uncertain.

Sixth, the wine revolution as a scientific and technological undertaking did not come about to save or even to improve jug wine. The decision to discourage the cultivation of inferior grapes was a political and not a scientific one: the need to curb the subsidies that drained the budget of the Ministry of Agriculture. At the base of the viti-vinicultural mutation lies the greater knowledge of grapes and wine components—their reactions to natural ecological forces as well as to man's influence through the use of chemical fertilizers, manufactured insecticides, and herbicides, and the vast array of mechanical devices functioning in vineyards and cellars. Without this enormous increase of knowledge and the people who discovered it, taught it, and absorbed it, there would have been no wine revolution. And any letup will surely compromise the progress made so far, leaving France in a weakened position within radically altered foreign markets.

Seventh, the wine revolution has created a superior drink that can no longer attract enough buyers within France's national boundaries. Creators of fine wines tend to believe that the lure of foreign markets, where they must face up to the world's best beverages, is a stimulant to further improve their own, however excellent it may already be—in short, a challenge to excellence. Partly to meet the challenge, partly to enjoy the higher prices of the richest markets, they have always exported on a fairly large scale, which does enrich the image of the wine makers' label. And they have been the first to profit from the formation of the European Economic Community. Since 1970 the wine industries of the member countries have been stimulated to participate in an economic experiment that has no European precedent, save the Roman Empire: a vast grouping of once independent states, in which national tariff barriers have gradually diminished and are scheduled to disappear in 1992. So far, France's appellation wines, from highest to lowest, have benefited from membership, but her millions of hectoliters of jug wine have not.

Finally, the massive transformation of the wine industry has had a marked effect on various types of growers. For southerners the changing situation has been traumatic. Algeria's declaration of independence in

1962 was certainly a step favorable to them; for more than a century, Algerian wine had competed with southern wine on the French domestic market. Now the native North Africans, forbidden to use alcohol by the Koran, have replaced many of the massive vineyards that Frenchmen once owned with the wheat fields they need to improve their diet, and the flood of Algerian wine entering duty-free into France has nearly dried up. But this development did not fully diminish the woes of southerners. Since 1970, when French viticulture came under the Common Agricultural Policy of the European Economic Community, wines from southern Italy have entered the French market in sizable quantity, albeit less than those from Algeria, and now they compete with French ordinary vintages. This new competition and the southern French reactions to it have been the cause of virtually annual violent protests and demonstrations in the south, one of the most violent ending in the death of a police officer and a vigneron in Lower Languedoc in 1976.

These protests have blended with an awakened regionalism among the new generation, indicating an upsurge of Occitanian consciousness among the thirty-one departments from Bordeaux to Nice where the Occitanian language has survived. Occitania is a broad area comprising Languedoc as well as Provence—in fact, much of France south of the Loire River. These authentic regionalists, many of whom are younger vignerons in the lower Midi, see in the government's policy of uprooting vines an effort to get rid not only of vines, but of people who are themselves deeply rooted in the sun-scorched earth. Their rhetoric of protest reflects their love for their region and their desire to continue the life of vine trainers as done by their parents and grandparents before them. "Volem viure al pais!" is their slogan in the Langue d'Oc, the language of Languedoc, and means "We want to live in our region!" To be sure, this revolt of the south must be seen as an early development of a larger rural renovation, for farmers of all types have been seeking greater recognition of their needs since the 1930s. It is noteworthy, however, that vignerons, chiefly southerners, were the initiators of this movement.

The current dilemma of southern vignerons reflects the fact that since the mid-nineteenth century all vignerons have been less isolated than other French peasants; they have been well integrated into the national market and are consequently subject to the influence of national and international trade. As producers of a commodity sold chiefly in urban markets, they live close to arteries of commerce and are forced to look beyond their narrow environs. Even if they communicate among themselves in their native regional languages, which is increasingly rare, French has long been the medium of their profession, and their major problem has continued to be one of resolving national policies in accordance with regional needs and concerns. Resolution, however, has become increasingly complex and elusive since 1970, when the EEC included viti-viniculture into the vast array of economic integration.

Midi growers in Languedoc-Roussillon have insistently and at times violently expressed their opposition to EEC policies, and the recent entry of Spain and Portugal has struck them as the final betrayal by a government basically hostile to their interests. All other growers, however, have welcomed the nearly free trade they enjoy in the member states, essentially the expanse of Europe west of the Iron Curtain. All the quality wine areas of France enjoying an appellation ship from 45 to 60 percent of their exports to this huge market. The present and future prosperity of France's wine industry is heavily dependent on exports. Perhaps southern growers are too pessimistic. Eighty-three percent of VDQS wine, most of it from Languedoc-Roussillon, went to the less affluent drinkers of the Common Market in 1981. And although rates of unemployment reach 9 to 10 percent, jobless compensation approaches normal wage levels, and the demand for *gros rouge* may recover.

At any rate, table-wine growers do not have the political leverage to force France's abandonment of the EEC. More and more of them have come to realize and to accept the inevitable, with the consequence that they are now in the precess of improving the quality of their wine. They at last are abandoning the street barricades, where they won nothing of substance, to return to their vineyards and cooperatives where lies their salvation. They now recognize that they must adapt the scientific elements and mental outlook of the wine revolution to augment quality rather than quantity. A recent classification of Midi wines, which appeared in the May 1988 issue of the prestigious *Revue du vin de France* is a tardy recognition of the progress already achieved toward excellence, and the surest means of changing for the better the tainted image of the premier land of *gros rouge*.

In our time, every facet of life is in a continuing revolution, and the thrust is toward enriching the quality of our existence. Well-made wine already enjoys a solid place in the scale of values with which we weigh, in almost Benthamite fashion, the pleasures and pains of daily existence. Happily for producers—and for drinkers—a truly worthy bottle easily tips the balance in favor of Bacchus.

INTRODUCTION

1. A selection of these sources can be found in Leo A. Loubère, Laura Frader, Jean Sagnes, and Rémy Pech, eds., *The Vine Remembers* (Albany, 1985).
2. For the early effects of the phylloxera crisis, see Leo A. Loubère, *The Red and the White* (Albany, 1978); Yves Rinaudo, *Les Vendanges de la République* (Lyon, 1982).
3. Harry Paul, *From Knowledge to Power: The Rise of the Science Empire in France, 1860–1939* (Cambridge, Eng., 1985), 187.
4. For an excellent study of recent experiments, see Etienne Montaigne, "Enjeux et stratégies dans la filière d'innovation du matériel végétal viticole," doctoral dissertation, University of Montpellier, 1988. On the question of innovation, see also M. J. Mulkey, *The Social Process of Innovation: A Study in the Sociology of Science* (London, 1972); R. C. Epstein, "Industrial Invention, Heroic or Systematic," *Quarterly Journal of Economics* 40 (1926): 126–76. For general histories of the wine industry, see the pioneering work of Roger Dion, *Histoire de la vigne et du vin en France* (1959), and Marcel Lachiver, *Vins, vignes et vignerons, histoire du vignoble français* (1988), a book of vast historical erudition. Of vast scientific erudition is Emile Peynaud, *Le Vin et les jours* (1988), chap. 2.

CHAPTER ONE *General Trends and Conditions since 1914*

1. G. Duby and Armand Wallon, eds., *Histoire de la France rurale*, 4 vols. (1977), vol. IV, 23ff.; M. Augé-Laribé, *Agriculture française pendant la guerre* (1925), 33–41, 76–81, 121–70, 212.
2. P. Prestwich, *Drink and the Politics of Social Reform: Anti-alcoholism in France* (Palo Alto, Calif., 1988), 167–73.
3. Ibid.

4. *Revue de viticulture*, 1914, passim.

5. G. Galtier, *Vignoble du Languedoc méditerranéen et du Roussillon*, 3 vols. (Montpellier, 1960), vol. I, 135.

6. Interview with René Engel of Vosne-Romanée.

7. Edmund Penning-Rowsell, *Wines of Bordeaux* (New York, 1969), 85–86.

8. C. Moreau-Berillon, *Au Pays du champagne. Le vignoble, le vin* (Reims, 1922), 279–93.

9. François Bonal, *Le Livre d'or du champagne* (Lausanne, 1984), 167–70; Patrick Forbes, *Champagne: The Wine, the Land and the People* (London, 1967), chap. 14.

10. Rémy Pech, *Entreprise viticole et capitalisme en Languedoc-Roussillon* (Toulouse, 1975), 244–69, 271, 336.

11. *Revue de viticulture* 60, no. 1424 (13 October 1921): 273; 70, no. 1810 (7 March 1929): 158–61; no. 1811 (14 March 1929): passim.

12. Pech, *Entreprise viticole*, 244–69, 271, 336.

13. J. L. Gyss, *Le Vin et l'Alsace* (1978), 42; Lucien Sittler, *La Viticulture et le vin de Colmar* (Colmar, 1956), 155.

14. Paul Bergeot, *Champagne, la coupe est pleine* (1980), 23–28; Henri and Rémy Krug, *L'Art du Champagne* (1979), 90.

15. P.-M. Doutrelant, *Les Bons vins et les autres* (1976), 87ff.

16. Gilbert Garrier, *Paysans du Beaujolais et du Lyonnais, 1800–1970*, 2 vols. (Grenoble, 1973), vol. I, 582–85; Jacques Loyat, *La Propriété foncière citadine . . . à Villié-Morgan* (Dijon, 1977), 71.

17. Gerald-Jack Gilbank, *Vignobles de qualité du sud-est du bassin Parisien* (1981), 270, 639–43.

18. René Pijassou, *Le Médoc: Un grand vignoble de qualité*, 2 vols. (1980), vol. II, 871–73; Nicholas Faith, *The Winemasters* (New York, 1978), 131.

19. Charles Vavasseur, "Le Vignoble de Touraine de 1880 à 1932," *Revue de viticulture* 76, no. 1974 (28 April 1932): 261–84.

20. Pijassou, *Le Médoc*, II, 926, 930–31; Philippe Roudié, "Campagnes girondines et vins de Bordeaux à l'époque contemporaine, 1850–1978," doctoral dissertation, University of Bordeaux III, 1980, 68off., 733–49, 758ff., recently published as *Vignobles et vignerons du bordelais* (1988); J. Masson, *La Crise viticole en Gironde* (Bordeaux, 1938), 68–69.

21. Galtier, *Vignoble du Languedoc*, I, 135–36.

22. R. Courtin, "La Viticulture devant les pouvoirs publiques," *Revue politique et parlementaire* 147 (10 June 1931): 461; Pech, *Entreprise viticole*, 443–60; Geneviève Gavignaud, *Propriétaires-Viticulteurs en Roussillon* (1983), vol. II, 607.

23. Charles Warner, *Winegrowers of France and the Government since 1878* (New York, 1960), chap. 6; *Revue de viticulture* 74, no. 1974 (1932): 263–82; Faith, *Winemasters*, 140ff.; Garrier, *Paysans du Beaujolais*, I, 619–20.

24. G. Dutraive, *L'Institut national des appellations d'origine des vins* (Lyon, 1954), 18ff.

25. Pijassou, *Le Médoc*, II, 942–55; Roudié, "Campagnes girondines," 807–18.

26. Louis Chapuis, *Vigneron en Bourgogne* (1980), 70–73.

27. *Journée viticole*, 18 September 1947.

CHAPTER TWO *The Viticultural Revolution*

1. Ernest Chancrin and Jean Long, *Viticulture moderne* (1955), 297.

2. J. P. Richardot, ed., *Papa Bréchard, vigneron du Beaujolais* (1977), 74–75, 80–82, 94, 157; Chapuis, *Vigneron*, 174–81; Rolande Gadille, *Le Vignoble de la Côte Bourguignonne* (1967), 34–36, 210–25.

3. Bonal, *Le Livre d'or du champagne*, 246.

4. Henri Enjalbert, *Les Grands vins de Saint-Emilion, Pomerol, Fronsac* (1983), 489–525; Pijassou, *Le Médoc*, II, 996ff., 1026; Roudié, "Campagnes girondines," 875–93.

5. My interviews with vignerons.

6. Chapuis, *Vigneron*, 130ff.

7. Ibid., 80.

8. Georges Chappaz, *Le Vignoble et le vin de Champagne* (1951), 216–17; Jeffrey Benson and Alastair MacKenzie, *Sauternes, A Study of the Great Sweet Wines of Bordeaux* (London, 1979), 21ff.

9. Richardot, ed., *Papa Bréchard*, 94; *Bourgogne viticole*, February 1982, 10–18; interview of M. Marcellin of the Chambre d'Agriculture des Pyrénées-Orientales, Perpignan.

10. J. Loyat, *Le Beaujolais nouveau et ancien. 150 ans de métayage* (Lyon, 1982), 54–56, 82–83; Daniel Faucher, *Paysan et machine* (1954), 64–65, 165, 213–27; D. Requier-Desjardins, *Petite exploitation agricole* (Lyon, 1978), 224; Galtier, *Vignoble du Languedoc*, I: 260, 287, II, 29–30; T. Rosa, "Mécanisation des vendanges," Office International de la Vigne et du Vin, *Bulletin* 49, no. 550 (henceforth listed as OIV, *Bulletin*); Jean Branas, *Viticulture* (Montpellier, 1974), 448; Garrier, *Paysans du Beaujoulais*, I, 590; A. Blanc et al., *Rapport sur les essais publiques contrôlés d'appareils de motoculture dans la vigne* (Montpellier, 1933), 90–105; *Revue de viticulture* 60, no. 1422 (29 September 1921): 221; no. 1423 (6 October 1921): 246–47; *Gironde agricole et viticole* 8, no. 93 (September 1932): 2–5; Roudié, "Campagnes girondines," 44, 911; Roudié, *Vignoble bordelais* (Toulouse, 1973), 44; Pijassou, *Le Médoc*, II, 1011–13.

11. M. Pastor-Barrue, *Viticulture en crise à Laure-Minervois* (1981), 147; R. Sceau, "Un Vignoble dynamique, le Beaujolais," *Revue de géographie de Lyon* 50, no. 2 (1975): 127–50; A. Berger and F. Maurel, *La Viticulture et l'économie du Languedoc* (Montpellier, 1980), 179.

12. Michel Gervais, *France sans paysans* (1965), 50–58.

13. A. J. Winkler et al., *General Viticulture* (Berkeley, 1974), chap. 21.

14. Hubert Piat, *Le Beaujolais* (1977), 32, note 1.

15. Chapuis, *Vigneron*, 171; Richardot, ed., *Papa Bréchard*, 159.

16. P. Vagny, "Mécanisation des vendanges, les automotrices stabilisent le marché," *Journée vinicole*, 31 October 1986, 6.

17. Bonal, *Le Livre d'or du champagne*, 299; L. Bourdier, "Les Progrès récents de l'oenotechnie," *Bulletin du Conseil Général du Groupement de Recherches Economiques et Financières*, no. 18 (August 1987): 101–105.

18. Thomas Matthews, "Harvest Machines Rattle Bordeaux," *The Wine Spectator*, 29 February 1988, 7; P. B. Bartoli et al., *L'Economie viticole française* (1987), 20; *The Friends of Wine* 25, no. 2 (April–May 1988): 70–71.

19. Richardot, ed., *Papa Bréchard*, 139; Loubère et al., *The Vine Remembers*, 177–82; R. Agulhon and P. Vagny, "Les Techniques d'application pour le désherbage d'été," *Vignes et vin*, no. 321 (July–September, 1983): 11–17.

20. Centre d'Etudes des Techniques Agricoles de Côte-d'Or, *Expérimentation et conduite de vignes à faible densité en Côte-d'Or* (n.p., March 1979), 1–36; D. Boubals and R. Pistre, "Résultats d'essais de vignes hautes à grand écartement obtenus dans l'Aude," *Progrès agricole et viticole* 157 (1962): 280–84.

21. Roudié, "Campagnes girondines," 914–22; Anthony Hanson, *Burgundy* (London, 1982), 283–321.

22. Jules Milhau, *Le Pouvoir d'achat des viticulteurs* (Montpellier, 1945), 126; Pech, *Entreprise viticole*, 202, 498, 501; Communauté Economique Européenne, *Conditions de commercialisation et de formation des prix des vins de consommation courante* (1969), 126.

23. Bonal, *Livre d'or du champagne*, 191; Colin, "Vignoble . . . Champagne," 83, 88.

24. Sittler, *Viticulture et le vin de Colmar*, 158–61; Gyss, *Vin et l'Alsace*, passim.

25. Charles Pomerol, ed., *Terroirs et vins de France* (1984), 22; Gadille, *Vignoble*, 253.

26. Roudié, "Campagnes girondines," 852; Pijassou, *Le Médoc*, I, 1000; Banque de France, *Le Vin de Bordeaux* (Bordeaux, 1977), 43.

27. René Barthe, "Economie et politique viticole en France, 1950–1965," doctoral dissertation, University of Montpellier, 1966, 28; Daniel Boulet et al., *Quelques tendances de l'économie viticole française*, Institut National de Recherche Agronomique (INRA), série *Notes et Documents*, no. 32 (October 1979): passim; INRA, "Quelques données pour analyser la crise viticole," série *Notes et Documents*, no. 16 (September 1976), 5ff.; *Vignoble du Languedoc-Roussillon méditerranéen* (n.p., n.d.), 406–407.

28. Pierre Bréjoux, *Les Vins de Loire* (1956), 25.

29. The Ministry of Agriculture has published the *Recensement général de l'Agriculture* for 1955, 1970, 1979–80, which are indispensable sources for viticulture. It has also published *Monographies agricoles départementales*, a volume for

each department. Some departments have published the data of its *Résultats généraux de l'enquête agricole de 1929*, and a sizable collection of data are available in their departmental archives; Chapuis, *Vigneron*, 271–72; Jean Duffort, *L'Organisation internationale du marché du vin* (1968), 30; Denis Requier-Desjardins, *Petite exploitation agricole et développement du capitalisme: L'exemple de la viticulture languedocienne* (Lyon, 1978), 145–47, 160–61; B. Delord, "Marché foncier et dynamique des exploitations . . . méridionales," *Société Languedocienne de Géographie, Bulletin* 11, no. 1 (January–June 1977): 76.

30. Robert Lifran, *Grandes exploitations et viticulture méridionale* (INRA, 1975), 46ff.; Robert Lifran, *Elargissement du marché et couches sociales dans la viticulture languedocienne*, INRA, série *Etudes et Recherches*, no. 30 (1977): 25; Galtier, *Vignoble*, I, 23, 138, 186.

31. Guy Mergoil, "La Structure du vignoble girondin," *Revue géographique des Pyrénées et du Sud-Ouest*, no. 2 (1961): 140; G. Caumes, "Le Vignoble Saint-Emilionnais. Les conditions de production," DES, University of Bordeaux III, 1965, 40–69; Jean-Paul Hermitte, "La Structure du vignoble à Gigondas," *Etudes vauclusiennes*, no. 13 (January–June 1975): 1–4; Gyss, *Vin et l'Alsace*, 47ff.; Ministère de l'Agriculture. Service Régional de Statistique Régional de Champagne-Ardennes, *Les Structures du vignoble de Champagne* (1970–71), 87; Colin, "Vignoble . . . Champagne," 77–78.

32. Gadille, *Vignoble*, 564; Gilbank, *Vignobles*, 55–58, 359–67.

33. Sceau, "Un Vignoble dynamique," 142. Professor Sceau has calculated a 30 percent decline using the formula $\frac{x-y}{x} \cdot 100 = r$. In all my calculations I have used the formula $\frac{x-y}{y} \cdot 100 = r$, recognized as standard by most demographers. x stands for the most recent figure, y for the earlier one.

34. Ministère de l'Agriculture, *Bourgogne rurale* (1980), 103; Communauté Economique Européenne, *Conditions de commercialisation et de formation des prix des vins de consommation courante* (1969), 15; Léopold Morel, *L'Economie dirigée en viticulture* (1939), 22ff.

35. *Journal officiel, avis*, "L'Avenir de la viticulture française," no. 4 (15 February 1978): 284ff.

36. P. Carrière, "Viticulture et espace rurale: L'assiette géographique du vignoble languedocien et son évolution récente," *Société Languedocienne de Géographie, Bulletin* 7, no. 2 (April–June 1973): 232–37.

37. Montaigne, "Enjeux et stratégies," 130–69.

CHAPTER THREE *Viniculture*

1. Paul, *From Knowledge to Power*, 202–207.

2. Jean Ribéreau-Gayon, *L'Oenologie d'hier et d'aujourd'hui* (Montpellier, 1955), 1–32; idem, *Les Sciences de la vigne et du vin à Université de Bordeaux* (Bordeaux,

1965), 1–64; Emile Peynaud, "La Qualité hier et aujourd'hui," in Raymond Dumay, ed., *Le Vin de Bordeaux et du haut-pays* (1977), 97–136.

3. Lucien Sémichon, "L'Etat actuel des recherches oenologiques," in *Congrès international de la vigne et du vin* (Bordeaux, c. 1928), 132ff.

4. Jean Ribéreau-Gayon and Emile Peynaud, *Traité d'oenologie*, 4 vols. (1972–77).

5. *La Vinification beaujolaise* (Villefranche, 1979), 7–37; P. André et al., "Méthode de vinification en macération carbonique," *Annales de technologie agricole* 16 (1967): 109–23; P. André, "Influences du foulage de la vendange sur la qualité des vins du Beaujolais," *Vignes et vins*, special issue (1966): 122–24.

6. *Symposium des vins des Côtes de Provence, 21–23 Juin 1966* (Draguignan, c. 1966), 64ff.; M. Flanzy et al., "Contribution à l'étude des boissons alcooliques," *Annales de technologie agricole* 4 (1955), 359–80; Flanzy, "Fermentation du jus de raisin en continue," ibid., 15 (1966): 311–20; INRA, *Le Vignoble des Côtes-du-Rhône* (1977), 48.

7. G. Marteau, "Etat actuel de l'oenologie du point de vue technologie," OIV, *Bulletin* 432 (1975): 523–32; Chabas and Vannobel {first names not given}, "Les Progrès constatés dans la technologie des équipements des caves vinincoles," *Bulletin technique d'information du Ministère de l'Agriculture* 373 (1982): 635–52.

8. *Midi vinicole*, 12 June 1978.

9. *Revue de viticulture* 64, no. 1650 (11 February 1926): 14; 75, no. 1939 (27 August 1931): 137; 75, no. 1948 (29 October 1931): 277–79.

10. John E. Baxevanis, *The Wines of Bordeaux and Western France* (Totowa, N.J., 1987), 148–49.

11. Hanson, *Burgundy*, 126–29.

12. Roland Pisani, *Le Vin en France à l'heure de l'Europe* (Montpellier, 1977), 194, 236–42; Jean Rozier and Eugène Gardia, *L'Etiquetage des vins. Réglementation française et communautaire* (1979), chap. 4.

13. Boulet et al., *Quelques tendances de l'économie viticole française*, 45–61.

14. Léon Douarche, *Le Vin et la vigne dans l'économie nationale française* (1943), 81.

15. *Revue de viticulture* 75, no. 1938 (20 August 1931): passim; Chapuis, *Vigneron*, 207; Richardot, ed., *Papa Bréchard*, 153–55.

16. Raymond Brunet, *Le Vignoble et les vins d'Alsace* (1932), 119ff.

17. Roudié, "Campagnes girondines," 631, 925.

18. *Journal officiel, avis*, no. 2 (11 January 1972): 25.

19. Camille Rodier, *Le Vin de Bourgogne* (3d ed., Dijon [1948]), 39–40; Gadille, *Vignoble*, 433–67; H. W. Yoxall, *The Wines of Burgundy* (New York, 1970), 130–31; Hanson, *Burgundy*, 101; Chapuis, *Vigneron*, 195; *Revue de viticulture* 75, no. 1933 (16 July 1931): 37; Gilbank, *Vignobles*, 146–47.

20. Paul Jamain, *La Vigne et le vin* (1901), 598–647.

21. M. A. Amerine and M. A. Joslyn, *Table Wines: The Technology of Their Production* (2d ed., Berkeley, 1970), 786–90.

22. Germain Laforgue, *Le Vignoble girondin* (1947), 235–47; Laforgul, *La Culture de la vigne dans le Bordelais* (1929), 76–79; Pijassou, *Le Médoc*, II, 1020–25; J. Benson and A. MacKenzie, *The Wines of Saint-Emilion and Pomerol* (London, 1983), 26–32; E. Feret and C. Cocks, eds., *Bordeaux et ses vins* (13th ed., Bordeaux, 1982), 365–66; E. Penning-Rowsell, *The Wines of Bordeaux* (5th ed., London, 1985), 37.

23. P. Maisonneuve, *Le Vigneron Angevin* (Angers, 1926), 263–314; A. Chauvigne, *Monographie de la commune de Vouvray et de son vignoble* (Tours 1908), 127–31.

24. Chappaz, *Le Vignoble . . . Champagne*, 353–56; Bergeot, *Champagne, la coupe est pleine*, 99–101; Krug, *L'Art du champagne*, 61–63.

25. Aline Fabre, "Le Vignoble des Côtes-du-Rhône," doctoral dissertation, University of Montpellier, 1966, 41–42.

26. Eugène Richard, *Le Marché du vin à Paris* (1934), 87.

27. Bonal, *Le livre d'or du champagne*, 198, 299–311.

28. C. Bourquin, *Connaissance du vin* (Verviers, 1970), 17, 29–30.

29. *Symposium des vins des Côtes de Provence, 21–23 Juin 1966*, 75ff. for Branas.

30. Doutrelant, *Les Bon vins*, 12–18, 95–98.

31. Piat, *Beaujolais*, 121–43.

32. Bourquin, *Connaissance*, 30.

33. Faith, *The Winemasters*, 122, 218–20.

34. Doutrelant, *Les Bon vins*, 12–13.

35. Hanson, *Burgundy*, 131–32.

36. Roudié, "Campagnes girondines," 1030–37.

37. Jean-Raymond Gayon, *Au Service du vin de Bordeaux* (Bordeaux, 1956), 38–58.

38. Pijassou, *Le Médoc*, II, 895–900; Gilbank, *Vignobles*, 370–71; *Vigneron du Midi*, August 1935; Penning-Rowsell, *Wines of Bordeaux*, 5th ed., 152; Frank Schoonmaker, ed., *Encyclopedia of Wine* (6th rev. ed., New York, 1975), 127–28; Bernard Blanchet, ed., *Code du vin et textes viti-vinicoles français et communautaires* (new rev. and enl. ed., Montpellier, 1970).

39. Pierre Bert, *In Vino veritas: L'affaire des vins de Bordeaux* (1975), 61ff.

40. *The Wine Spectator*, 15 February 1988, 5.

CHAPTER FOUR *The Attack on Fraud*

1. Joseph Capus, *L'Oeuvre du Comité National des Appellations d'Origine* (1942), passim; idem, *L'Evolution de la législation sur les appellations d'origine* (1947), passim.

2. G. Lafforgue, *Le Vignoble girondin* (1947), 4–51; Gérard Dutraive, *L'Institut National des Appellations d'Origine des Vins* (Lyon, 1954), 4–34.

3. Bonal, *Le Livre d'or du champagne*, 206–10.

4. Roudié, "Campagnes girondines," 630–718, 778–87, 828, 844; Penning-Rowsell, *Wines of Bordeaux*, 81–86, 106, 190, 289.

5. M. Peyre, "Le Vignoble de Bourgogne. La question des Appellations," *Revue des études rhodaniennes* 11, no. 1 (1935): 88–97; Rodier, *Vin de Bourgogne*, 107; Françoise Grivot, *Le Commerce des vins de Bourgogne* [1964], 200.

6. Gilbank, *Vignobles*, 279–83, 287.

7. Sceau, "Un Vignoble . . . Beaujolais," *Revue de géographie de Lyon* 50, no. 2 (975): 127–50; Piat, *Beaujolais*, 76–77, 129.

8. Maisonnevue, *Vigneron Angevin*, 353–56.

9. Institut National de la Recherche Agronomique, *Le Vignoble des Côtes-du-Rhône* (1977), 3–9, 26, 93–98.

10. *Revue de viticulture* 70 (7 February 1929): 90–99; 76 (14 April 1932): 229–37; Paul Piard, *Des Syndicats vers la corporation* (1937), 259–80.

11. Sheldon Wasserman, *The Wines of the Côtes-du-Rhône* (New York, 1977), 171–81.

12. "L'Evolution du vignoble d'appellation d'origine contrôlée de 1950 à 1970," *Bulletin de l'INAO des Vins et Eaux de Vie*, no. 112, special issue (1971): 2–6.

13. Pijassou, *Le Médoc*, II, 940.

14. Bartoli et al., *Economie viticole française*, 230, 255.

15. Chapuis, *Vigneron*, 283.

16. Yves Masurel, "Le Commerce des vins de Provence orientale," *Acta Geographica*, fasc. 51 (September 1964): 7–13; *Symposium des vins des Côtes-de-Provence, 21–23 Juin 1966*, 47–49; Roger Livet, "Le Vignoble de Provence," *Méditerranée, revue géographique* 5, no. 1 (January–March 1964): 13–43.

17. Faith, *Winemasters*, 152–53, 195; Guy Mergoil, "La Structure du vignoble girondin," *Revue géographique des Pyrénées et du Sud-Ouest*, no. 2 (1961): 119–40.

18. Jean Clavel and Robert Baillaud, *Histoire et avenir des vins en Languedoc* (Toulouse, 1985), 110.

19. Raymond Azibert, *La Confédération générale des vignerons* (Carcassonne, 1925), 5, 43, 78–114, 137–39.

20. *Vigneron du Midi*, July 1935, September–October 1936.

21. Warner, *Winegrowers of France*, chaps. 6–11.

22. Léopold Morel, *L'Economie dirigée en viticulture* (1939), 26–86, 116–18.

23. *Revue de viticulture* 82, no. 2126 (26 March 1935): 207; 82, no. 2140 (4 July 1935): 13–29; 91, no. 2357 (31 August 1939): 219; "Entre Saône et Loire," no. 69 (1974): 36; Lafforgue, *Vignoble girondin*, 46–47.

24. Galtier, *Vignoble*, I, 157, 306–13.

25. Jaume Bardissa, *Cent ans de guerre du vin* (1976), 38–40.

26. René Barthe, *Vingt-cinq ans* (n.p., n.d.), 7–22, 33–34, 40.

27. Duffort, *L'Organisation internationale du marché du vin*, chap. 11.

28. G. Carrière, "Viticulture et espace rural," *Société Languedocienne de Géographie, Bulletin* 96, no. 2 (April–June 1973): 221–40.

29. *Journal officiel, avis*, no. 2 (11 January 1972): 12; no. 3 (15 February 1987): 176–83; Jean Sagnes, "Viticulture et politique: Edouard Barthe, député de l'Hérault, 1881–1949," in *Hommage à Robert Laurent* (Montpellier, 1982), 217–46.

30. Communauté Economique Européenne, *Conditions de commercialisation*, 4–5, 84–91.

CHAPTER FIVE *Cooperatives among Individualists*

1. *Annuaire des caves coopératives de France*, 1st to 6th eds.; Christian Delbos and Max Furestier, "Caves coopératives et commercialisation du vin en Sommiérois et Vaunage (Gard)," *Société Languedocienne de Géographie, Bulletin* (2d ser.) 4, no. 2 (April–June 1970): 167–81; Pierre Carrière, "Les Coopératives vinicoles en Languedoc-Roussillon," ibid. (3d ser.), 13, no. 2 (April–June 1979): 1–9; Galtier, *Vignoble*, I, 336–45.

2. INRA, *Le Vignoble des Côtes-du-Rhône* (1977), 34–38, 41–44.

3. Daniel Boulet and J. P. Laporte, *Contribution à une analyse économique de l'organisation coopérative en agriculture*, Ecole Nationale Supérieur Agronomique, Station d'Economie et de Sociologie Rurales, série *Etudes et recherches*, no. 13 (1975): 345–61.

4. A. Reparaz and Claude Berard, "Viticulture et coopération vinicole . . . le cas du Var," *Méditerranée* 23, no. 4 (1975): 37–57.

5. Michel Angé-Laribé, *Syndicats et coopératives agricoles* (1926), 143–46.

6. Chapuis, *Vigneron*, 274.

7. *Revue de viticulture* 70, no. 1806 (7 February 1929), 85–88; no. 1807 (14 February 1929): 105; 75, no. 1951 (19 November 1931): 335; Gadille, *Vignobles . . . côtes*, 381; Hubert Clique, *Les Caves coopératives de vinification en Bourgogne* (1931), 26–77, 90–96.

8. Auguste Moison, *Tavel, la renaissance d'un cru* (Uzès, 1974), 29–54.

9. Chappaz, *Le Vignoble . . . Champagne*, 395–98; J. P. Peyon, "La Coopération viticole en Champagne," *Travaux de l'Institut de Géographie de Reims*, nos. 27–28 (1976): 29–55; "L'Evolution du vignoble d'appellation d'origine contrôlée de 1950 à 1970," *Bulletin de INAO*, no. 112, special issue (1971), table 1.

10. *Annuaire des caves coopératives*.

11. CEE, *Conditions de commercialisation*, 143–54, 172.

12. Y. Rinaudo, "Une filière du pouvoir local: La coopération viticole dans le Var," *Revue de l'économie sociale* (1986): 23–32.

13. Sceau, "Un Vignoble dynamique, le Beaujolais," *Revue de géographie de Lyon* 50, no. 2 (1975): 133–37.

14. Reparaz and Bérard, "Viticulture et coopération," 37–57.

15. Confédération Nationale des Coopératives Vinicoles, "Statistiques et indicateurs de la coopération vinicole," June 1987. Typed manuscript kindly sent to me by the CNCV.

16. Ibid.

17. Boulet and Laporte, *Contribution à une analyse*, 170–76.

18. Pastor-Barrue, *Viticulture en crise*, 223–25, and my interviews.

CHAPTER SIX *The Economics of Wine*

1. Alain Berger, *Nouvelle économie de l'espace rurale* (1975), 37–39.

2. Jean Boyreau, *Profits et salaires dans la viticulture girondine* (Bordeaux, 1921), 7–10.

3. Barthe, "Economie et politique viticole," 161–63.

4. Loyat, *Le Beaujolais nouveau et ancien*, 136–44.

5. *Journal officiel, avis*, no. 2 (11 January 1972): 17–18; Gilbank, *Vignobles*, 356.

6. Roland Jouandet-Bernadat, *Les Comptes du département de la Gironde* (Bordeaux, 1963), I, 47–53.

7. Pijassou, *Le Médoc*, II, 956–78, 1038–47.

8. Roudié, *Campagnes girondines*, 991–1011; Faith, *Winemasters*, 170, 222–23, 241.

9. Colin, "Vignoble . . . Champagne," 39–42.

10. A. Berger and F. Maurel, *La Viticulture et l'économie du Languedoc du XVIIIe siècle à nos jours* (Montpellier, 1980), 185–88; Benno Sternberg-Sarel, "La Crise de la monoculture viticole," *Etudes rurales* 9 (April–June 1963): 55; *Revue de l'économie méridionale* 26, no. 101 (1978): 15–34.

11. J.-P. Chabrol and Claude Marti, *Caminarèm* (1978), 51.

12. Philippe Lacombe, "Les Stratégies d'adaptation des exploitations agricoles à la croissance économique. Languedoc-Roussillon . . . , " doctoral dissertation, University of Montpellier, 1972, 412–15; Pierre Bartoli, "La Prime de reconversion et le vignoble régional," *Economie méridionale* 27 (1979): 57–70.

13. *Annuaire statistique, 1985* (1986), 445.

14. Jules Milhau, *Etude économétrique du prix du vin en France* (Montpellier, 1935), 11–50; Berger and Maurel, *Viticulture . . . Languedoc*, 79–85; Barthe, "Economie et politique viticole," 54–62.

15. R. Badouin, "La Coexistence d'une situation de pénurie et d'un état de surproduction sur les marchés vinicoles," *Economie méridionale* 19, no. 78 (June 1972): 1–4; Badouin, "L'Economie viti-vinicole," ibid., 22, no. 90 (April 1975): 1–12; *Revue de l'économie méridionale* 26, no. 101 (1978): 35–39; Duf-

fort, *L'Organisation internationale du marché du vin*, 74–140; Communauté Economique Européenne, *Conditions de commercialisation*, 196–200.

16. Pastor-Barrue, *Viticulteurs en crise*, 296.

17. Communauté Economique Européenne, *Conditions de commercialisation*, 81–83; Daniel Boulet and R. Faillenet, *Eléments pour étude du système de production, transformation, distribution du vin* (Montpellier, 1973), 56; Organisation des Nations Unies Pour l'Alimentation et l'Agriculture, *L'Economie viticole mondiale*, Monographies des Produits, no. 43 (Rome, 1969), 11.

18. Milhaud, *Etude économétrique*, 67.

19. Requier-Desjardins, *Petite exploitation agricole*, 109–217.

20. Morel, *L'Economie dirigée en viticulture*, 11; André de Cambiaire, *L'Autoconsommation agricole en France* (1952), 125–26.

21. Jules Milhau, *Le Pouvoir d'achat des viticulteurs* (Montpellier, 1945), passim.

22. R. Bonnes, "Les Principaux aspects du problème de la qualité en matière viticole," doctoral dissertation, University of Montpellier, 1954, 22, 49–50; Douarche, *Le Vin et la vigne dans l'économie nationale française*, 42–44.

23. Duffort, *L'Organisation internationale du marché du vin*, 48; J. Dubos, "Evolution de la consommation par capita du vin en fonction de son prix et des caractéristiques," OIV, *Bulletin* 47, no. 520 (1974): 486–516.

24. R. Badouin, "La Coexistence d'une situation de pénurie," *Economie méridionale* 19, no. 78 (June 1972): 1–4.

25. INRA and ONIVIT, *La Consommation du Vin en France* (November 1980), 4 vols. See vol. 1, pp. 1–23, for the résumé.

26. INRA and ONIVINS, "Notes de synthèse," 29 May 1985, 1–17; poll cited in note 25; Chabrol and Marti, *Caminarèm*.

27. D. Boulet and R. Faillinet, *Eléments pour l'étude du système de production, transformation, distribution du vin* (1973), 48–51.

28. Office International de la Vigne et du Vin, *Symposium international sur la consommation du vin dans le monde, 1976*.

29. INRA, *Quelques données pour analyser la crise viticole*, INRA, série *Notes et Documents*, no. 16 (1976), 38; D. Boulet et al., *La Consommation du vin: Facteurs d'évolution. Enquête exploratoire sur Montpellier et Toulouse*. INRA série *Etudes et Recherches*, no. 34 (1978), résumé not paginated.

30. H. Dautriat, "Recherches sur les motivations d'achat des vins de Bordeaux," *Revue juridique et économique du Sud-Ouest*, série *Économique* 11, no. 3 (1962): 615–70; Roudié, "Campagnes girondines," 1676.

31. Communauté Economique Européenne, *Conditions de commercialisation*, 67–68, 71.

32. *Journal officiel, avis*, no. 4 (15 February 1978), annexes 35–37.

33. S. Lavigne et al., *Le Vignoble des Côtes du Rhône* (1977), 84–90.

34. E. Evina, "Les côtes-du-rhône digère leur croissance," *Revue vinicole internationale*, no. 3659 (August–September, 1988): 77–84.

CHAPTER SEVEN *The Commerce of Wine*

1. *Symposium des vins . . . Provence*, 64.
2. Eugène Richard, *Le Marché du vin à Paris* (1934).
3. *Marchand de vin* (1977), passim.
4. A. Berger et al., *Le Négoce des vins en France* (1980), 3 vols (vols. 1 and 2 list the firms, vol. 3 provides a summary); Gérard Le Pelletier de Woillemont, *La France et le commerce international du vin* (Toulouse, 1971), 9, 37.
5. Lavigne, *Vignoble des Côtes-du-Rhône*, 103–106; J. Dupuy, "Le Vignoble de Gigondas," DES, University of Grenoble, 1974, passim.
6. Bernard Revel, *Vins de l'Aude* (Villelongue d'Aude, 1979), 24–45; Michel Bouille et al., *Le Minervois* (Montpellier, 1987), 57–74.
7. Richardot, ed., *Papa Bréchard*, 265.
8. Bergeot, *Champagne, la coupe est pleine*, 126–29; D. Boulet and J. P. Laporte, *L'Evolution de la concentration et de la concurrence dans le secteur des champagnes et mousseux en France* (Montpellier, 1976), 42–69.
9. Krug, *L'Art du champagne*, 131–40.
10. Henri de Farcy, "La Part des transports dans le coût de commercialisation des produits agricoles," *Economie rurale* 51 (January–May 1962): 32; Duffort, *L'Organisation internationale du marché du vin*, 56; Office des Nations Unies pour l'Alimentation et l'Agriculture, *L'Economie viti-vinicole mondiale*, annual (Rome, 1969-).
11. Prestwich, *Drink and the Politics of Social Reform*, 211–17.
12. *Vigneron du Midi*, July 1935, December 1936, February 1938, January 1939.
13. Richardot, ed., *Papa Bréchard*, 312–14.
14. Doutrelant, *Bon vins et les autres*, 89, 107–17.
15. Piat, *Le Beaujolais*, chap. 15; Garrier, *Paysans du Beaujolais*, I, 601.
16. Forbes, *Champagne*, chap. 13.
17. Pijassou, *Le Médoc*, II, 1055.
18. Roudié, "Campagnes girondines," 861ff., 1051–59.
19. CIV Bordeaux, *Rapport annuel d'activité*, 1978–86.
20. Pastor-Barrue, *Viticulture en crise*, 250–51.
21. Revel, *Vins de l'Aude*, 108–17.
22. Prestwich, *Drink and the Politics of Social Reform*, 278–81.
23. Douarche, *Le Vin et la vigne*, 33–35; Douarche and Charles Penic, *L'Exportation des vins de France* (Montpellier, 1939), 17–20, 42–84; B. Landeche, *L'Exportation des vins de France* (Bordeaux, 1930), 9; *Annuaire statistique*, yearly.
24. Douarche, *Le Vin de France, son exportation sur les marchés étrangers* (Agen, 1927), 3–4; *Revue de viticulture* 82, no. 2132 (9 May 1935), 38–40.
25. F. Muglioni, *Les Accords commerciaux sur les vins* (1935), 51–56.
26. Piard, *Des Syndicats vers la corporation*, 38–40; Jean Masson, *La Crise viticole en Gironde* (Bordeaux, 1938), 86–87.

27. Bonal, *Livre d'or du champagne*, 185.

28. Germaine Marquette, "Le Commerce intérieur des vins de Bordeaux aux alentours de 1960," *Revue juridique et économique du Sud-Ouest*, série *Économique* 14, no. 1 (1965): 141–48, 182.

29. Banque de France, *Le Vin de Bordeaux*, I, 1–47, annex 3; Roudié, "Campagnes girondines," 856–926; Pijassou, *Le Médoc*, II, 1050–56.

30. France, Ministère de l'Agriculture, *La Bourgogne rurale* (1981), 99; "Entre Saône et Loire," no. 9 (1974): 38; Piat, *Beaujolais*, 155, 217–56.

31. Organisation des Nations Unies pour l'Alimentation et l'Agriculture, *L'Economie viticole mondiale*, 12.

32. France, Ministère du Commerce, *Tableaux généraux du commerce extérieur*, annual in 1950s; Food and Agriculture Organization of the United Nations, *Trade Yearbook*, annual; Centre Français du Commerce Extérieur, Direction des Agroalimentaires, *Statistiques des exportions de vins et spiritueux*, annual. This center has published numerous studies on foreign wine markets.

33. "Dossier export," *L'Information internationale des vins et spiritueux*, nos. 143 (March 1983), 145 (May 1983), 147 (July–August 1983), 149 (October 1983).

34. Asa Briggs, *Wine for Sale: Victoria Wine and the Liquor Trade* (Chicago, 1985), chap. 6.

35. *Revue vinicole international*, année 101 (April 1980) and passim.

36. *Journal officiel, avis*, no. 2 (11 January 1972): passim.

37. Georges Hatton, *Le Commerce extérieur de la France* (1968), 248.

38. Lavigne, *Le Vignoble des Côtes-du-Rhône*, annex 21.

39. *Journal officiel, avis*, "L'Avenir du vin?," no. 4 (15 February 1978): 298–300.

40. Henri de Farcy, "Trop de vin?" *Etudes*, August–September 1976, 169–71; Office International du Vin, *Symposium international sur la consommation du vin dans le monde*, special issue of *Bulletin* (1977), 161, *Annuaire statistique*.

41. J. Dubos, "Evolution de la consommation per capita du vin," OIV, *Bulletin* 47–250 (June 1974): 489–95.

42. "Federal Alcohol Administration Act," *United States Statutes at Large*, 74th Congress, 1935–36, vol. 49, part 1, Public Laws (1966): 977–85.

43. Colin, "Vignoble . . . Champagne," 56–57.

44. Antonio Niederbacher, *Wine in the European Communities* (Luxembourg, 1983), 29–30.

45. Bonal, *Le livre d'or du champagne*, 241–42, 347.

CHAPTER EIGHT *Conditions of Life: Propertied Growers*

1. Duby, ed., *Histoire de la France rurale*, IV, 208–16.

2. Richardot, ed., *Papa Bréchard*, 84–86; Roudié, "Campagnes girondines," 723–27.

3. Léon Foillard and Tony David, *Le Pays et le vin de Beaujolais* (Villefranche, 1929), 3, 42, 95–98; Raymond Dumay, ed., *Vins de Loire* (1979), 65.

4. Christine Amiel et al., *Jours de vigne* (Villelongue d'Aude, 1981), 73.

5. Loubère et al., *The Vine Remembers*, chaps. 1, 4.

6. Duby, ed., *Histoire de la France rurale*, IV, 212.

7. Gadille, *Vignoble de la côte bourguignonne*, 629–33.

8. Eunice Fried, *Burgundy: The Country, the Wines, the People* (New York, 1986), 175–79. Quotation from p. 176; Chaleil, *Mémoire du village*, 315. A useful introduction to rural life is Giovanni Hoyois, *Sociologie rurale* (1968).

9. Ministère de L'Agriculture, *Monographies agricoles départementales*, no. 83, *Le Var* (1958), 35–41; *Le Vaucluse*, passim; Enquêtes et Etudes Statistiques, *Statistiques agricoles*, annuals; *Journal officiel, avis*, no. 2 (11 January 1972): 7; no. 3 (15 February 1978): 271.

10. Gadille, *Vignoble*, 590–94; Fried, *Burgundy*, chap. 12; Loyat, *Le Beaujolais*, 43–52, 57–60; Sceau, "Un Vignoble . . . Beaujolais," *Revue de géographie de Lyon* 50, no. 2 (1975): 125–50.

11. Garrier, *Paysans du Beaujolais*, I, 664–65; Renée Mauric Payan, "Rapports entre les structures agricoles et sociales et la coopérative," DES, University of Lyon III, 1976, chap. 1; Gilbank, *Vignobles*, 122ff.

12. M. Rajchenbach, "Preignac, commune des Sauternais," DES, University of Bordeaux, 1971, 33–38.

13. Roudié, *Campagnes girondines*, 866–74, 1147–91, 1204–1205, 1213–32.

14. INRA, *Exploitations viticoles et viticulteurs* (Montpellier, 1980), 16; R. Lifran and C. Cibenel, *Typologies d'exploitation et couches sociales viticoles en Languedoc* (Montpellier, 1980), INRA, série *Etudes et Recherches*, no. 52, passim; R. Lifran, *Elargissement du marché et couches sociales dans la viticulture languedocienne* (Montpellier, 1977), INRA, série *Etudes et Recherches*, no. 30, passim.

15. Pastor-Barrue, *Viticulture en crise*, 106–204; Amiel et al., *Jours de vigne*, passim.

16. Bonal, *Livre d'or du champagne*, 219–23; Colin, "Vignoble . . . Champagne," *Travaux de l'Institut de Géographie de Reims*, no. 15: 76–77; Bergeot, *Champagne*, 158–62; Pierre Dessoliès et al., *Structure et population du vignoble Champenois* (Reims, 1957), 63–65, 93.

17. Numerous interviews, some of which have been published in Loubère et al., *The Vine Remembers*, chap. 3.

18. Gerard Nau, *Vin de Saumur, ses vignerons, son folklore* (Montreuil-Belloy, 1976), 45.

19. Richardot, ed., *Papa Bréchard*, 131, 232–49; Chapuis, *Vigneron*, 85–89.

20. Amiel et al., *Jours de vigne*, 50–52.

21. *Champagne viticole*, no. 191 (December 1932).

22. *Indépendant* (Perpignan), June 1961, September 29, 1977 (wine riots); Cabrol and Marti, *Caminarèm*, gives a vivid description as do Bardissa, *Cent ans de*

guerre du vin, and Pastor-Barrue, *Viticulteurs en crise*; Emmanuel Maffre-Baugé, *Vendanges amères* (1987); Michel Le Bris, *Occitanie: Volem viure!* (1971); Comités d'Action Viticoles, eds., *La révolte du Midi* (1976), 23.

23. *Le Monde*, 8 July 1977, 11.

24. Roudié, "Campagnes girondines," 1022–26.

25. *Le Monde*, 22 May 1984, 6; private correspondence.

26. Bonal, *Livre d'or du champagne*, 223; *Revue du vin de France*, no. 316 (December 1986–January 1987): 41–45.

27. Laura Frader, "La Femme et la famille dans les luttes viticole de l'Aude," *Sociologie du Sud-Est* 21 (July–October 1979): 33–54.

28. C. Amiel et al., *Jours de vignes*, 24–26, 53–55, 92, 135ff.; Richardot, ed., *Papa Bréchard*, 166.

29. Loubère et al., *The Vine Remembers*, chaps. 1, 3, 4.

30. "Caractéristiques générales de la population agricole féminine," *Bulletin d'information du ministère de l'agriculture*, no. 1054 (20 February 1984): 4–6; Louise Tilly and Joan W. Scott, *Women, Work and Family* (New York, 1978), 124, 135, 222.

CHAPTER NINE *Conditions of Life: Laborers*

1. Françoise Langlois, *Les Salariés agricoles en France* (1962), 111–15.

2. Paul Marres, "Le Prolétariat viticole. Aspects humains de la crise viticole," *Société Languedocienne de Géographie, Bulletin* (2d series) 6 (1935): 125–40.

3. Pech, *Entreprise viticole*, 337.

4. Ibid., 488; Jacques Girault, "Agriculture du Var en 1930," unpublished text given to me by M. Yves Rinaudo; Yves Rinaudo, "Les Paysans du Var, fin XIXème siècle—debut du XXème siècle," doctoral dissertation, University of Aix-Marseille, 1978, vol. I, 581ff., recently published as *Les Vendanges de la République* (Lyon, 1982).

5. Roudié, *Vignoble bordelais*, 54–56.

6. Ministère de l'Agriculture, Statistique Agricole de la France, *Résultats généraux de l'enquête de 1929* (1936), 534ff.; Geneviève Gavignaud, *Propriétaires-Viticulteurs en Roussillon*, II, 497; Berger and Maurel, *Viticulture et l'économie du Languedoc*, 178–79.

7. Pastor-Barrue, *Viticulteurs en crise*, 195–201.

8. Loyat, *Beaujolais*, 55, 152–65.

9. Ministère de l'Agriculture, Service Régional de Statistique Régional de Champagne-Ardennes, *Les Structures du vignoble de Champagne* (1970–71), based on the *Recensement Général de l'Agriculture, 1970–1971*, 85–86; Colin, "Vignoble . . . Champagne," in *Travaux de l'Institut de Géographie de Reims*, no. 15 (1973): 71–73, 78–84; Bonal, *Livre d'or du champagne*, 233–34; Krug,

L'Art du champagne, 158–59; Galtier, *Vignoble du Languedoc*, II, 119–20; Sternberg-Sarel, "La Crise de la monoculture viticole," 47–57.

10. Chapuis, *Vigneron*, 163.

11. Gadille, *Vignoble*, 615–20.

12. Roudié, *Campagnes girondines*, 731, 948–50, 1356–66; Mme Ladonne-Boye, "Les Graves, région géographique," DES, University of Bordeaux, 1946, 109–10; Pijassou, *Le Médoc*, II, 1014–28.

13. Roudié, *Vignoble bordelais*, 56.

14. *Journal officiel, avis,* (11 January 1972): 2.

15. Duby and Wallon, eds., *Histoire de la France rurale*, IV, 236–46; J. Harvey Smith, "Work Routine and Social Structure in a French Village: Cruzy (Hérault) in the 19th Century," *Journal of Interdisciplinary History* 5 (1975): 357–82.

16. Jean Sagnes, "Le Mouvement ouvrier dans . . . l'Hérault durant l'entre-deux-guerres," doctoral dissertation, University of Paris VIII, 1983, vol. III, 680–94, 730–45, vol. IV, 838–920. Recently published under the title *Politique et syndicalisme en Languedoc: L'Hérault . . .* (Montpellier, 1986).

17. Philippe Gratton, "Mouvement des grèves agricoles en France de 1898 à 1935," *Le Mouvement social*, no. 71 (1970): 3–38.

18. Edward Shorter and Charles Tilly, *Strikes in France* (Cambridge, Mass., 1974), 374–75.

19. Germain Lafforgue and Paul Thiery, *La Culture de la vigne dans le bordelais* (1929), 88–89; Pijassou, *Le Médoc*, II, 848–53, 927–30; Boyreau, *Profits et salaires dans la viticulture girondine*, 94–131; Loyat, *Beaujolais*, 122–26, 174ff.; Garrier, *Paysans du Beaujolais*, I, 598.

20. The sections on women in chapters 8 and 9 owe much to the work of Laura Frader. I recommend her following studies for more detailed information: "La Femme et la famille dans les luttes viticoles de l'Aude," *Sociologie du Sud-Est* 21 (July–October 1979): 33–54; "The Working Class of the Wine Industry of Lower Languedoc, Coursan, 1850–1919," Ph.D. dissertation, University of Rochester, 1978; "Peasants and Protest: Agricultural Workers and Revolutionary Syndicalism in the Aude," unpublished manuscript. Also useful for information on southern women is C. Amiel et al., *Jours de vigne*, for more recent developments. My information about women's work for the post-1914 period has come from numerous interviews.

21. Langlois, *Les Salariés agricoles*, 16–38, 59, 90–93, 111–15.